T0212302

Intercultural Communication, Identity, and Social Movements in the Digital Age

This book examines the complex and multidimensional relationship between culture and social media, and its specific impact on issues of identity and social movements, in a globalized world.

Contemporary cyber-culture involves communication among people who are culturally, nationally, and linguistically similar or radically different. Social media becomes a space for mediated cultural information transfer which can either facilitate a vibrant public sphere or create cultural and social cleavages. Contributors of the book come from diverse cultural backgrounds to provide a comprehensive analysis of how these social media exchanges allow members of traditionally oppressed groups find their voices, cultivate communities, and construct their cultural identities in multiple ways.

This book will be of great relevance to scholars and students working in the field of media and new media studies, intercultural communication, especially critical intercultural communication, and academics studying social identity and social movements.

Margaret U. D'Silva is a professor of communication and Director of the Institute for Intercultural Communication at the University of Louisville. She is President (2019–2021) of the International Association for Intercultural Communication Studies. Widely published, she recently co-edited, with Ahmet Atay, *Mediated Intercultural Communication in a Digital Age* (2019, Routledge).

Ahmet Atay is an associate professor at The College of Wooster. He is the author of *Globalization's Impact on Identity Formation: Queer Diasporic Males in Cyberspace* (2015, Lexington Books) and co-editor of nine books. He recently co-edited *Millennials and Media Ecology: Culture, Pedagogy, and Politics* (2019, Routledge); *Mediated Intercultural Communication in a Digital Age* (2019, Routledge); and *Examining Millennials Reshaping Organizational Cultures: From Theory to Practice* (2018, Lexington Books).

Routledge Research in Communication Studies

For more information about this series, please visit: www.routledge.com/
Routledge-Research-in-Communication-Studies/book-series/RRCS

Intercultural Communication, Identity, and Social Movements in the Digital Age

Edited by Margaret U. D'Silva
and Ahmet Atay

Routledge
Taylor & Francis Group

NEW YORK AND LONDON

First published 2020
by Routledge
605 Third Avenue, New York, NY 10017

and by Routledge
2 Park Square, Milton Park, Abingdon, Oxon, OX14 4RN

First issued in paperback 2022

Routledge is an imprint of the Taylor & Francis Group, an informa business

Publisher's Note
The publisher has gone to great lengths to ensure the quality of this reprint
but points out that some imperfections in the original copies may be apparent.

Library of Congress Cataloging-in-Publication Data
Library of Congress Control Number:2019952512

ISBN: 978-1-03-240091-4 (pbk)
ISBN: 978-1-138-30325-6 (hbk)
ISBN: 978-0-203-73127-7 (ebk)

DOI: 10.4324/9780203731277

Typeset in Sabon
by Apex CoVantage, LLC

Contents

PART II
Intercultural Communication and Online Social Movements

Tables

Contributor Biographies

Huda Mohsin Alsahi is a final year PhD student in Political Science and Sociology at Scuola Normale Superiore in Italy, under the supervision of Professor Donatella Della Porta. Her research interests include the intersection of gender and politics in the Arab Gulf States and the political use of information and communication technologies. She has been a visiting scholar at the department of Gender Studies at the University of California, Los Angeles, and the winner of the 2017 Graduate Paper Prize from the Association for Gulf and Arabian Peninsula Studies (AGAPS). Moreover, she had written several articles about the status of gender in the Arab Gulf States that appeared in the *Journal of Arabian Studies* and the publications of Istituto Affari Internazionali, among others.

Dr. Ahmet Atay (PhD, Southern Illinois University–Carbondale) is Associate Professor of Communication at the College of Wooster. His research revolves around cultural studies, media studies, and critical intercultural communication. In particular, he focuses on diasporic experiences and cultural identity formations of diasporic individuals; political and social complexities of city life, such as immigrant and queer experiences; the usage of new media technologies in different settings; and the notion of home. He is the author of *Globalization's Impact on Identity Formation: Queer Diasporic Males in Cyberspace* (2015) and the co-editor of nine books. His scholarship appeared in number of journals and edited books.

Dr. Olga Baysha (PhD, University of Colorado at Boulder) is an assistant professor at the National Research University "Higher School of Economics" (Moscow, the Russian Federation). Her research centers mainly on political and cultural aspects of globalization with an emphasis on new media and global social movements for justice and democratization. Dr. Baysha is especially interested in analyzing inherent anti-democratic tendencies of the discourses of westernization employed by post-Soviet social movements. Dr. Baysha is the author of two books: *The Mythologies of Capitalism and the End of the Soviet Project* (Lexington, 2014) and *Miscommunicating Social Change: Lessons from Russia and Urkaine* (Lexington, 2018).

Dr. Fathi Bourmeche (PhD, University of Sfax, Tunisia) is an assistant professor in the Department of English at the Faculty of Letters and Humanities, Sfax. His research and teaching interests touch upon various aspects in cultural studies, focusing on the major themes affecting the changing nature of different societies, including media, ethnicity, politics and elections. He is also interested in studying recent migration trends and their impact on host societies, with particular attention to the American and British contexts. Dr. Bourmeche has recently published *The Falklands War: An Analysis of Prime Minister Margaret Thatcher's War Speeches; Eastern Europeans in British newspapers from 2004 to 2007: New others in British multicultural society; and Eastern Europeans in British press from 2004 to 2014.*

Dr. Margaret U. D'Silva (PhD University of Kentucky) is Professor of Communication and Director, Institute for Intercultural Communication at the University of Louisville. Dr. D'Silva was an invited plenary speaker for conferences in Chicago, USA (2018), Taipei, Taiwan (2012), and Vladivostok, Russia (2013), and invited presenter in Oslo, Norway (2008). She has co-edited three academic books, including *Mediated Intercultural Communication in a Digital Age* with Ahmet Atay for Routledge. She has authored and co-authored several articles and book chapters. She was co-investigator on a $397,000 National Institutes of Health grant. Professor D'Silva has served as editor of the journal *Intercultural Communication Studies.* She has served as chair of the APAC Division of the National Communication Association and is currently the president of the International Association for Intercultural Communication Studies.

Dr.Monserrat Fernández-Vela (PhD, University of New Mexico) is a fulltime professor in the Communication School at Central University of Ecuador. Her areas of interest are related to social justice and social change in Latin America, the critical analysis of power/knowledge and education/communication, the construction of discourses of otherness in intercultural communication, the impact of new technologies on human networks in education, and the design and evaluation of communication/education curricula in higher education. Her doctoral research focuses on the discourse of human rights, and human rights education read from a Latin American educommunicational perspective. Her work has a multidisciplinary approach that combines communication, education, and sociology. She has written articles about journalism, educommunication related to peace and conflict, and education.

Dr. Katie Day Good (PhD, Media, Technology, and Society, Northwestern University) is an assistant professor in the Department of Media, Journalism and Film at Miami University in Oxford, Ohio. Her research focuses on the historical and contemporary development of civic, educational, and intercultural media. She is the author of *Bring the World to the Child: Technologies of Global Citizenship in American Education, 1900–1946* (MIT Press) and has published articles in *New Media & Society, Media, Culture and Society, Communication and Critical/Cultural Studies, Technology and Culture*, and other venues.

Dr. Renee Middlemost is a lecturer in communication and media at the University of Wollongong, Australia. Her research focuses on fan/audience participatory practices and how these intersect with celebrity and popular culture. Her recent work has been published in *Celebrity Studies; M/C Journal*, the *Australasian Journal of Popular Culture*. She is the co-founder of FSN Australasia and a co-editor of *Participations*.

Dr. Nina Grønlykke Mollerup is postdoc at the Saxo Institute, University of Copenhagen. She was trained as an anthropologist and holds a PhD in communication. Her research interests include journalism, activism, refugees, revolution, conflict, violence, technology, and sustainability. Her work has mainly focused on Egypt, Syria, and Scandinavia. She has published in journals like *International Journal of Communication* and *Journalism Practice*.

Alex Rister is a PhD student in texts and technology at the University of Central Florida and is simultaneously pursuing a graduate certificate in gender studies. She has a MA in Communication from UCF's Nicholson School of Communication and Media as well as an MA in English from the University of North Florida. Alex is an assistant professor of the Practice at Embry-Riddle Aeronautical University, Worldwide, where she teaches courses in the Department of English, Humanities & Communication. Alex's research focuses on activism and social justice, especially on issues related to women and gender.

Dr. Nathian Shae Rodriguez (PhD, Texas Tech University) is an assistant professor of digital media in the School of Journalism & Media Studies at San Diego State University and core faculty in the Area of Excellence "Digital Humanities and Global Diversity." He specializes in critical-cultural and digital media studies. His research focuses on minority representation in media; specifically, LGBTQ and Latinx portrayals, identity negotiation, and issues of masculinity. Dr. Rodriguez has ten years of professional radio experience in on-air talent, sales, promotions, and social media marketing. Dr. Rodriguez has published many book chapters and journal articles centered on identity negotiation and media.

Jennifer Sandoval is an associate professor and the Program Coordinator for Communication and Conflict at the Nicholson School of Communication and Media at the University of Central Florida. She has a PhD in Communication and Culture from the University of New Mexico and a Master's of Dispute Resolution from Pepperdine School of Law. Dr. Sandoval brings her experience as a mediator, project manager, trainer, and consultant to the classroom and her research program at UCF. She is interested in the communication of marginalized identity in various contexts. Her research focuses on the communicative elements involved in the intersection of identity, the body, and health. Additionally, she examines the rhetoric of choice and assistive reproductive technology, as well as looks at reproductive health access for the LGBT community. Dr. Sandoval also continues work with community based-participatory research projects focusing on health intervention in underserved and underrepresented populations.

Dr. Yuyun W. I. Surya (PhD, University of Auckland) is a lecturer in the Department of Communication at Universitas Airlangga, Indonesia. Her research and teaching interests are in the areas of online media and multiculturalism, and focuses on ethnic and minority identity, intercultural communication, online journalism, and cyberculture. She has published a book (*Online Journalism in Indonesia: The Use of Interactive Elements in Six Online Newspapers*, published by Lambert Academic Publishing Germany, 2010) and a book chapter ("Sorry I Judge Your Ethnicity" in IGAK Wibawa (Ed) Minority Issue in Indonesian Cinema Post New Order Era, published by Communication Department Universitas Airlangga, 2009). She has presented her papers in international conferences and has been involved in several research projects.

Acknowledgements

This project is a product of years of thinking about the links between media and intercultural communication and years of teaching courses on media and intercultural communication. We want to thank our students who inspired us. This project is also inspired by years-long conversations we had about much wanted collaboration.

First and foremost, we would like to thank Routledge who trusted us with this important project. We are grateful to our former and current amazing editorial team. Your help is really appreciated. Thank you for continuously encouraging us.

Our gratitude goes to Chelsea Pruett, Katherine Wiedeman, and Madison Thompson for their editorial assistance.

Most importantly, we thank our families for their continued support and encouragement.

Margaret thanks her mom, Irene D'Silva, for her unwavering support through all these years, and her partner, Murali Rao, and their two sons, Nikhil Rao and Neil Rao, for love and laughter.

Ahmet thanks his parents, Ayla and Kemal Atay, and his partner for their unconditional support.

Introduction

Cultural Identity and Activism in Digital Spaces

Margaret U. D'Silva and Ahmet Atay

We are witnessing powerful and complex changes in how global citizens communicate with each other. Social media and other forms of digital communication, the harbingers of this change, have been increasingly used to accomplish everyday tasks as well as complex deeds. What is captivating about this process is that it simultaneously involves intercultural contexts and participants as well as mediated forms of expression. Through digital communication platforms and social media, individuals and organizations are constructing, performing, and expressing cultural identities. They are also communicating their political and ideological standpoints as well as organizing online communities for social activism.

Editing this, our second book, has involved many mediated exchanges of pithy comments attached to the authors' chapters. We only met face-to-face once to write and critique each other's work. Our collaboration has been a productive mediated intercultural communication experience that has taught us the power of social media in generating ideas, organizing large documents, and working through cultural differences. With our early education and upbringing in different nation states, Margaret in India and Ahmet in Cyprus, we brought our cultural ways of knowing and writing to these interactions. Underlying all our exchanges, however, is a profound appreciation that social media is a transformative force in how we communicate interculturally. This book is one example of such digital intercultural collaboration.

As transnational scholars, our main goal was to curate global pieces that tackle the different aspects of intercultural identity and social activism within digital domains. Therefore, we used a number of international listservs and platforms to publicize our call for chapters. Our efforts and the resulting book demonstrate the importance of new media technologies in the lives of transnational communication scholars. Digital communication with our chapter authors from distant and not-so-distant spaces has been quick and effective. Our authors' geographic locations span the globe: Australia, Denmark, Ecuador, Indonesia, Italy, Russia, Saudi Arabia, Tunisia, and the United States. Collectively, these authors examine different global cultural issues, identity performances, and social movements.

Online intercultural exchanges through the World Wide Web have allowed global participants to connect with each other with phenomenal ease, as did the contributors of this book. As the editors of this book, we constructed a working community that is committed to studying digital intercultural communication. Virtual communities developed online have enabled strong and weak links among citizens of the world; however, these mediated ties have an often unrecognized history that goes back to a time before the advent of computers. Pen pal exchanges, for instance, allow for mediated intercultural exchanges between citizens of various nation states (see Good). Building on the traditional ways of disseminating information and linking people, new media technologies, such as social network sites and online platforms, aim to connect people within nation-states as well as globally. Thus, this web of connections and exchanges facilitates continuous intercultural encounters between people who may or may not know each other. For example, we can easily follow social movements in different parts of the world by simply watching the updates on our smartphones or newsfeeds (see Alsahi).

Some of the most common examples of digital intercultural communication forms or narratives include social movements around the cyber world, philanthropic interventions, and the identity performances of immigrants. This cyber-culture centers on the communication among people who are culturally, nationally, and linguistically similar, or radically different.

Online communication enables greater exposure to social issues and allows narrative activism to flourish despite obstacles. Social media exchanges occur through multiplayer video games, Facebook, Twitter, and a host of other digital platforms. These social media platforms also allow the members of traditionally oppressed groups to find their voices, express their issues, cultivate communities, and perform social activism in physical and digital contexts (see Middlemost; Mollerup; and Rister and Sandoval). These technologies also create homes away from home for immigrants, cosmopolitans, and global nomads, thereby allowing them to construct their cultural identities in multiple ways and express the facets of their identities (see Rodriguez). Because this cyber-culture involves communication among those who are culturally, nationally, and linguistically similar, or radically different, studying social media in relation to intercultural communication is both crucial and timely. This book attempts to illustrate and embody these cultural and digital tensions, forces, and opportunities.

In a digital age, the mediated information exchanges among people of different cultures involve complex cultural information transfers (Atay & D'Silva, 2019). Online interactions may obstruct or facilitate intercultural relationships across cultures. Some social media spaces create avenues for civil discourse, while others generate spaces for uncivil deliberations, thereby impeding successful intercultural communication. Online communication, however, is not always smooth or effective, and intercultural conflicts may even occur in online domains. This is a dark side of intercultural communication, as differing viewpoints, political rifts, and cultural conflicts can create chasms between individuals and groups of people. Estranged from each other for political, religious, and other reasons, online communicators may engage in inconsiderate and divisive discourse, disrupting communities and creating cultural cleavages (see Baysha). Social media uses its own platform of engagement through Internet language, which can lead to potentially challenging interactions.

When used intentionally and effectively, however, social media can play an important role in furthering social justice causes, building solidarity, and cultivating an awareness of environmental and political issues both nationally and globally. One striking use of social media is that when unfettered by crushing oppositional powers, it can be used to draw attention to difficult problems (e.g., Alsahi; Bourmeche; Surya). All these momentous changes in global communication, particularly in social media, have compelled researchers to review the current notions of culture, communication, social movements, and identity. Considering that most of our intercultural communication is mediated or digitalized, there is a clear need to continue to bridge the gaps between intercultural communication and new media scholarship. We hope that this book contributes to these conversations in meaningful ways.

This book examines the relationship between social media and intercultural communication with specific attention paid to identity issues and social movements. The chapter authors have used qualitative, interpretive, and critical and cultural perspectives to study identity and social activism in specific geographic locations.

This book's interrelated goals are to:

- Analyze how social media simultaneously facilitates a vibrant public sphere and creates cultural and social cleavages.
- Examine the history of social media and cultural practices to understand how social media influences and contributes to our intercultural communication.
- Examine how social media constructs identities and enables individuals to express their cultural identities or disables them from doing so.
- Analyze how global social movements as cultural and political processes impact mediated and intercultural communication and create a symbiotic relationship between the two.
- Explore different case studies about mediated intercultural communication by fusing the theoretical frameworks from intercultural communication and media studies.
- Look at different contemporary issues relevant to intercultural communication scholarship such as immigration, social movements, and intercultural/international relationships from a social media perspective.

- Examine both the negative and positive influences of social media on intercultural communication as these influences interact with social movements.
- Focus on the issues of diversity, oppression, and identity in the context of media and intercultural communication.

This book is divided into two sections and in each, the authors examine different case studies or cultural issues regarding social movements and cultural identity constructions in cyberspace.

Part I: Intercultural Communication, Online Community, and Identity

The authors in this section focus on how intercultural communication occurs in digital contexts. Together, the authors explore the ways in which new media technologies and digital platforms offer opportunities for identity construction and create spaces for different groups of people to engage in social issues.

Katie Day Good, in "From Pen Pals to ePals: Mediated Intercultural Exchange in a Historical Perspective," traces the history of pen pal exchanges that have facilitated cross cultural exchanges in the last century. She argues that, as a significant form of global communication in bygone years, these exchanges represent an idealized and enduring communicative practice from the Machine Age to the Digital Age. In this piece, she draws a connection between pen pal exchanges and ePal chats as she analyzes the intercultural communication dimensions of these mediated interactions.

While Good writes about the intercultural encounters among people from disparate locations, Nathian Shae Rodriguez focuses on space differently and examines the narratives of people dispersed from their place of origin. In "Western Media's Influence on Identity Negotiation in Pre-asylum 'Gay' Men," Rodriguez interviewed gay refugees from the Middle East now living in the United States to understand the complex relationship between their identity negotiation and media use. In this chapter, he postulates that the exposure to themes about gay people in Western media, unlike what is offered in Middle Eastern media, motivates gay men to authenticate this aspect of their identity.

Similar to Rodriguez, Renee Middlemost, in her chapter titled "'Serving Activist Realness': The New Drag Superstars and Activism Under Trump," explores issues around queer culture in digital spaces. She highlights the ways in which the popularity of the stars from the reality television show *RuPaul's Drag Race* offers these celebrities an opportunity to champion important causes. Drag is activism, she says, and celebrity drag personalities such as Bob the Drag Queen and Sasha Velour are using their celebrity status to draw attention to marriage equality and trans inclusivity in the current, difficult political climate.

Fathi Bourmeche's chapter "Brexit and EU Migration on the BBC and CNN: Britishness Versus EU Identity" also focuses on political issues by investigating CNN's and BBC's coverage of Brexit. In his analysis, he discovered that the issue was framed in terms of its repercussion on the British and global economies. According to Bourmeche, Brexit was also framed in terms of its impact on British and EU identity as well as the outlook for Britain's future should it no longer be part of the UK.

In this section's concluding chapter, "Who Am I? Who Are They?: Otherness in the Human Rights Discourse of the United Nations Facebook Pages," Monserrat Fernández-Vela presents a critical discourse analysis of the Facebook pages of three important UN agencies: UN Women, UNHCR, and OHCHR. Fernández-Vela uses the frameworks of otherness, power and knowledge, positionality, and discursive practices. While the main discourse of these Facebook pages centered around human rights, poverty, health, gender, and refugees, the pages also appealed to a Western audience.

Part II: Intercultural Communication and Online Social Movements

In this section, the chapter authors articulate how activists in different parts of the world use new media technologies to perform activism, create social awareness, and garner support for their causes. While some online practices are supportive of intercultural engagement, others can be disruptive, create fissures among participants, and damage social movement agendas.

Nina Grønlykke Mollerup, in her chapter titled "Tents, Tweets, and Television: Communicative Ecologies and the *No to Military Trials for Civilians* Grassroots Campaign in Revolutionary Egypt," writes about her extensive ethnographic fieldwork in Egypt, examining the "No to Military Trials for Civilians" campaign and how it garnered media attention. With communication ecologies as her framework of analysis, she argues that the campaign's vast array of communicative practices resulted in garnering corporate media attention to create a political awareness of the cause.

Olga Baysha's chapter, "Unfriending Is Easy: Intercultural Miscommunication on Social Networks," focuses on a conflict in a different geographical region and examines SNS unfriending during the Maidan conflict in the Ukraine. In her research, Baysha found a high rate of unfriending of opponents and cultural others. This unfollowing resulted in a more homogenous online environment and the deepening of existing cultural fissures.

In the chapter titled "Analyzing the *Women to Drive* Campaign on Facebook," Huda Mohsin Alsahi examined the role of the "Women2Drive" Facebook page in mobilizing protests among the women in Saudi Arabia. The movement used online spaces to create a grassroots campaign that incorporated religion into intersectional feminism, garnering viewers and supporters outside of Saudi Arabia. In her chapter, Alsahi advocates for intersectional feminism and asks for the inclusion of religion in transnational feminist agendas. For Alsahi, online platforms, such as Facebook, open up alternative spaces for women to create feminist collaborations.

Alex Rister and Jennifer Sandoval's chapter, titled "Does This Lab Coat Make Me Look #DistractinglySexy?: A Critical Discourse Analysis of a Feminist Hashtag Campaign," also engages with feminist alliances in online spaces. The authors studied public tweets with the hashtag "#distractinglysexy," which was being used in comments about women in science at an international conference. Using humor, sarcasm, historical pictures, and inspiration, the tweets constituted a counternarrative about women in science, particularly in digital spaces.

Like some of the previous authors, Yuyun W. I. Surya explores the intercultural dimensions of online activism and resistance on Facebook. In her chapter "Papuan Political Resistance on Social Media: Regionalization and Internationalization of Papuan Identity," Surya examines the "Orang Papua" Facebook group. She finds that the group's Facebook page articulates the Papuan political resistance to Indonesian oppression. The graphic images and descriptive captions on social media allow Papuans to generate a political affiliation with Melanesia and raise international awareness about human rights violations in Indonesia.

References

Atay, A., & D'Silva, M. U. (Eds.). (2019). *Mediated intercultural communication in a digital age*. New York City, NY: Routledge.

Part I

Intercultural Communication, Online Community, and Identity

1 From Pen Pals to ePals

Mediated Intercultural Exchange in a Historical Perspective

Katie Day Good

Introduction

In the late 1980s and early '90s, a flurry of electronic exchanges took place between schoolchildren in the United States and the dissolving Soviet Union. Logging onto bulletin board systems from computers in classrooms and public libraries, students in California, New York, and West Virginia posted friendly greetings and, as one educator put it, "reached across an ocean, a continent, and the remnants of an Iron Curtain to communicate with their peers in Moscow" (Watson, 1990, p. 109). Their Russian counterparts, many relying on computers and modems donated by Western technology companies or private foundations, answered back with their own greetings and, in one reported case, urgent questions about cars and blue jeans. Hailed by the *Los Angeles Times* as a grassroots movement in peace education and a "computer-age Glasnost," these youthful experiments in electronic goodwill symbolized both the openness of American society and the educational and democratizing promise of its globalizing telecommunications presence in personal computers and the emergent Internet (Melvin, 1988; Reppert, 1990). In the celebratory accounts of the Internet that proliferated during its subsequent commercialization phase in the mid-1990s, no single image more aptly conveyed the revolutionary promise of the technology than that of schoolchildren clustered around desktop computers, connecting with peers in faraway places, exchanging ideas, and becoming the "global citizens" who would one day lead the global information economy (Anonymous, 1993; Frazier, 1996).

I argue that these computer-mediated intercultural exchanges, which have become a mainstay of education in the 21st century, were not so much signs of an unprecedented digital revolution as they were a culmination of nearly a century of organized efforts, many initiated in the United States, to harness networked communication technologies to promote cross-cultural dialogue and American political ideology among youth. Tracing the roots of pen pal correspondences—the Progressive-era, paper-based precursor to contemporary intercultural exchanges that take place online—I show how an ideal that I call *mediated intercultural exchange* both emerged and endured within educational and popular discourse from the Machine Age to the Digital Age. These grassroots, international exchanges of media texts among children have constituted an influential and overlooked form of global communication in the last century. They have also offered American educationalists, policymakers, and industry leaders a durable trope for imagining the benefits of a world increasingly interconnected by technology.

Mediated intercultural exchange refers to the transfer of media and/ or material objects between citizens of different nations and cultures for the stated purpose of making contact across geographic and cultural barriers, exchanging cultural knowledge, and conveying messages of international amity or goodwill. While conducted in the name of education, cosmopolitanism, and international peacebuilding, such cultural practices have historically also served governments and corporations as mechanisms for promoting particular communication technologies and political ideologies. The ways in which American students engaged in this practice in the early 20th century spanned multiple networks and devices, including writing letters to pen pals overseas through the postal system, broadcasting messages of goodwill over the radio, and exchanging cultural tokens of friendship—such as scrapbooks, school supplies, or dolls—with schoolchildren overseas through transoceanic shipping routes (Dowling, 1928, pp. 174–180; Fletcher, 1937).[1] In the digital age, these sorts of multi-mediated exchange practices continue to thrive in both physical and virtual form, and they remain as diverse as the technologies available and the participants involved. Popular programs include ePals, or pen pal exchanges conducted over email; telecollaboration, or the use of web technologies to complete shared projects online between classrooms in different countries; and coordinated swaps of symbolic objects, such as handmade paper dolls called "Flat Stanleys," through the postal system or in the suitcases of travelers. In many cases, students virtually track and chronicle the journeys of these physical objects with digital tools such as blogs, email, and social media (Good, 2016; Guth & Helm, 2010; O'Dowd, 2007).

The thread uniting these diverse cultural exchange practices across eras, technologies, and modalities is their shared emphasis on engaging youth through networks of international communication to foster intercultural dialogue and understanding. In ways that resonate strikingly with millennial discourses about the digital age, the first decades of the 20th century were hailed by social observers as a new era defined by rapid technological advancement, ubiquitous communication, and global connectivity—an "age of super-contact" and a "shrinking world" (Dowling, 1928, p. 102; Popp, 2011, p. 459). Commentators variously celebrated and fretted over the global proliferation of new technologies of communication and transport, including motion pictures, newspapers and magazines, radio, telephones, airplanes, and automobiles. These technologies enabled ordinary people to not only consume unprecedented amounts of information about the world but also to directly contact and communicate with others in new ways and across vast distances (Czitrom, 1982; Fischer, 1994).

For educators and policymakers, the influx of immigration and the outbreak of the First World War heightened concerns about preparing young people to become not only patriotic citizens of the nation with shared American values but also informed and internationally aware "world citizens" who could defend democracy and free-market capitalism in an increasingly multicultural society and tumultuous international landscape (Carr, 1928; Center, 1933; Stratton, 2016). As former President William Howard Taft wrote in the introduction to *A Course in Citizenship and Patriotism*, a wartime curricular guide for teachers created by the peace education organization the American School Peace League, the war presented American schools with a dual obligation to not only transform the nation's immigrants into "law-abiding, patriotic citizens [who will contribute . . .] prudential virtues, and civic activity, to the general welfare," but also to "impress upon the youth [. . .] the idea that we are not the only people in the world; that we should earnestly cultivate friendship and sympathy with other peoples" (Cabot, Andrews, Coe, Hill, & McSkimmon, 1918, pp. xiii–xiv).

In this climate, pen pal exchanges emerged as a popular teaching tool and symbol of the utopian potentials of a more interconnected world. Through "this friendly intercourse," wrote Josephine Doniat (1904), an Illinois high school teacher, on the rise of international correspondences between students in the United States and Europe at the turn of the century,

> the student gains a fund of information about the manners and customs of the foreign nation, and as he grows to respect and even love his partner, he realizes that foreign modes of life, while they may be different, are not, on that account, inferior to his own.
>
> (p. 77)

As the prominent peace educator Florence Brewer Boeckel observed over two decades later, the surge of global connectivity brought about by modern technologies of communication and transport was felt not only in the high-level domains of geopolitics and commerce but also in the everyday lives of ordinary youth:

> With the coming of steamboats and locomotives fast mails were built up, and now, by telegraph, cable, and by radio it is possible to send a message all the way around the earth in a few moments. It is not

only grown people who send messages back and forth on business, but from children too letters are being sent in all directions, asking questions about what it is like to live in other countries.

(Boeckel, 1928, p. 92)

Boeckel (1928) was one of many educators to highlight both the technological modernity and grassroots accessibility of pen pal exchanges, marking them as an emerging form of communication that could bring peace and stability to the "closely related world" of the new century (p. 1). For years before the media theorist Marshall McLuhan would make his famous proclamations in the early 1960s about the advent of a "global village" of nations intimately interconnected through new electronic media, educators were already praising the exchange of letters and other cultural materials through the mail for "cultivating good international relations at the John-Doe level," or creating democratic pathways and practices of global interaction beyond the gated domains of mass media, international trade, or diplomacy (de Zafra, Jr., 1953, p. 305; Hawk, 1936; MacDonald, 1939; McLuhan, 2001).

Recovering the history of international pen pals and other mediated intercultural exchanges enriches our understanding of the techno-utopian discourses and assumptions that have historically underpinned the expansion of communication networks and practices from the industrializing West to the non-Western world. Traditionally, histories of long-distance international communication have focused on communicators who were predominantly male and professional, and messages related to matters of colonial administration, commerce, mass media, or geopolitics (Mattelart, 1994; Thussu, 2006; Winseck & Pike, 2007). According to Carolyn Marvin (1990), these dominant figures in the telegraph era envisioned the value of a networked planet in terms of its capacity not for genuine cross-cultural dialogue but rather for Anglo-Saxon values and notions of progress to travel more efficiently from the civilized center of the West to the "less-fortunate periphery" (Marvin, 1990, pp. 192–193). It is only recently, with the advent of the Internet, that amateur media users—particularly women and youth—and multilateral media flows are gaining scholarly attention for their role in fostering more democratic, participatory, and dialogic forms of international communication (Hull, Stornaiuolo, & Sahni, 2010; Jenkins, Shresthova, Gamber-Thompson, Kligler-Vilenchik, & Zimmerman, 2016).

Turning toward neglected historical practices of mediated intercultural exchange in early 20th-century schools reveals that efforts to associate emerging technologies with ideals of global citizenship and intercultural goodwill are not unique to the Internet age, nor are they politically neutral. Teaching young Americans to engage in personalized, youthful, and authentic communication across borders has long aligned with the nation's interests in expansionism and empire, even as these practices have also been touted by educators as uniquely progressive teaching devices for eradicating prejudice and promoting peace. The historically fraught nature of these exchanges can thus help to illuminate some of the contradictions underpinning the World Wide Web and contemporary virtual exchange practices in education, which are both hailed for their participatory and global nature and criticized as yet another tool of American hegemony and electronic imperialism (Ess, 2002; Fabos & Young, 1999; Zembylas & Vrasidas, 2005).

Origins of Pen Pals

Contemporary exchanges of media between schools have roots in the international correspondence movement, a turn-of-the-century effort led by European educators to coordinate educational letter writing between university and secondary school pupils in England, France, Germany, and the United States (Doniat, 1904; Magill, 1902; Stoker, 1933). As early as the 1890s, educators praised international correspondence for enlivening the study of foreign languages and geography and promoting an unprecedented sense of mutual awareness, neighborliness, and friendship among students in different nations. As one German schoolmaster wrote in 1899,

> Since so many thousands are corresponding with each other, we may say that the different countries which, up to this date, were used to consider each other as mortal enemies, only thirsting for each other's blood, . . . are linked together by new ideas, by peaceful thoughts, by mutual respect and love.
>
> (Thiergen, 1899, p. 7)

International letter writing between strangers gained visibility in American culture during the First World War, as churches and voluntary organizations sent relief supplies to allied countries in Europe and received letters of thanks in return. Some of these correspondences continued for years (Roehm, 1928, p. 57; Wells, 1935). But American participation in the school correspondence movement remained limited until after war's end, when teaching international understanding and "world friendship" emerged as a new priority for progressive educationalists (Carr, 1928; Dowling, 1928; Stoker, 1933).

The first large-scale effort to promote international correspondence between students in the United States and abroad began in 1919, when the George Peabody College for Teachers in Nashville, Tennessee, established the Peabody National Bureau of Educational Correspondence. The initial aim of the Peabody program was to facilitate letter exchanges between students in the United States and France to commemorate and build on the wartime alliance between the two nations. Within its first year, the bureau matched an estimated 18,000 pairs of American and French students, taking care to ensure that there would be an even geographic distribution of letter-writers so that a single class of French students would receive letters from various parts of the United States and vice versa (Anonymous, 1920; Oliver, 1919). The program grew quickly with the endorsement of a number of leading educational agencies and associations, including the National Education Association (NEA) and the US Bureau of Education. By the mid-1920s it expanded to coordinate correspondences between students in the United States and China, Japan, Germany, Spain, and parts of Latin America.

Promotional literature for the Peabody program emphasized the importance of international correspondence as both an edifying social practice for children and a promising new form of citizen diplomacy. Receiving a letter from abroad, written in French and marked with a foreign postage stamp, was the first opportunity that most American children had to see "living French with a personal throb in it," wrote the program's first director, A. I. Roehm (Roehm, 1928, p. 57). Whereas earlier international correspondence programs emphasized the exchange of staid, formal letters containing academic facts and information, the Peabody program advanced a more "modern" approach to correspondence that allowed for some inclusion of popular culture, individual experience, and everyday life. Children were encouraged to stuff their letters' envelopes with visual and token materials of personal and local interest such as postcards, pressed flowers, and photographs. This "wealth of enclosures" would ensure that correspondents not only gained academic knowledge of the country but also vivid impressions and appreciation of its people and culture (Dorsey, 1920, p. 21). As the US Commissioner of Education Philander P. Claxton wrote during the program's launch in 1919, the combination of personalized textual, visual, and material correspondence would be key to its effectiveness:

> Along with the letters, there will be a fine exchange of historical, artistic, geographical, manufactural, commercial, and home-life material and information, clippings, picture postals, kodak [*sic*] views, etc., leading up to the deepest exchanges of human sympathies and ideals, that will reinforce international good will.
>
> (Claxton, 1919, pp. 2, 8)

But the newfound emphasis on cultivating personalized cultural exchanges among youth was tempered with reminders about the seriousness of international correspondence as an extension of state diplomacy. To advance the mission of promoting peace and preventing future wars, program officials maintained that proper representation of oneself and one's nation was a matter of utmost importance. Children participating in the Peabody program in France were told to behave as "cultured, careful and correct English letter-writers" (Roehm, 1928, pp. 58–59). Additionally, boys were matched exclusively with boys, and girls with girls, in an effort to prevent improper romantic ties from forming (Anonymous, 1920). In apparent tension with other statements celebrating the authentic, individualized nature of international correspondence, some Peabody officials warned students against using an overly informal tone and instructed them to focus instead on exchanging "real information about the foreign country [. . .] not merely the description of everyday happenings" (Oliver, 1919, p. 74). As Charles Garnier, the inspector general of the French Ministry of Public Instruction and administrator of the Peabody program in France wrote, educational correspondence was "not simply fun and play":

> [I]t must not, cannot be an everyday, irrelevant, hasard [*sic*] exchange like "phoning to the next village neighbor." [. . .] When we correspond with another country, we must always write what we know and what we think worth sending across the ocean, worth being told to the son of another republic and it must be what is best in our beliefs and thoughts.
>
> (Garnier, 1929, pp. 248–249)

Garnier was one of many educational and government officials in the aftermath of World War I to cast international correspondence as powerful form of junior diplomacy, suggesting that students' letter-writing could be potentially as influential to the future of international relations as the dialogue between high-level officials of the state (Dowling, 1928, p. 176; Stoker, 1933, p. 206). Garnier encouraged the young American writers to imagine their efforts as akin to those of the US Secretary of State Frank B. Kellogg, who was, at the time of his writing, soon to arrive to France to sign the Kellogg-Briand Pact renouncing war and promoting the peaceful settlement of international disputes. Although students wrote with a "humble steel pen or fountain pen," Garnier wrote, if they behaved as proper citizens and ideal representatives of their nation, their pens would "at once, in your very fingers, be changed into gold and be worth being put side by side with Kellogg's pen as helping to spread good will and peace" (1929, p. 249). Such comments from both sides of the Atlantic testified to an emerging view that the international communications of children, though carried out in the personalized and playful form of handwritten letters and pictures, could nevertheless influence nations' perceptions of each other. They should therefore be carefully guided by adults and aligned with dominant definitions of good citizenship.

Praised as vivid supplements to textbooks and other visual aids, these early pen pal letters and their visual enclosures served as important global texts in the interwar classroom. Missives from abroad were enthusiastically scrutinized and studied by students, while teachers displayed them on bulletin boards and filed them away for future use as authoritative reference materials on foreign languages and customs. Representatives of the Peabody program cited the power of children's correspondence materials of all types—such as "pictures of farms, of villages and towns, little songs and poems, a pressed plant or flower, or specimens of handiwork," and even the exotic postage stamps on the envelopes themselves—to "vitalize interest" in people and places abroad (Roehm, 1928, pp. 57–59).

In the interwar period, the terms "pen pal" and "pen friend" began to replace the more formal moniker of "international correspondence" that had defined the first interschool exchanges earlier in the century. Whereas the international correspondence movement stressed restrained, academic, and closely supervised discourse among school pupils, the informal and child-oriented terminology of pen pal programs reflected a concerted turn among educators and peace advocates towards elevating young people's individual voices, interests, and everyday experiences in the promotion of internationalism. Edna MacDonough, a graduate of Wellesley College, founded the International Friendship League in 1930, a Boston-based pen pal matching agency that reportedly facilitated the exchange of five million letters within its first decade. She touted her program's correspondences as "entirely unsupervised and [. . .] therefore unstereotyped," arguing that fostering candid conversations between youth would lead them to recognize their inherent sameness or "likeness in ideals," thus offering a needed corrective to the tendency of mass culture, movies, and newspapers to focus on the "peculiarities and differences" of foreigners (Fieldston, 2015, pp. 58, 93; MacDonough, 1932). In a similar vein, in 1942 the Peabody program changed its earlier stance of discouraging overly personal letters and instructed teachers instead that "personal attachment [. . .] must never be crowded out of the correspondence, no matter what we educators may wish to outline for these young people in the way of topical information on social conditions, in order to make the correspondence 'educational'" (Roehm, 1942, pp. 227–228).

Far from hindering the diplomatic power of international correspondence, advocates of pen pal exchanges believed that moving toward a more informal, child-driven style of pen friendship would be more effective for laying the groundwork for mutual understanding and world peace. During and after World War II, children's pen pal exchanges were deemed particularly useful devices for teaching Americans to see the human impact of distant conflicts and to galvanize their interest in current affairs, newspapers, and maps (Barnes, 1950; Braden, 1948; Cunningham, 1945; Goy, 1948). In 1939, Mary MacDonald, a high school teacher in Monson, Massachusetts, credited her students' European pen pals for sparking their interest in the war overseas and developing their literacy of news and mediated information:

They are getting the point of view of children who are in the heart of world-troubles and yet have wishes and ambitions like their own. They are hunting in the newspapers for items of those countries where their "pen pals" live. They give oral topics on the customs they have learned. Estonia is now a real place on the map. Latvia is more than a name.

(MacDonald, 1939)

In addition to improving American students' awareness of foreign cultures and conflicts, pen pal exchanges could fortify their patriotism. After World War II, educators noted that writing to a pen pal helped students appreciate the unique advantages of American life and the role of the United States in liberating the world from authoritarianism and war. Tommie Barnes, a high school English teacher in Tulsa, Oklahoma, wrote in 1950 that pen pal exchanges taught her students that "Americans have an obligation to be modest and considerate" in their interactions with foreigners and, at the same time, made them "feel that they can help spread the American way of life" to other countries. Barnes was one of many teachers in the post-WWII period to describe the value of pen pals by citing passages from letters in which foreign children expressed their gratitude to Americans for their role in the war and admiration for life in the United States. "You must realize the Nazitime to be like a bad dream, which now our country awoke from," wrote a German boy to one of Barnes's students. "The effect is we must now have a new beginning. Therefore it is very important for us to hear something of peace-loving nations based on a democratic foundation because we must learn from the bottom" (Barnes, 1950, pp. 289–290). Or as a Dutch boy wrote to a student in Naidene Goy's class in Hinsdale, Illinois, in 1948:

[W]e shall always be thankful for everything the Americans have done for us. [. . .] I often remember that good time when the Yankees were here. They were very good and kind boys indeed and I often wondered about the great friendship shown between officers and men. What a difference between them and the Germans!

Another student in Goy's class received the following comments from his Swedish pen pal: "Here in Sweden we have food and other necessary things enough although we cannot buy as much as we want of some sorts. We receive much from the USA, but you cannot probably export sufficient quantities" (Goy, 1948, pp. 320–321). By singling out these types of comments from foreign children in their reports on the value of pen pal correspondences, teachers reinforced an emerging postwar view that cultural exchange was beneficial not only for spreading American ideals and friendship abroad but also for teaching young Americans to appreciate their country's unique role in settling international disputes, its booming free market economy, and its democratic way of life (Bu, 1999).

In step with the US government's precipitous increase in delivering international aid and humanitarian assistance to other nations after the Second World War, many American schools "adopted" schools or individual students in war-affected countries and initiated written correspondence in conjunction with sending gifts of school supplies, food, and clothing. These unilateral gifts of material assistance, described as gestures of goodwill, reinforced ideas about the United States as steward and safe-keeper of democracy and stability in the international arena. They presented a problematic convergence of pen pal correspondence with charity, blurring the lines between cultural exchange and economic aid and contributing to narratives of the United States as a paternalistic superpower with a duty to assist and uplift other countries and thwart the spread of communism (Fieldston, 2015). This view was central to a 1953 essay about the far-reaching educational and societal benefits of the "pen-pal movement" by Carlos de Zafra, a New York high school educator who had, in his own childhood, corresponded with a pen pal in France. He wrote that schools across the United States should participate in pen pal exchanges with war-affected countries, as his own classes had done by "adopting" pen pals in Belgium and Japan and sending them "boxes of homey presents, extra food and clothing, and strong, encouraging friendship just when they needed them most." Providing both friendship and material support was important, he wrote, because of "the desperate current need of America to cultivate every possible friend and bit of good will in every cranny of the globe, for nothing less than civilization itself may depend on our doing so" (de Zafra, Jr., 1953, p. 305).

The historian Elena Albarrán (2008) argues in her study of pen pal programs in post-revolutionary Mexico that children "assumed the mantle of nationalism" from adults in their correspondence with peers abroad. By prompting students to represent their country in terms of its holidays, traditions, industries, and typical foods, pen pal exchanges encouraged youth to think of their nation as a cohesive entity while cultivating cosmopolitan interests and identities that complemented a patriotic and unified nationalism (Albarrán, 2008, pp. 238–243). In the postwar United States, too, pen pal programs reflected a tension between internationalism and nationalism, often positioning the cultivation of "international understanding" as a means of defending American freedoms from the Soviet threat. In 1946 and 1948, President Harry Truman signed the Fulbright and Smith-Mundt Acts, respectively establishing cultural exchange as both a domestic educational priority and a centerpiece of American foreign policy in the Cold War (Belmonte, 2010, pp. 26–33; Bu, 1999). These priorities were salient in the NEA's 1948 handbook, *Education for International Understanding in American Schools*, which informed teachers that incorporating an internationalist view into instruction, including through cultural exchange activities such as international correspondence and exchanges of student visitors, was critical for "maintaining peace not from the point of view of domestic security and well-being alone but also from the point of view of the security and well-being of the world in general" (National Education Association, 1948, p. 2).

International educational exchange practices among schoolchildren thus became freighted with the politics of the Cold War. "The term educational exchange became," according to Bu,

> [A] synonym for cultural relations in postwar America. In the competition with the Soviet propaganda, "educational exchange" became an important instrument to project favorable images of the United States symbolized by its abundance of material wealth, consumer culture, technological know-how, individual freedom, and political democracy. A unilateral approach to exporting American culture, values, and technology was increasingly emphasized. Hence "exchange" became a misnomer, although "mutual understanding" remained the watchword.
>
> (1999, pp. 393–394)

Indeed, while pen pals' accounts of daily life were lauded for promoting "mutual understanding," they were simultaneously valorized for educating both US citizens and foreigners alike about the dangers of communism and benefits of free-market capitalism. In contrast to state-issued Soviet propaganda, American pen pal letters represented the nation from the bottom up, serving as personalized testimonials of the benefits and freedoms of life in the United States. They were often cited in conjunction with American information libraries, created under the Office of War Information during World War II and housed in US embassies and consulates around the world, as important sources of cultural information for people abroad who were eager to learn about life in the United States (Brown, 1956; Kraske, 1985).

As Cold War tensions between the United States and the Soviet Union escalated in the 1950s and early 1960s, pen pal exchanges gained an unprecedented level of cultural visibility as the US government began officially promoting them as not only an edifying hobby but also an accessible and urgently needed form of citizen diplomacy that could bring developing nations into the Western sphere of influence. In 1956, President Dwight Eisenhower established the People-to-People program, a partnership between the newly formed US Information Agency (USIA) and nongovernmental committees led by prominent business leaders, educators, and cultural figures. The program's objective was to support local and citizen-driven cultural exchange activities, including international pen pal and stamp exchanges, sister city affiliations, and exchanges of artists, athletes, scholars, and students. Part of the soft power strategy of the United States to contain the global spread of communism through the export of American cultural products and propaganda, the People-to-People program aimed to involve ordinary citizens in the USIA mission of utilizing a range of "communication techniques" to "submit evidence to peoples of other nations [. . .] that the objectives and policies of the US are in harmony with and will advance their legitimate aspirations for freedom, progress, and peace" (Eisenhower, 1956; Hagerty, 1956; United States Information Agency, 1954). While mobilizing the power of the state behind the program, Eisenhower stressed that it would be carried out by ordinary citizens and communities, not the government. As Secretary of State John Foster Dulles described it, the People-to-People program was "a valuable device to create a sense of public participation in the government's Cold War policies" (Klein, 2003, p. 51).

While the program's professed goal was to foster "understanding between peoples," its rhetoric revealed a strategic intent to strengthen American influence around the world (Klein, 2003, pp. 49–50). A predecessor to the program was Letters from America Week, a nationwide pen pal drive launched in 1950 by the Common Council for American Unity, an organization that sought to promote interethnic and civic unity in the United States by celebrating the universality of democratic principles (Gleason, 1984, p. 348; Wall, 2008, pp. 265–270). The campaign urged American descendants of immigrants to serve as "spokesmen" for the United States by writing letters to friends and relatives abroad. As a brochure for the program stated, "You will be performing an act of natural friendliness and at the same time serving your country and the cause of peace and freedom in the world." The campaign emphasized the importance of average citizens and their "personal accounts" of American life in bolstering the image of the United States around the world and counteracting the influence of Soviet propaganda. As President Eisenhower said in support of the program,

> Each American who writes to someone abroad is an ambassador of good will and understanding. No statements about the "American Way of life" made by government officials have a better impact on the people of other lands than the personal accounts of individual Americans writing from their local communities about their schools and homes and work."
>
> (Anonymous, 1956, 1957; The Common Council for
> American Unity, n.d.)

The Letters from America campaign was emblematic of Eisenhower's vision of "individual Americans acting through person-to-person communication in foreign lands," a strategy which, as he stated in a letter to People-to-People committee leaders in 1956, was key "if our American ideology is eventually to win out in the great struggle being waged between two opposing ways of life" (Hagerty, 1956).

The notion that American pen pals could serve as both initiators of international friendship and foot soldiers of freedom and democracy resounded throughout US educational discourse and popular culture during the late 1950s and early 1960s. Newspapers ran stories about adults and children who acted as "do-it-yourself diplomats," using their home addresses as unofficial clearinghouses to respond to a flood of mailed requests from foreigners eager to learn about the American way of life (de Zafra, Jr., 1953; Donovan, 1958; Roberts, 1959). Pen pal agencies and social welfare programs recruited young people to join the cause through advertisements in comic books, children's periodicals, and a pen pal kiosk at Freedomland, an American history-themed amusement park in New York (Anonymous, 1962; National Social Welfare Assembly, 1965). Stories about the high global demand for American pen pals complemented narratives about the desirability of American products and popular culture around the world. The World Pen Pal Program (WPPP), a nonprofit correspondence bureau operated out of the World Affairs Center at the University of Minnesota and a member organization in the People-to-People program's Letter Writing Committee, worked with the USIA and the newly established Peace Corps to recruit potential pen pals abroad and match them with American students, scouts, clubs, and religious groups. In 1964, the WPPP matched over 58,000 young people in dozens of countries. The organization invited young Americans to write letters, particularly to peers living behind the Iron Curtain and in developing countries, to do their part to advance the growth of global democracy. In its newsletter, the program celebrated the geopolitical savvy of its American pen pals by printing letters from young participants like "Steve B.," a 16-year-old boy from Danville, California, who wrote to the WPPP asking to be connected with a pen pal living in a region of strategic importance to the United States:

> As a US citizen, I would like a pen pal, so I could do my part to help the image of the US abroad. I can write in French, and my main interest lies with the peoples of the newly-emerging areas of Africa, the Middle East, and the Orient. Later on I hope to serve in the Peace Corps. Now I would greatly appreciate this opportunity to serve my country.
>
> (World Pen Pal Program, 1964)

In pen pal literature, participants like "Steve B." were the poster children for emerging mid-century ideals of American-led internationalism and world citizenship. They were proficient in foreign languages, knowledgeable of current affairs, and compelled by a sense of patriotic duty to befriend peers abroad in order to spread American values and promote stability in the international world.

The early 1960s saw a resurgence of the techno-utopian discourses that had characterized discussions of long-distance communication in the early part of the century, as commentators grappled with the social implications of a new crop of media and information technologies, including television, satellites, and computers, that were increasingly networked and global in reach (McLuhan, 1962). At the 1964 World's Fair in Queens, New York, the Unisphere, a stainless steel monument to global interdependence, was erected to represent the themes of "Peace Through Understanding" and "Man's Achievements on a Shrinking Globe in an Expanding Universe." The sense of a rapidly contracting planet was exhibited and celebrated throughout the fair, most famously in the Walt Disney ride, "It's a Small World," which was hosted in the Pepsi-Cola Pavilion with admission proceeds benefiting UNICEF. The United States, embarrassed by the Soviet display of technology during the 1958 Brussels Universal Exposition, welcomed high-tech exhibits from companies such as IBM, Coca-Cola, and General Electric that showcased the globalizing and democratizing power of American technological innovations and consumerism (Samuel, 2010). Among these displays was the Parker Pen Pavilion, sponsored by the Parker Pen Company of Janesville, Wisconsin. Working in partnership with the People-to-People program, the Pavilion's main attraction was a computer dubbed the "Pen Pal Picker Machine." Fairgoers were invited to enter their age, sex, and interests into the computer and were instantly matched with a compatible pen pal abroad (Anonymous, 1964; "Junior People-To-People," 1962; McLendon, 1964). They were then given a complimentary postcard with their new pen pal's name and address, and were encouraged to write to the pen pal on site using any of 90 writing desks, attended by a fleet of multilingual hostesses, some of them former airline stewardesses, called "Penettes" (Samuel, 2010, pp. 101–102). Revamping the practice of international correspondence with high-tech and sexualized signifiers of the jet and computer age, the exhibit epitomized Eisenhower's vision of leveraging citizen-based international communications as a weapon of modern ideological warfare.

Connecting over a million pen pals between 1964 and 1965, the Pen Pal Picker Machine was hailed by its promoters and the press for facilitating closer and more customized contact among the world's citizens than had ever been possible before (Anonymous, 1965; Johanning, 1965). One of several computer-based attractions at the fair, the exhibit heralded the arrival of a new age of information in which pen pals would be able to reach each other not simply through pen and paper, but through the assistance of digital technology. The Pen Pal Picker Machine showcased the revolutionary accessibility and democratizing potential of an increasingly high-speed and global communications system while at the same time reasserting the uniquely powerful role of the United States within it. While signaling towards a future of instantaneous cross-cultural connectivity enabled by computers, the exhibit also testified to the enduring role of handwritten and homegrown media, exchanged among ordinary citizens, in cultivating grassroots international friendships and peace in alignment with American educational and political ideals.

Conclusion

The People-to-People program and 1964 World's Fair popularized a premise that had guided American international correspondence initiatives for decades: that an increasingly internationalized and interdependent world needed ordinary citizens, particularly young people, to learn to communicate with each other across borders to promote peace, democracy, capitalism, and stability. In this task, Americans saw themselves as uniquely suited for initiating the conversation. The history of international pen pal practices outlined in this chapter, though necessarily incomplete, serves to highlight some of the tensions and contradictions that have endured in discussions of school- and citizen-based international exchanges of media from the Machine Age to the Digital Age. Over time, American educators and policymakers have supported an evolving range of practices that can broadly be categorized as forms of *mediated intercultural exchange*, or long-distance transfers of letters, images, and other cultural materials among citizens of different nations for the purpose of building international friendships and advancing national interests.

The alignment between mediated intercultural exchanges and American geopolitical priorities was evident in the 1980s and '90s, when a host of new virtual exchange projects encouraged computer-mediated dialogue among schoolchildren to improve relations between countries in the West and behind the Iron Curtain. Prominent among these was the New York State–Moscow Schools Telecommunications Project, launched in 1988 by the Copen Family Foundation and the New York State Department of Education, which connected students in a dozen classrooms in the United States and the USSR via email and video speakerphones donated by Mitsubishi (Berenfeld, 1993; Melvin, 1988; Watson, 1990). A more recent example can be seen in the cyber-diplomacy initiatives supported by the US State Department since the early 2000s. These include Civil Society 2.0, which promotes technology use and digital literacy among global nonprofit and civic organizations, and Exchange 2.0, which supports "technology-enabled international interaction" and project-based exchanges among students in different countries and provides resources to "help teachers use the Internet to 'reach out' globally" (iEARN-USA, n.d.; tech@state, 2010). Positioning cross-cultural communication, technological literacy, and social media dialogue among school-aged youth as a springboard for furthering international understanding in the Internet age, such exchange initiatives are reflective of the kinds of digitally mediated citizen diplomacy that former Secretary of State Hillary Rodham Clinton termed, in a video address on YouTube, "twenty-first century statecraft" (US Department of State, 2009). Likewise, telecommunications and technology companies, such as AT&T, Microsoft, and Apple, have embraced international "exchange projects" and the rhetoric of international understanding and global citizenship education to promote their products and services to educators (Fabos & Young, 1999).

Like the pen friends of yore, today's electronic correspondents are depicted as future-ready cultural ambassadors and influential global communicators. Through their youthful explorations of global communication networks and exchanges of personal media to generate intercultural dialogue, these electronic ambassadors continue to symbolize the democratic potentials of a highly mediated "global village." They also continue to lend a friendly and optimistic image to educational, governmental, and industrial visions of a more interconnected future and global information economy in which the United States retains a dominant voice and role.

Note

1. An account of these varied historical practices of exchange appears in the author's book, *Bring the World to the Child: Technologies of Global Citizenship in American Education* (Cambridge, MA: MIT Press, 2020).

References

Albarrán, E. J. (2008). *Children of the revolution: Constructing the Mexican citizen, 1920–1940* (Doctoral dissertation). Retrieved from ProQuest Digital Dissertations (Order No. 3310948).

Anonymous. (1920). American pupils correspond with French children. *School Life*, 5(7), 15.

Anonymous. (1956, May 14). Truth by mail. *New York Herald Tribune*, p. 12.

Anonymous. (1957, May 19). Americans advised to write overseas. *New York Times*, p. 79.

Anonymous. (1962, September 12). Diplomacy and amusement. *Tyrone Daily Herald*, p. 4.

Anonymous. (1964, March 17). Pen pals at the fair. *Christian Science Monitor*, p. 15.

Anonymous. (1965, May 8). Penfriend program near million mark. *Janesville Daily Gazette*, p. 11.

Anonymous. (1993, August 14). Internet brings youth together. *The Daily Times*.

Barnes, T. (1950). Letters abroad: Schoolwide project at Will Rogers High. *The Clearing House*, 24(5), 289–290.

Belmonte, L. A. (2010). *Selling the American way: US propaganda and the Cold War*. Philadelphia, PA: University of Pennsylvania Press.

Berenfeld, B. (1993). Linking east-west schools via telecomputing. *Technological Horizons in Education*, 20(6).

Boeckel, F. B. (1928). *Through the gateway.* New York: Macmillan.

Braden, H. E. (1948). Arsenal high students' letters build world pen-friends. *The Clearing House, 22*(7), 396–397.

Brown, S. J. (1956, July 15). Sally seeking pen pals for pals overseas. *Chicago Daily Tribune,* p. N10.

Bu, L. (1999). Educational exchange and cultural diplomacy in the Cold War. *Journal of American Studies, 33*(3), 393–415.

Cabot, E. L., Andrews, F. F., Coe, F. E., Hill, M., & McSkimmon, M. (1918). *A course in citizenship and patriotism.* Boston, MA: Houghton Mifflin.

Carr, W. G. (1928). *Education for world-citizenship.* Palo Alto, CA: Stanford University Press.

Center, S. S. (1933). The responsibility of teachers of English in contemporary American life. *The English Journal, 22*(2), 97–108.

Claxton, P. P. (1919). American school boys and girls to correspond with French. *School Life, 3*(6), 1, 8.

The Common Council for American Unity. (n.d.). *Be a spokesman for the United States.* Art For World Friendship Records, 1946–1969. Swarthmore Peace Collection (Box 5, Folder: "Pen Pals"), Swarthmore College, Swarthmore, PA.

Cunningham, A. L. (1945). Corresponding with British children. *The English Journal, 34*(10), 560–562.

Czitrom, D. (1982). *Media and the American mind: From Morse to McLuhan.* Chapel Hill, NC: University of North Carolina Press.

de Zafra, Jr., C. (1953). Our pupils can build millions of international friendships. *The Clearing House, 27*(5), 305–307.

Doniat, J. C. (1904). International correspondence of pupils: Its history, purpose, and management. *The School Review, 12*(1), 70–77.

Donovan, J. (1958, July 20). Old magazines win friends for U. S. *The Baltimore Sun,* p. F3.

Dorsey, S. M. (1920). Notices from superintendent's office. *Los Angeles School Journal, 3*(23), 20–22.

Dowling, E. (Ed.). (1928). *World friendship: A series of articles written by some teachers in the Los Angeles Schools and by a few others who are likewise interested in the education of youth.* Los Angeles, CA: Committee on World Friendship.

Eisenhower, D. D. (1956, September 11). Remarks at the people-to-people conference. *Dwight D. Eisenhower Presidential Library, Museum, and Boyhood Home.* Retrieved from www.eisenhower.archives.gov/research/online_documents/people_to_people/BinderT.pdf

Ess, C. (2002). Computer-mediated colonization, the renaissance, and educational imperatives for an intercultural global village. *Ethics and Information Technology, 4*(1), 11–22.

Fabos, B., & Young, M. D. (1999). Telecommunication in the classroom: Rhetoric versus reality. *Review of Educational Research, 69*(3), 217–259.

Fieldston, S. (2015). *Raising the world: Child welfare in the American century.* Cambridge, MA: Harvard University Press.

Fischer, C. S. (1994). *America calling: A social history of the telephone to 1940.* Berkeley, CA: University of California Press.

Fletcher, L. (1937, May 2). Hands across the sea. *The Atlanta Constitution,* p. 9G.

Frazier, D. (1996). *Internet for kids.* Alameda, CA: SYBEX, Inc.

Garnier, C. M. (1929). A call to the schoolboys and girls of America. *The French Review, 2*(3), 247–249.

Gleason, P. (1984). World War II and the development of American studies. *American Quarterly, 36*(3), 343–358.

Good, K. D. (2016). Tracking traveling paper dolls: New media, old media, and global youth engagement in the Flat Stanley Project. In E. Gordon & P. Mihailidis (Eds.), *Civic media: Technology, design, practice* (pp. 421–428). Cambridge, MA: MIT Press.

Goy, N. (1948). Pen pals in foreign lands. *The English Journal, 37*(6), 320–321.

Guth, S., & Helm, F. (Eds.). (2010). *Telecollaboration 2.0: Language, literacies and intercultural learning in the 21st century*. Bern, Switzerland: Peter Lang.

Hagerty, J. C. (1956, May 31). Press release, the White House. *Dwight D. Eisenhower Presidential Library, Museum, and Boyhood Home*. Retrieved from www.eisenhower.archives.gov/research/online_documents/people_to_people/BinderV.pdf

Hawk, H. C. (1936). Winfield High's homeroom project in international understanding. *The Clearing House, 11*(3), 149–152.

Hull, G. A., Stornaiuolo, A., & Sahni, U. (2010). Cultural citizenship and cosmopolitan practice: Global youth communicate online. *English Education, 42*(4), 331–367.

iEARN-USA. (n.d.). *A teacher's guide to exchange 2.0: Technology-enabled international interaction*. Retrieved from www.connectallschools.org/exchange-guide-international-collaboration

Jenkins, H., Shresthova, S., Gamber-Thompson, L., Kligler-Vilenchik, N., & Zimmerman, A. (2016). *By any media necessary: The new youth activism*. New York, NY: NYU Press.

Johanning, D. (1965, May 8). Penettes have exciting weekend at world's fair. *Janesville Daily Gazette*, p. 11.

Junior People-To-People. (1962, September 30). *Boston Globe*, p. 10.

Klein, C. (2003). *Cold War orientalism: Asia in the middlebrow imagination, 1945–1961*. Berkeley, CA: University of California Press.

Kraske, G. E. (1985). *Missionaries of the book: The American library profession and the origins of United States cultural diplomacy*. Westport, CT: Greenwood Press.

MacDonald, M. (1939). More real letters. *The English Journal, 28*(9), 753.

MacDonough, E. (1932). International friendship by the way of youth. *World Affairs, 95*(3), 169–170.

Magill, E. H. (1902). History of the international correspondence in the United States of America. *Modern Language Notes, 17*(7), 227–229.

Marvin, C. (1990). *When old technologies were new: Thinking about electric communication in the late nineteenth century*. New York, NY: Oxford University Press.

Mattelart, A. (1994). *Mapping world communication: War, progress, culture*. Minneapolis, MN: University of Minnesota Press.

McLendon, W. (1964, April 4). Pen pal picker machine makes friendships. *The Washington Post*, p. A17.

McLuhan, M. (1962). *The gutenberg galaxy: The making of typographic man*. Toronto, Canada: University of Toronto Press.

McLuhan, M. (2001). *Understanding media: The extensions of man* (2nd ed.). Abingdon, Oxon: Routledge.

Melvin, T. (1988, December 4). A computer project links students with Soviet partners. *New York Times*, p. WC1.

National Education Association. (1948). *Education for international understanding in American schools: Suggestions and recommendations.* Washington, DC: National Education Association of the United States.

National Social Welfare Assembly. (1965). Friends across the seas. *The Flash*, (151). Art for World Friendship Records, 1946–1969. Swarthmore Peace Collection (Box 8, Folder: "Media Coverage, 1965"), Swarthmore College, Swarthmore, PA.

O'Dowd, R. (Ed.). (2007). *Online intercultural exchange: An introduction for foreign language teachers.* Clevedon, England: Multilingual Matters.

Oliver, T. E. (1919). The national peabody foundation for international educational correspondence. *The Modern Language Journal*, 4(2), 73–76.

Popp, R. (2011). Machine-age communication: Media, transportation, and contact in interwar America. *Technology and Culture*, 52(3), 459–484.

Reppert, B. (1990, January 14). Computer age glasnost: Satellite links up Americans and Soviets via personal computers. *Los Angeles Times*, p. 3.

Roberts, P. (1959, February). The foreign policy of my daughter Ellen. *Harper's Magazine*, 218(1305), 40–43.

Roehm, A. I. (1928). Organization and educational objectives of French-American educational correspondence. *The French Review*, 2(1), 57–60.

Roehm, A. I. (1942). Learning foreign languages and life by new techniques including international educational pupil-correspondence. *Peabody Journal of Education*, 19(4), 227–229.

Samuel, L. R. (2010). *End of the innocence: The 1964–1965 New York world's fair.* Syracuse, NY: Syracuse University Press.

Stoker, S. (1933). *The schools and international understanding.* Chapel Hill, NC: University of North Carolina Press.

Stratton, C. (2016). *Education for empire: American schools, race, and the paths of good citizenship.* Oakland, CA: University of California Press.

tech@state. (2010, November 15). *What is civil society 2.0?* Retrieved April 4, 2017, from http://tech.state.gov/profiles/blogs/what-is-civil-society-20

Thiergen, O. (1899). On international correspondence between pupils. *The School Review*, 7(1), 4–10.

Thussu, D. K. (2006). *International communication: Continuity and change* (2nd ed.). London, UK: Hodder Education.

United States Department of State. (2009). *21st century statecraft*. Retrieved from www.youtube.com/watch?v=x6PFPCTEr3c

United States Information Agency. (1954). Mission of the United States Information Agency. *Dwight D. Eisenhower Presidential Library, Museum, and Boyhood Home.* Retrieved from www.eisenhower.archives.gov/research/online_documents/people_to_people/BinderR.pdf

Wall, W. L. (2008). *Inventing the "American way": The politics of consensus from the new deal to the civil rights movement.* New York, NY: Oxford University Press.

Watson, B. (1990). The wired classroom: American education goes on-line. *The Phi Delta Kappan*, 72(2), 109–112.

Wells, C. A. (1935). Hobby par excellence! *The Rotarian*, 46(3), 2, 37.

Winseck, D. R., & Pike, R. M. (2007). *Communication and empire: Media, markets, and globalization, 1860–1930.* Durham, NC: Duke University Press.

World Pen Pal Program. (1964). *Annual report*. Art for World Friendship Records, 1946–1969. Swarthmore Peace Collection (Box 5, Folder: "Pen Pals"), Swarthmore College, Swarthmore, PA.

Zembylas, M., & Vrasidas, C. (2005). Globalization, information and communication technologies, and the prospect of a "global village": Promises of inclusion or electronic colonization? *Journal of Curriculum Studies, 37*(1), 65–83.

2 Western Media's Influence on Identity Negotiation in Pre-asylum "Gay" Men

Nathian Shae Rodriguez

In a viral video, members of the militant extremist group ISIS (also known as Daesh), threw two men off a tower in Syria as punishment for the act of "liwat"—the term used for men accused of homosexuality in Sharia law (Prince, 2015). After going viral, the video was broadcast on news outlets worldwide. People witnessed the men falling to their death and a crowd of spectators throwing stones at the bodies. Similar incidents took place in Iraq in 2016 and 2017 with video and pictures also released to the media (Charlton, 2017; Wyke, 2016). Locals argued that ISIS did not kill the men as a message to gays in the Middle East, but rather as a message to the West (Haddad, 2016). Massad (2002) argues that while same-sex intimacy has long been present in the Middle East, a "gay" identity is a Western concept that has brought about attention, and thus harassment, to individuals practicing same-sex intimacy.

Many examples of Middle Eastern men who have sex with other men (MSM) being persecuted exist; however, the aforementioned instances highlight the most malevolent. Many academics have characterized such acts to be instigated by a postcolonial shift away from Western colonizing influences (Awwad, 2010; Haddad, 2016). The argument here is not to suggest that eliminating Western influence is to persecute MSM, but rather to argue that transgressions in this global region directly affect the identity negotiation of gay men. This identity negotiation involves both western ideals of gay culture and the construction and maintenance of same sex desire in the Middle East. Specifically, this chapter investigates how Western media influences a gay identity in MSM who fled Iraq, Iran, Syria, Lebanon, and Saudi Arabia to seek asylum in the United States. Employing a lens of social identity as conceptualized by Jenkins (1994, 2014), interviews with eight self-identifying gay men are utilized to answer this research question.

Jenkins (1994) conceptualizes identity as an interdependent process of highlighting similarities and differences between individuals and social groups that he refers to as the internal and external moments of the dialectic of identification. Individuals continuously negotiate their social identity through identification (internally how individuals identify themselves) and categorization (how external others identify them). This chapter first explores the influence of the West on gay identities in the Middle East, focusing specifically on Western media. It then outlines the theoretical tenets of social identity and uses the theory as a schema to examine the lived experiences of MSM from regions in the Middle East. Although the men recount their personal narratives before they sought refuge in the United States, their lived experiences help contextualize the role of Western media in gay identity formation and asylum seeking.

Western Influence and Gay Identity

There are three kinds of general primary identities that are acquired at birth—blood, place, and religion—forming a broad category of identity existing as allegiance to a respective ruler (Lewis, 1998). This allegiance may evolve through annexation, transfer of power, migration, or naturalization. Historically in the Middle East, these two identities—"the involuntary identity of birth and the compulsory identity of the state" (Lewis, 1998, p. 7)—were the only two that existed. Due to modernity, a new type of identity is evolving between the two because of a Western influence. This third identity is rooted in time and space but is malleable and modifies with social interactions—both physical and mediated. Some scholars have directly credited the Western influence on this modernized identity for fostering a homosexual or gay identity in the Middle East (Altman, 2002; Massad, 2002). They argue persecution is due to the global discourse produced by human rights advocates; therefore, a gay identity in the Middle East is a product of globalization (Altman, 2002). Western media provides the lexicon and perspective for those individuals in non-Western regions to vocalize their sexual identities.

Massad (2002) refers to this globalized product as the "gay international," which fosters a discourse that "both produces homosexuals, as well as gays and lesbians, where they do not exist, and represses same-sex desires and practices that refuse to be assimilated into its sexual epistemology" (p. 363). Arguably, this Westernized identity forces many Middle Eastern men who engage in same-sex intimacy into coming out and identifying as gay. It generates attention in the eyes of the state and "self-inflicts persecution" (p. 363). Universal categories of gay cannot be ascribed to global communities, making gay men one monolithic group. Scholars and global communities alike should consider temporal, spatial, and cultural differences.

Although this chapter focuses on countries within the Middle East, it is important to note that Western influence on a gay identity is not limited to this region. Altman (1996) has observed global queering in what he has coined a "global gay"—"internalization of a certain form of social and cultural identity based upon homosexuality"—in Asian and other non-Western societies derived from American fashion and intellectual style (p. 77). His concept has been challenged as anecdotal due to a lack of empirical studies demonstrating changes in social organization, political systems, and economics (Jackson, 2001), all of which have created gay spaces in non-Western countries.

Evidence of global queering exists, in fact, in many spaces around the globe. Lionel Cantú's (2009) study on Mexican men found the absence of a "gay" or "homosexual" identity. The words used by Mexicans were *activo* (top) and *pasivo* (bottom). In Mexican culture, focus is not placed on the concept of homosexuality itself, but rather the position an individual performs in sexual intercourse. The receiving partner is stigmatized as effeminate and less than a man. A new term, *internacional* (international), had been used within the early 2000s to identify a man who was versatile, both the insertive and receptive partner. The term *internacional* highlights foreign cultural influence, specifically from the United States.

The stigmatization of the receptive partner also occurs in Cuba (Peña, 2007), Nicaragua (Lancaster, 1999), and several Arab and Islamic countries (Massad, 2002; Roscoe, 1997). Specific to the Middle East, sexuality is reduced to the role a man performs in sexual intimacy (Murray, 1997). The role of the top is seen as dominant, whereas the role of the bottom is seen as submissive and reserved for women. Although there are many historical accounts of men engaging in same-sex intimacy, the activity was not considered a long-term sexual identity (Najmabadi, 2005), but rather a phase in life—particularly during adolescent years (Labi, 2007).

As of December 2018, same-sex intimacy is punishable by law in 74 countries (Stewart, 2018). The highest concentration of countries with such laws are in the Middle East and North African (MENA) region, where harsh sanctions—including imprisonment, fines, forced psychiatric treatment, physical abuse, and death—are imposed (Asal & Sommer, 2016; Rodriguez, 2016). Specific sanctions vary by country and are determined by local forms of legal, political, moral, and religious codes or conventions (Fortier, 2002).

Western Media and the Middle East

Research on the penetration of Western media in the Middle East has primarily focused on "the unique sociocultural and political context" of the region, juxtaposing the intricate relationship of local media and government with regional and international media (Mellor, 2013, p. 202). The earliest of these transnational studies focused primarily on Western media influences on Arabic-speaking audiences (Abdel-Rahman, 1985). Since then, there has been a shift to research how audiences react to Middle Eastern–produced media as well (Mellor, 2013).

It has been argued that communication research in Middle Eastern countries has primarily centered on a "technological determinism that has focused on the impact of news over entertainment" (Armbrust, 2012,

p. 48). However, entertainment media, music, and pop culture are just as penetrating and ubiquitous in most Middle Eastern countries (Hafez, 2013). Previous research has demonstrated that Middle Eastern audiences who consumed satellite television programs from the West or Westernized Middle Eastern–produced shows had more favorable views about the West, whereas those who consumed terrestrial media with traditional programming held more traditional gendered views (Al-Shaqsi, 2002).

This media effect can also be attributed to distrust among some Middle Eastern audiences toward government-controlled media. Mellor (2013) argues that propaganda has been inserted into regional media since its inception, causing a sentiment of distrust. He credits this to the war in the Middle East in the early '90s when a radio station, *Voice of the Arabs*, was discovered to be spreading misinformation about the Gulf War. Audiences turned to the BBC for a different perspective. More recently, there has been a split between local and Western news media outlets preferred among Middle Easterners in both their native countries and in diasporas in the West.

For those who identify with, or are questioning, a gay identity, trust may be placed in foreign media where a sense of acceptance in the West is fostered, aiding in the construction of identities. Gay migrants use media to inform themselves on more accepting global areas, visualizing the West as a gay sanctuary (Puar, 2002, 2008). Media also allow for the dissemination of global gay content (Rodriguez, 2016) and the ability for immigrants living abroad in diasporic communities to remain in contact with people and issues in their home country (Papaioanou & Olivos, 2013). The Internet creates a novel and efficient way to navigate "cultural, racial, and class differences as well as physical space" (Manalansan, 2006, p. 234).

The Internet also gives way to a sexual migration of sorts (Carillo, 2004) by providing a platform from which individuals can browse global websites with gay content and, arguably, recruiting gay migrants (Wesling, 2008). The Internet, specifically, gives these individuals access to a life outside their homeland and allows them a lens of sexual desire and pleasure (Manalansan, 2006), often adding tension between tradition and modernity. The sexual migration process is in contrast to a standardizing process where migrants move for economic opportunity, the intentions of heterosexual reproduction, or safety.

Although globalization and communication technology have positioned global citizens to engage in addressing injustices and disseminating information, there are still issues of access and safety. Not everyone is connected, but everyone is affected, and in fact, those without value to the network or without access are disconnected (Castells, 2010). This disconnection, of course, occurs in differing degrees depending on geographic location, social economic status, and regulations among others. Restrictions are placed on Internet usage and content by government bodies.

There is also a danger in using digital media in some areas of the world. The media in Middle Eastern countries, particularly, are closely scrutinized and controlled by governments, either by overt communication laws or through direct ownership (Warf & Vincent, 2007).

For some, however, the opportunity for identity formation and asylum seeking far outweigh the scrutiny and dangers of the Internet, as well as other forms of media. Individuals living in the Middle East, specifically, have limited locally mediated spaces to explore their same-sex desires. Thus, Western media provide a situation for identity construction and maintenance that is not afforded to them in mediated or physical spaces by providing contextual information on gay identities and social interaction with other LGBTI-identifying people (Manalansan, 2006; Puar, 2002, 2008; Wesling, 2008).

Social Identity

Identity negotiation simultaneously involves both individual and social factors (Jenkins, 1994; 2014). Jenkins (2014) contends that globalization has made individuals conscious of living in a global, rather than a local, context and positions three main corollaries of globalization in relation to identity: (1) globalization has made society more diverse; (2) globalization encourages greater homogeneity; and (3) globalization has made it likely that more individuals will routinely confront others with dissimilar ways of doing things. The current study examines how global communication influences identity negotiation in a localized social space of pre-asylum life.

In order to better understand social identity, we must first conceptualize "identity." At its most fundamental, identity is "the human capacity—rooted in language—to know 'who's who' (and hence 'what's what')" (Jenkins, 2014, p. 5). Identity is a symbolic representation of the self. All human identities are social identities; identifying ourselves and others is a matter of meaning and meaning always involves interaction (Jenkins, 2014).

Identity is better understood not as an object but rather as a process, termed identification—"the specification of what things are and what they are not, entailing at the same time some specification of their properties" (Jenkins, 2000, p. 7). Identification can occur between individuals, between collectivities, and between individuals and collectivities. It is directly linked to a contextual classification of self and others that is both interactional and social, and serves as "the basic cognitive mechanism that humans use to sort out themselves and their fellows, individually and collectively" (Jenkins, 2014, p. 13). Two interdependent processes are necessary for classification and identification: similarities and differences.

The condition of similarities and differences corresponds to what Jenkins (1994) calls the internal and external moments of the dialectic of identification. A constant back-and-forth exists between how individuals identify themselves (internal process of identification) and how others identify them (external process of categorization), resulting in social identity. Both group identification and categorization are interdependent, and individuals are subjected to both processes. For gay refugees, this means that each is subject to an internal identification process of themselves juxtaposed with an external categorization process by others. This social identification process is always in flux and, most importantly, contextual. Individuals have a self-image, as well as a social/public image that they reconcile and internalize.

The gay men interviewed were socialized in the Middle East and were exposed to local, regional, transnational, and global media in their respective native countries. As mentioned earlier, the practice of same-sex intimacy has always been performed in this region of the world; however, the concepts of gay or homosexual as categories of identity were not indigenous to the Middle East (Najmabadi, 2005; Massad, 2002). It is important to examine how various forms of media, as well as mediated platforms, influence how these gay males identify—or not—with these categories. How do gay refugees/asylum seekers use communication, both mediated and interpersonal, to negotiate their identity pre-asylum? Where do mediated and interpersonal communication interact, and where do they diverge, in the process of identity negotiation?

Methodology

A purposive sample of gay refugees/asylum seekers was gathered using snowball sampling, taking advantage of the social networks of those gay refugees and asylum seekers that could be identified through recruiting methods such as emails and public posts. They, in turn, provided escalating leads to potential participants. As a result, the subsequent sample comprised six Middle Eastern gay males (see Table 2.1).

While unstructured interviews were utilized to collect data, a list of questions was referenced to guide the process. This combination of techniques

Table 2.1 LGBTI Refugees/Asylees Interviewed

Name	Native Country	Asylum Status
Ibrahim	Iraq	Applied
Mahdi	Iran	Granted
Reza	Iran	Granted
Marwan	Syria	Granted
Nassim	Lebanon	Granted
Atif	Saudi Arabia	Applied

Note: N = 6. Each individual consented to being recorded. Pseudonyms were assigned to maintain anonymity.

allowed for probing and follow-up questions while still maintaining an organic and extemporaneous flow of the interview (Denzin & Lincoln, 2017). Each interview, conducted face-to-face in English, lasted approximately one hour. The interviews were recorded on an audio recorder and pseudonyms were assigned.

The audio was transcribed and a textual analysis was performed employing open, inductive coding that followed Owen's (1984) qualitative method guidelines for distinguishing themes: repetition, recurrence, and forcefulness. Repetition is defined as the reiteration of the same authentic words, phrases, or sentences within and across the transcribed discourse; recurrence as the reiteration of similar ideas or underlying meanings in the transcribed discourse; and forcefulness as vocal inflection, shifts in volume, or deliberate pauses which serve to emphasize any of the aforementioned communication in the transcriptions (Hotta & Ting-Toomey, 2013). Member checks were then performed with the six interviewees, where the men were asked to review the interpretation of the data retrieved from his respective interview.

Results and Discussion

The analysis revealed themes of gay categorization, traditional media's reification of homophobia, Internet and social media use, and asylum.

Gay Categorization

In the Middle East, there has long been a practice of men having sex with other men, although not viewed as an orientation or identity (Labi, 2007; Najmabadi, 2005). Reza, a refugee from Iran who now lives in California, served as the informant for the study and a participant. His internalization of what it meant to be gay was something he struggled with for a long time and, ultimately, something he negotiated between Western and traditional Iranian categorizations:

> I was always accused of being westernized, even when I was trying to accept myself. I was not trying to say, "this gay lifestyle is from the western tradition and I want to get married and then have tons of sexual relationship with boys." That's what they think, this is gay life to them, there . . . not all. There are lots of people who want to live their lives like normally. They want to accept their self, celebrate their sexuality.

Reza's commentary resonates Western influence. Some individuals living in his home country of Iran do not identify as gay. Their nationality, culture, and religion may be more salient for them. The men still engage in same-sex intimacy in secret, but do not consider it to be a facet of their overall identity. Massad (2002) argues this Western-imposed identity has brought about attention, and thus harassment, to individuals practicing same-sex intimacy.

One participant explored his sexuality in secret while living in Dubai. Ibrahim's life changed after his first sexual experience with an American visitor: "After that I started hooking up normally, regularly. In Dubai they have nightclubs, underground nightclubs, gay nightclubs. Mostly men, of course gay men." Ibrahim's experience, however, differed from others interviewed. Most utilized media to investigate their internal feelings of same-sex desires, although they never acted on those desires in their homeland. The fear of repercussions from being categorized as gay was enough to dissuade any physical actions.

There are not many positive words for homosexuals in the Middle East. In Nassim's native country of Lebanon, "Gay is like a good word, but they say, fag—that's a fag." Reza added that in Iran,

> There are so many slang, which all of them are offensive or very negative. Fag, that's the word that most of people use . . . if you talk, nobody say, oh, you're homosexual. They will say you are faggot or kuni.

Mahdi, also from Iran, stated:

> Because there are a lot of conflicts—like religious conflicts, cultural conflicts, and traditionally this was not something acceptable—the terms that have been used traditionally are all negative and pejorative. Actually, it's interesting because in Iran the official media is actually moving away from the really pejorative terms to nicer terms to refer to these people, although there the officials still use the pejorative terms.

Faris and Rahimi (2015) noted a recent trend of Iranians crafting new words in the Farsi language such as "degarbashan jensi (queer), hamjans garaa (a positive reference to homosexuality as a viable sexual orientation), and degarbash setizi (homophobia)" in order to better localize and communicate the Iranian LGBTI experience (p. 68).

Derogatory terms are still widely used in the native countries of the interviewees. These pejorative conceptualizations of gay often have a harmful effect on gay men growing up in the Middle East because of their emotional and psychological repercussions. Marwan recounts how he came to terms with being gay:

> When I was introduced to my sexuality, back then I always knew myself as a pervert because this the language they use and mostly when they translate, let's say a western movie with the mention of the word gay, they always use "abnormal" when they translate it to

Arabic. I never knew it as me, gay . . . and then the Internet came and Wikipedia explained the whole concept of homosexuality, and gayness and things. And gay, like a word does not exist. You don't use it and speak it out loud. If you say gay, whisper it!

Because there is not a positive Arabic or Farsi equivalent for the word gay, people simply use the English word gay.

Mahdi explained that "Gay is very common among people who are more educated maybe or more in touch with the media." Pre-conceptualized Western frameworks are often imported and localized in order to negotiate an understanding of homosexuality (Korycki & Nasirzadeh, 2014).

This reoccurring theme of not having a native word for gay is important to note. The interviewees clearly expressed having a gay identity but not having a way in which to express it. They turned to Westernized concepts in order to shape meaning around their sexuality. It was through mediated interactions that the gay men were able to internalize a categorization of gay that was more in line with how they felt. The word had different connotations depending on context; it was contingent upon the speaker and the receiver.

Another interesting observation was the presence of patriarchal gender roles. The interviewees were socialized within a greater heteronormative system in their respective home countries. Gay men still value as well as regulate masculinity among other gay males, a process referred to as "mascing" (Rodriguez, Huemmer, & Blumer, 2016). Nassim explained:

Actually, men have to be men. If I'm gay, it means like I'm a man but I'm gay. I like gays, but I like masculine gays. If someone is feminine, he's not mine. I can be friends with him or whatever, but like for me, sexually—no. I have to be with a man. That's it, or I can go sleep with a girl, maybe.

Nassim demonstrates the way he both categorizes and internalizes how a male should act, which is hegemonic in nature. Hegemonic masculinity can be viewed as a socially constructed pattern of masculine performances characterized by dominance, sexual prowess, strength, and aggressiveness (among others), which works to create a hierarchy of power that subordinates women and effeminate men (Connell, 1995; Rodriguez et al., 2016). External categorizations and internal identification are not mutually exclusive; they influence one another in the social identity process (Jenkins, 2014). Nassim also identified the consequences for not behaving appropriately within his social context. Punishment in his home country of Lebanon is self-inflicted by gay men "acting gay":

Sometimes we, the gays, make fun of them because they're not supposed to do that, because they got hit or someone will spit on them.

> You have to do that at home because you're in a country that it's illegal to do that.

Marwan provided a similar comment: "Because if you're a man you should represent the society in a certain way and you should not cross the line of gender role. So, you should always look masculine and stuff like that." In Nassim and Marwan's respective countries, as in many other Middle Eastern countries, there are different categorizations for gender. Each category has its own expectations of appropriate behavior and interaction (Jenkins, 2014). If an individual does not act according to his/her gender categorization, they are othered and sanctioned.

Traditional Media's Reification of Homophobia

The government still controls a majority of the traditional media in Middle Eastern countries (Warf & Vincent, 2007) and homophobia is reinforced within it (HRW, 1999). Marwan provides an example from his native country of Syria:

> Since the satellites came in there were people more exposed to the thing, they started to tell the Sodom and Gomorrah story. It's the same in the Quran but in a more violent way. They'd call us sodomites and other pervert names. Then TV started to introduce, after the unrest in 2012 and 13, gay characters—but the gay characters only came through effeminate boys. There were no real representations of what is gay, or how complicated is the character. It was only effeminate boys who's looking for sex, or they were infected with HIV and they were dying.

In a similar fashion, Reza said he mainly used television and radio as a way to entertain himself. The government regulates the traditional media in Iran and most of the programming was, and still is, Islamic-based. He recounted watching satellite channels from Turkey, Europe, and the United States as a source of information for both gay understanding and Western concepts:

> All of my family, we know English, we are watching these TV channels. I don't remember from when, but I know the word gay and everybody knows. I mean almost everybody in Asia they know the word of gay also. And then also this things that you are watching like Ricky Martin, Elton John, we were all teenagers and they will say, "You know, Ricky Martin is gay" or something like that and laugh at him.

Reza's account highlights how gay men were ridiculed in social settings. Reza was laughing with his cousins about gay celebrities, but secretly watching gay content on European satellite channels: "I remember I was curious. So, I found the TV channel, I think it was called Pink TV. So that was just like a gay channel, TV channel, for French people. And there was one from Italy just was gay TV." Reza's commentary points to the diversification of traditional media, something that is often, and incorrectly, credited solely to digital media.

Mahdi, also from Iran, never perceived the programing as Western because the shows he was exposed to were broadcast on Iranian television with Iranian actors:

> It was never portrayed as something Western because it always included information about people in Iran. Because this is the Farsi Service, all the people who are involved are Iranian, actually. They're either Iranian-Americans or just ones who moved here [US]. So, when you watch those programs, you rarely get the stance that they are promoting a Western culture, although the government and the official media in Iran might try to impose on people that this is Western-fed. I never got that feeling.

Mahdi's assessment of news programs, however, was not the same as entertainment programming:

> The media just exaggerates old pieces of news, just trying to portray it as something negative. It's like, "Oh, that country just ratified gay marriage." They don't promote it, but they just include it in the news as to condemn the Western culture. But you still, when you're gay, you just connected to that and say, "Hey, well it's legal in that country whether my own government accepts it or not." You know that it's happening somewhere else.

Mahdi's comment supports Armbrust's (2012) argument that technological determinism has encouraged academics to focus on news over entertainment in the Middle East. Although there is value in both news and entertainment, Mahdi highlights that news coverage directly addresses the gay issues that are most salient in the West, encouraging them to also be significant in non-Western countries. Mahdi also points out that no matter how the news media frame the story, the information is still processed at an individual level and gay men make note of areas where being gay is acceptable. Media helped them identify more accepting locations to flee (Puar, 2008).

Social Media and Internet

Being gay was not portrayed in positive terms through local traditional media in a majority of the interviewees' respective Middle Eastern countries. Most turned to the Internet and social media to find information on gay concepts. Mahdi used the Internet to look up definitions, practices, and further investigate his internal struggles with his sexuality:

> We still didn't have Internet access at home, but I went to school, we had Internet access there. At that time, there were no filters or anything and I was so excited. So, one of the things that I did was to run a search on Iran and homosexual, because I already knew the term. There was this whole lot of information on websites that Iranian and gay Iranians, who were living outside of Iran, had put together. So that was my first exposure to the term, and that was actually the first time that I realized there are people like this living abroad and they have a life.

Mahdi's commentary demonstrates the exact moment when he first encountered a different type of categorization for homosexuals. This categorization was more in line with how he identified himself, so he gravitated toward media that helped strengthen his gay identity. External categorizations that are more or less the same as an existing group identity will generally reinforce each other (Jenkins, 1994).

Ibrahim did not have an Arabic word to describe his internal attraction to other men. "Just, I knew that I liked men, I didn't have any kind of word. I called it sometimes my big secret." Ibrahim used the Internet to watch pornography, not only satisfy his sexual arousal, but to also learn more about being gay. It was a process of observation, symbolism, and imagination. He soon realized that there was more to gay culture than just sex:

> I watched porno, yeah, pornography, but I did not know that there was actually a whole community there. I just knew it was just sexual, that's it. If I knew there was a gay community I would definitely be more attracted to there, but I did not grow up with that. I did not realize that that actually exists. So, it was late, like in my 20s, I figured it out.

Ibrahim stated that the Internet was censored and most of the pornographic sites were blocked. "I used to get a VPN, bypass the whole block thing. I used to download pictures, movies, whatever it is." Aside from pornography, Ibrahim also began to explore gay websites and online chatrooms. Websites can foster a sense of safety and community for gays living in areas of the world that are less tolerant of their sexuality (Kuntsman, 2007). Ibrahim used the Internet to communicate with other gay men:

> I downloaded an application or program on my laptop called *Paltalk*. It contains rooms from all over, and more specifically in the Middle

East. There was the gay and lesbians' rooms in the Middle East and in the gulf region. So, I found a room of 500 men just [chuckles] flashing their thing on cams and looking for other men to fuck with them. This was like heaven just opens right in front of me.

He also named another website, *ManJam*, as a popular site where Middle Eastern men would chat, exchange pictures, and arrange sexual encounters. Men in Iraq and the United Arab Emirates messaged him more than any others. Ibrahim had once been tricked online and forced to attempt sex with a prostitute and recounted the risks of real-world contact:

> This is very risky and there are people who have profiles telling you to be aware, don't just go to that person—not before seeing his picture, before talking to him on the phone—you have to have several issues and several things to do before you actually go to that person and talk to them.

Surveillance by regimes of power, most often governments, is an important identity issue for gay men in regards to their security (Warf & Vincent, 2007). Reza was also cautious with his Internet use:

> In high school, still I was very scared, because I know, "Okay, the government is tracking which website I'm visiting." Usually they block or filter those websites, but some of them are open so I could go. But I was very nervous, I was scared. "Oh my god, now police will come and arrest me because they know I watched these gay websites."

Like Ibrahim, Reza used virtual private networks (VPNs) as he became more experienced with the Internet. He was then able to access Facebook and YouTube and search the Internet with less fear of being caught. This aligns with the research of Papaioannou and Olivos (2013), who found that Libyans also used Facebook to bypass government regulations and censorship. Nassim used the Internet to search for gay-friendly areas in cities he planned to visit:

> Because I'm a hair stylist I used to travel to Italy, to Spain, to London. Before I go there, I search for the gay places and the gay community where they are and I go . . . even my friends told me about that too, but I looked for my own search. I looked at Australia mostly. They put lots of advertisements and I think there are lots of magazines out there online and they advertise themselves as a country where they celebrate equality. I felt like, "Yeah, that could be a place for me because of all this media that I'm reading and all this equality thing."

In agreement with Puar's research (1994), Nassim used media to find places in other countries that were more accepting of him. Although his peers made suggestions, his concern for safety led him to conduct his own research and trust the media rather than his friends. Like Nassim, Marwan used his home Internet connection in Syria to search for global regions that were more accepting of gays. He was, however, looking for permanent places to make a new life, not just visit.

English and Computer Literacy

One of the main catalysts for Internet and social media use was English literacy. Mahdi started taking private lessons at age 6 and learned English before he learned Farsi. This not only gave him an advantage in school, but also aided in his personal inquiries online. Mahdi, like most of the refugees interviewed, came to terms with his sexuality through Western terms and concepts: "I didn't know until I was 18, the term itself. I knew English, so I knew the technical term, which was homosexual. But I had no idea that there is a term called gay." Like Mahdi, Reza started learning English at an early age in Iran:

> I started learning when I was six or seven years old because we had some relatives that's like me. They came to US many years ago as a student and then they went back. So, then my parents asked them to teach us English. They said, "Oh, you have to go to western countries for your education."

For him, it was something his family instilled as requisite for a well-educated individual. Marwan's experiences in Syria were similar. His English skills and computer literacy helped him better understand being gay and internalize his desires:

> I was always in search for things that would accept me, so Arabic was not the best language to express myself, my sexuality, so I escaped to English and I started to learn it from a young age. I studied English translation too, so that helped me more to understand the culture and understand these articles—or the books. And I started with Wikipedia, so I understand sexuality more, and gender expression, and gender orientation, and stuff.

It is important to note that the Internet is not easily accessible to everyone. Marwan explained that the Internet penetrated Syria in 1998 and was utilized mainly by business professionals and others who were permitted, "They could be given permission by the secret police in Syria, or the government itself, because they need to monitor you and everything that you do, so it was not available for everybody." There was also the additional matter of cost, "It was so expensive. I think if we compare to dollars, or convert to dollars it's something—for a 265 kilobytes connection for DSL, it was more than $200 of comparing with the income and the country's conversion rate." Marwan stated that DSL was introduced in the capital city in 2005 and then it slowly spread to other provinces. Reza's province received DSL in 2006. Cost and access continue to be issues that most individuals, not just gays, face globally.

Conclusion

The above accounts are indicative of Western media influence on identity negotiation in the Middle East, particularly in the gay community. The men's primary identities, which are directly shaped by primary socialization between the gay men and authoritative figures during their formative years, are deeply rooted in the men's first encounters within a social world (Jenkins, 1994). They are "robust and resist easy change or manipulation" (Jenkins, 2000, p. 14). Pejorative categorizations of gay men are manifested in national laws and governmental organizations, policed by community members, and reified in local media, which is controlled by regimes of power. The pejorative meanings are depicted as normative, internalized by the men, and used in the identification process. Primary identity provides the foundational identity from which one negotiates further identities in relation to future interactions, specifically in secondary socialization (Jenkins, 2000).

Western media introduced new categorizations of gay during the men's secondary socialization, before the commencement of social adulthood (Jenkins, 2000). It was during this period of secondary socialization in their adolescence that they began to utilize media in an effort to explore their same-sex desires. Whether it was within their established institutions of education or informally among peers, the gay men were introduced to digital spaces—Internet and social media—that allowed them to interact with content and other individuals, providing counter narratives of categorization to those they previously encountered. The new Western categorizations were internalized and, through a process of identification, were exercised in shaping their identity.

International media—specifically Western media—still has an enormous amount of influence on how individuals in non-Western regions of the world think about gay issues. Western entertainment media, broadcast via satellite or online, inform audiences in Iraq, Iran, Lebanon, Saudi Arabia, and Syria on gay culture. International news, no matter how the content is framed, can make gay issues salient for those individuals in global regions where being gay is relegated to negative and pejorative categorizations.

Although gay is a social identity category, it is not uniform. It is contextual and dependent upon social interactions within cultural, temporal, and spatial circumstances. Mediated platforms were able to provide alternative categorizations of identifying as gay, but only for those who knew English and were computer literate. All of the interviewees indicated that they learned English in their early, formative years. This gave the gay men an advantage of information and pleasure seeking, as well as the ability to directly communicate with Western gays. This elevated status directly influenced the formation of gay identities. Status intrinsically brings with it questions of equity and access. Although all individuals are affected, only those with higher status are connected (Castells, 2010).

Examining a marginalized population, such as gay refugees, highlights the role mediated and interpersonal communication play in researching, finding, and ultimately adopting gay identities in MSM who fled Iraq, Iran, Syria, Lebanon, and Saudi Arabia. The fact that these men identified as gay and rejected the negative, and consequential, categorizations in their homeland underscores the salience and importance of a gay social identity. The interviewees purposely fled their respective countries to seek asylum in spaces where they felt categories were more in line with their same-sex desires and feelings.

Gay refugees, as a population, are extremely marginalized and difficult to access. Those willing to speak about their experiences, however, provided extensive, nuanced, and vital information on media consumption, identity negotiation, and asylum seeking. Previous research has emphasized religion's role in anti-gay attitudes and behaviors found in some Islamic countries in the Middle East (Asal & Sommer, 2016; Fortier, 2002; Jaspal, 2016; Labi, 2007; Mohammadi, 2018). Although questioned about the intersection of religion and media, and its impact on their sexuality, the interviewees did not devote very much time or attention to the matter. All of the men mentioned conservative interpretations of the Quran have been used to condemn same-sex intimacy in their native homelands and expressed their fear that others have used, and continue to use, the religious text to justify violence against gays.

The intent of this chapter was not to portray a dichotomy of positive and negative in relation to a gay-friendly West versus a homophobic Middle East, nor is it to generalize a monolithic identity among MSM in the entire Middle East. Rather, the study highlights the collective awareness and identity uncovered through the lived experiences of MSM who were born and raised in several countries in the Middle East affected by Western media and communication.

References

Abdel-Rahman, A. (1985). *The issue of developmental media in the Arab world.* Cairo, Egypt: Dar Al Fikr.

Al-Shaqsi, O. S. (2002, July). *Cultivation analysis: A Middle Eastern perspective.* International Association for Media and Communication Research, the 23rd Conference and General Assembly, Barcelona (pp. 21–26).

Altman, D. (1996). Rupture or continuity? The internationalization of gay identities. *Social Text, 48*(1), 77–94.

Altman, D. (2002). Globalization and the international gay/lesbian movement. In D. Richardson & S. Seidman (Eds.), *Handbook of lesbian and gay studies* (pp. 415–425). Thousand Oaks, CA: Sage Publications.

Armbrust, W. (2012). History in Arab media studies: A speculative cultural history. In T. Sabry (Ed.), *Arab cultural studies: Mapping the field* (pp. 32–54). London, UK: I. B. Tauris.

Asal, V., & Sommer, U. (2016). Sodomy law in comparative perspective. *The Wiley Blackwell Encyclopedia of Gender and Sexuality Studies.* doi:10.1002/9781118663219.wbegss378

Awwad, J. (2010). The postcolonial predicament of gay rights in the queen boat affair. *Communication & Critical/Cultural Studies, 7*(3), 318–336. doi:10.1080/14791420.2010.504598

Cantú, L. (2009). *The sexuality of migration: Border crossings and Mexican immigrant men.* New York, NY: NYU Press.

Carillo, H. (2004). Sexual migration, cross-cultural sexual encounters, and sexual health. *Sexuality Research and Social Policy, 1*(3), 58–70.

Castells, M. (2010). The new public sphere: Global civil society, communication networks, and global governance. In D. K. Thussu (Ed.), *International communication: A reader* (pp. 36–47). New York, NY: Routledge.

Charlton, C. (2017, Mar 29). Executed for being gay: ISIS barbarians throw gay man off roof and pelt his corpse with rocks in public execution. *The Sun.* Retrieved from www.thesun.co.uk/news/3203292/isis-gay-execution-throw-man-roof/

Connell, R. W. (1995). *Masculinities: Knowledge, power and social change.* Berkeley, CA: University of California Press.

Denzin, N. K., & Lincoln, Y. S. (2017). *The Sage handbook of qualitative research* (5th ed.). Thousand Oaks, CA: Sage Publications.

Faris, D. M., & Rahimi, B. (Eds.). (2015). *Social media in Iran: Politics and society after 2009.* Albany, NY: SUNY Press.

Fortier, A. M. (2002). Queer diaspora. In D. Richardson & S. Seidman (Eds.), *Handbook of lesbian and gay studies* (183–197). Thousand Oaks, CA: Sage Publications.

Haddad, S. (2016, April, 1). The myth of the queer Arab life. *The Daily Beast.* Retrieved from www.thedailybeast.com/articles/2016/04/02/the-myth-of-the-queer-arab-life.html?via=desktop&source=twitter

Hafez, K. (2013). The methodology trap: Why media and communication studies are not really international. *Communications: The European Journal of Communication Research, 38*(3), 323–329.

Hotta, J., & Ting-Toomey, S. (2013). Intercultural adjustment and friendship dialectics in international students: A qualitative study. *International Journal of Intercultural Relations, 37*(5), 550–566.

HRW. (1999). The internet in the Mideast and North Africa: Free expression and censorship. *Human Rights Watch, New York.* Retrieved from www.hrw.org/sites/default/files/reports/midintnt996.PDF

Jackson, P. A. (2001). Pre-gay, post-queer: Thai perspectives on proliferating gender/sex diversity in Asia. *Journal of Homosexuality, 40*(3–4), 1–25.

Jaspal, R. (2016). Islam and homosexuality. *The Wiley Blackwell Encyclopedia of Gender and Sexuality Studies.* doi:10.1002/9781118663219.wbegss543

Jenkins, R. (1994). Rethinking ethnicity: Identity, categorization and power. *Ethnic and Racial Studies, 17*(2), 197–223.

Jenkins, R. (2000). Categorization: Identity, social process and epistemology. *Current Sociology, 48*(3), 7–25.

Jenkins, R. (2014). *Social identity* (4th ed.). New York, NY: Routledge.

Korycki, K., & Nasirzadeh, A. (2014). Desire recast: The production of gay identity in Iran. *Journal of Gender Studies, 25*(1), 1–16.

Kuntsman, A. (2007). Belonging through violence: Flaming, erasure, and performativity in queer migrant community. In K. O'Riordan & D. J. Phillips (Eds.), *Queer online: Media technology and sexuality* (pp. 101–120). New York, NY: Peter Lang.

Labi, N. (2007, May). The kingdom in the closet. *The Atlantic.* Retrieved from www.theatlantic.com/magazine/archive/2007/05/the-kingdom-in-the-closet/305774/

Lancaster, R. (1999). That we should all turn queer?": Homosexual stigma in the making of manhood and the breaking of a revolution in Nicaragua. In R. Parker & P. Aggleton (Eds.), *Culture, society and sexuality: A reader* (pp. 97–115). London, UK: UCL Press.

Lewis, B. (1998). *The multiple identities of the Middle East.* New York, NY: Schocken.

Manalansan, M. F. (2006). Queer intersections: Sexuality and gender in migration studies. *International Migration Review, 40*(1), 224–249.

Massad, J. (2002). Re-orienting desire: The gay international and the Arab world. *Public Culture, 14*(2), 361–385.

Mellor, N. (2013). Countering cultural hegemony: Audience research in the Arab world. *Journal of Arab & Muslim Media Research, 6*(2/3), 201–216. doi:10.1386/jammr.6.2–3.201_1

Mohammadi, N. (2018). Life experiences of sexual minorities in Iran: Limitations, adaptations and challenges. *Quality & Quantity, 52*(2), 719–737. doi:10.1007/s11135-017-0484-9

Murray, S. O. (1997). The will not to know: Islamic accommodations of male homosexuality. In W. Roscoe & S. O. Murray (Eds.), *Islamic homosexualities: Culture, history, and literature* (pp. 14–54). New York, NY: New York University Press.

Najmabadi, A. (2005). *Women with mustaches and men without beards: Gender and sexual anxieties of Iranian modernity.* Berkeley, CA: University of California Press.

Owen, W. F. (1984). Interpretive themes in relational communication. *Quarterly Journal of Speech, 70*(3), 274–287.

Papaioannou, T., & Olivos, H. E. (2013). Cultural identity and social media in the Arab Spring: Collective goals in the use of Facebook in the Libyan context. *Journal of Arab & Muslim Media Research, 6*(2/3), 99–114. doi:10.1386/jammr.6.2–3.99_1

Peña, S. (2007). "Obvious gays" and the state gaze: Cuban gay visibility and US immigration policy during the 1980 Mariel boatlift. *Journal of the History of Sexuality, 16*(3), 482–514.

Prince, S. (2015, August 14). Watch: ISIS throws 2 "gay men" off roof & stones them. *Heavy*. Retrieved from http://heavy.com/news/2015/08/new-isis-islamic-state-video-but-who-is-better-than-god-in-judgment-establishing-a-limit-upon-the-people-homs-syria-gay-homosexual-man-executed-executed-uncensored-full-youtube-video/

Puar, J. K. (1994). Writing my way "home," traveling South: Asian bodies and diasporic journeys. *Socialist Review*, 24(4), 75–108.

Puar, J. K. (2002). Queer tourism: Geographies of globalization. *GLQ: A Journal of Lesbian and Gay Studies*, 8(1/2), 1–6.

Puar, J. K. (2008). "The Turban is not a hat": Queer diaspora and practices of profiling. *Sikh Formations*, 4(1), 47–91.

Rodriguez, N. S. (2016). Communicating global inequalities: How LGBTI asylum-specific NGOs use social media as public relations. *Public Relations Review*, 42(2), 322–332. doi:10.1016/j.pubrev.2015.12.002

Rodriguez, N. S., Huemmer, J., & Blumer, L. E. (2016). Mobile masculinities: An investigation of networked masculinities in gay dating apps. *Masculinities and Social Change*, 5(3), 241–267. doi.org/10.17583/mcs.2016.2047.

Roscoe, W. (1997). Precursors of Islamic male homosexualities. In S. Murray & W. Roscoe (Eds.), *Islamic homosexualities: Culture, history, and literature*. New York, NY: NYU Press.

Stewart, C. (2018, December 12). 2019 goal: Eliminate two more countries' anti-gay laws. *Erasing 76*. Retrieved from https://76crimes.com/2018/12/12/eliminate-two-countries-anti-gay-laws/

Warf, B., & Vincent, P. (2007). Multiple geographies of the Arab Internet. *Area*, 39(1), 83–96.

Wesling, M. (2008). Why queer diaspora? *Feminist Review*, 90(1), 30–47.

Wyke, T. (2016, January 17). ISIS release horrific video showing bound man being hurled off the top of a building to his death after he was accused of being gay. *Daily Mail*. Retrieved from www.dailymail.co.uk/news/article-3403505/Horrific-moment-ISIS-throw-man-building-hands-feet-tied-accused-gay.html

3 "Serving Activist Realness"

The New Drag Superstars and Activism Under Trump

Renee Middlemost

Introduction

> Two queens stand before me. . . . This is your last chance to impress me, and save yourself. The time has come . . . for you to lip synch . . . FOR. YOUR. LEGACY!
>
> Good luck, and don't f!?k it up.
>
> (RuPaul, *RuPaul's Drag Race All Stars*)

Delivered at the climax of each episode, RuPaul's signature line is a timely reminder of the potential of drag activism in contemporary culture. In the era of Trump, it can be argued that *any* act of political resistance is a form of activism. This chapter will establish the success of *RuPaul's Drag Race* (2009–) in bringing drag culture into mainstream consciousness, and how this exposure might be utilized as a way to spark social change. The popularity of the program has been central to the elevation of contestants' profiles beyond their participation in the show. A case study of season 8 and 9 winners of *RuPaul's Drag Race* (*RPDR*), Bob the Drag Queen and Sasha Velour, examines how they have used their participation in the program, and subsequent victories, to position themselves as drag activists. While already enjoying successful drag careers in New York prior to their appearance on the program, both Bob the Drag Queen and Sasha Velour used their victories to declare their commitment to LGBTIQ[1] advocacy. By using satire to play with stereotyped gender roles, drag activists have historically used performance to gain media attention, organize, and call for change when the rights of LGBTIQ people are threatened. The role of local (national) identity is central to both Bob the Drag Queen's and Sasha Velour's creation of a dynamic fan community that can be mobilized around philanthropic causes. New York maintains a central role in the history of drag activism as a place where queer art and activist culture intersect and flourish. This chapter will review how drag performers use digital media to galvanize fans around causes of significance for the broader LGBTIQ community. Drag activism presents an opportunity for a new generation of performers to create and carry on the legacy of early

LGBTIQ activist pioneers, creating a community that is inclusive of difference, and less "f-ed up" for future generations.

Social Television, Social Media, and Activism

The movement of *RPDR* across platforms is indicative of the modern transmedia texts. Indeed, as Gudelunas (2017, pp. 231–232) has argued, audience engagement with the program has very little to do with the television medium; thus, fan engagement with the program across platforms such as Twitter and Instagram demonstrates the "unfolding consumption" (Hills, 2008, para. 19) of media texts. Research focused on social television has grown from academic studies evaluating the ability of digital media to facilitate communication across borders, and influence social change. Selva defines social television "as the social practice of commenting on television shows with peers, friends, and unknown people, who are all connected together through various digital devices" (2016, p. 160). Selva's empirical study found that social television engagement is seen by many audiences as an everyday part of active political participation: "the combination of television and social media enhances the whole experience of audiencehood and constitutes an innovative pathway to the constitution of publics, to political engagement, and to collective shared identity" (p. 169).

The role of social media in the creation and maintenance of celebrity is significant. Celebrities have been at the forefront of social media use not only for the promotion of their individual brand, but to promote causes that are meaningful to them. Both Bennett (2014), and Click, Lee, and Holladay (2017) have analyzed the connection nurtured by Lady Gaga with her fans via social media, and how this connection is cultivated by her use of confessional address (Redmond, 2008). Redmond (2008) states that "Stars and celebrities confess, and in so doing confirm their status as truthful, emotive, experiential beings who—as devotional fans—we can invest in" (p. 110). The use of confessional address allows fans to feel close to the celebrity, and resulting online fan communities can then be directed towards philanthropic causes that the celebrity favors (Bennett, 2014, pp. 138–152). Confessional address also adds to the perception of celebrity authenticity (or "realness," in drag terms) which is essential to their ability to gain, and communicate with fans in a meaningful fashion. As Marwick and Boyd (2011) contend of social media, celebrity, and the impression of authenticity is part of a continually unfolding "performative practice," which "involves presenting a seemingly authentic, intimate image of self while meeting fan expectations and maintaining important relationships" (p. 140).

The engagement between Bob the Drag Queen, Sasha Velour and their fans across multiple social media platforms, in addition to acting roles, production of online art, and guest columns for magazines, illustrates how modern drag performers can operate as both activists and transmedia authors. Bob the Drag Queen and Sasha Velour's online activity is informed by prior celebrity interventions which use social television exchanges as a starting point for political discourse. Ellcessor (2018) reinforces the substance of these exchanges, observing that "*connected celebrity activism* is a matter of ongoing, seemingly authentic, technologically-facilitated performances that forge connections between a celebrity's persona, projects, interactions, causes, and activist organizations" (original emphasis, p. 256). As the following sections demonstrate, social media is central to the ongoing success of *RPDR* and its alumni, particularly those who, like Bob the Drag Queen and Sasha Velour are undertaking connected celebrity activism. As O'Halloran (2017) suggests, political change can (and has) occurred both on and offscreen as a result of the grassroots conversations fostered among fan communities online.

'Herstory'—*RuPaul's Drag Race*

RPDR debuted in 2009 on the Logo TV Channel, the first network targeted toward the LGBTIQ community in the United States. While it is commonly categorized as reality television, *RPDR* is a hybrid of generic categories constructed around the whims of creator and host, RuPaul Charles. For over 30 years, RuPaul has performed across film, television, and music, and is the author of several books. RuPaul positions *RPDR* as a way to support new drag performers, as they compete to carry on her legacy as members of the "Drag Race Hall of Fame." On *RuPaul's Drag Race*, the queens refer to each other by their stage names, and feminine pronouns, both in and out of drag. I have followed this convention throughout this chapter, despite the noted problematic binary it presents (Gonzalez and Cavazos, 2016).

In each season, contestants compete for the title of "America's Next Drag Superstar"—the winner receives a cash prize ($100K in recent seasons, up from $20K in season 1); a bejewelled tiara and sceptre; a year's supply of cosmetics; a holiday; and a variety of other prizes from corporate sponsors. The opportunity to appear on *RPDR* is invaluable for drag performers, as the program has a devoted and active fan base both online and offline. Fan participation in online forums devoted to *RPDR* is a key feature of program's success as a transmedia product:

> From its first season, *RPDR* embraced digital extensions across various platforms including social media sites, elaborate experiential events that brought the casts of various seasons to multiple cities, and other sustained brand experiences that made RPDR about far more than just an hour-long reality television program.
>
> (Gudelunas, 2017, p. 232)

As a result of international television exposure, *RPDR* contestants experience enhanced opportunities to perform at home and abroad. Despite its progressive appearance, extensive criticism has been leveled at *RPDR* during its time on air. Vesey (2017) contends that contestants are predominantly tested for their potential to extend RuPaul's musical legacy due to the judge's preference for a prescribed "glamour drag" aesthetic, mandated as "a way to sell your records" (p. 597). Gonzalez and Cavazos (2016) also observe the tenuous balance that *RPDR* must negotiate, between "the normalization of drag queens and their lifestyles, [while] still perpetuating a heteronormativity that furthers the societal ideology at-large" (p. 664). Despite these critiques, the program has continued to expand its fan base and as I will argue, this currency can be leveraged by performers into support for their personal philanthropic causes.

Unlike most reality shows concluding their eleventh season, the program's following has increased each year, resulting in several spin off shows such as *RuPaul's Drag Race: Untucked, RuPaul's Drag Race: All Stars, RuPaul's Drag U,* and *Gay for Play Game Show Starring RuPaul. RPDR: Untucked* and *RPDR: All Stars* are straightforward paratexts based on the original series—focusing on the backstage drama between the queens, and a high stakes competition to reaffirm their status as "fan favorites," respectively. *RuPaul's Drag U* was a short-lived (2010–2012) series featuring previous contestants administering drag tips and life skills to women; and *Gay for Play Game Show Starring RuPaul* (2016–) as the title indicates, is a pop culture quiz game show, featuring both alumni of *RPDR* and celebrity guests. *RPDR: All Stars* in particular has increased the popularity of the main franchise, as fan favorites with devoted online followings return to the competition. Fans are enticed into believing there is an opportunity for past favorites to "right the wrongs" of their original season by winning *All Stars*. Indeed, *All Stars* champions, Chad Michaels (*All Stars* 1), Alaska Thunderfuck (*All Stars* 2), and Trixie Mattel (*All Stars* 3) were all widely tipped to win their original season, and maintained large fanbases after their initial elimination. In 2016, *RPDR* won its first Emmy Award for Best Reality Television Host, demonstrating the growing mainstream appeal of the program. In her acceptance speech, RuPaul revised her earlier derision of the honor, stating, "Earlier this year I was quoted saying I'd rather have an enema than an Emmy. But thanks to the Television Academy, I can have both!" (de Moraes, 2017, para. 4) In 2017, *RPDR* won three Emmys, including Best Host for RuPaul; and in 2018 RuPaul won for hosting at both the Critics' Choice Awards and the Emmys, in addition to Outstanding Reality Competition Series, Directing, Hair Styling, and Costume Emmy Awards. The recognition of *RPDR* at industry awards ceremonies demonstrates the acceptance of the series and its influence on mainstream media culture.

After broadcasting for eight seasons on the Logo TV Network, for season 9 (2017) *RPDR* moved to VH1. VH1 is an American cable television network owned by Viacom; originally aimed at an older demographic than sister channel MTV, VH1 has, in recent years, moved towards reality television programming. RuPaul had previously hosted a popular talk show on VH1, *The RuPaul Show*, from 1996 to 1998. The move to VH1 highlighted the changing nature of *RPDR* in relation to three key issues. First, *RPDR* is no longer confined to a niche LGBTIQ channel, enabling access to a much larger audience. Second, the move to VH1 is suggestive of *RPDR*'s move to cultivate greater mainstream appeal without addressing prior critiques centered around the casual use of transphobic language and the problematic representations of race and class (see Goldmark, 2015; Hargraves, 2011; Vesey, 2017). Finally, when the move to VH1 is coupled with the courting of mainstream appeal, *RPDR* appears to now overtly cater to the cis audience, with revelatory segments discussing queer history (Kelly, 2017). While seemingly unprompted, these segments appeared more frequently during season 9. The discussion between contestants conveniently educates a cis audience about key events and history that would be well known to the LGBTIQ community, such as the legacy of the 1969 Stonewall riots, the suppression of gay rights in Russia, the discrimination faced by trans people in the drag scene, and impact of the Pulse Nightclub massacre. As Daggett (2017) contends, "An affective connection is generally forged with reality stars through confessionals and personal stories, but in *RPDR* these stories serve a larger pedagogical and political goal" (p. 280). Season nine of *RPDR* was the most watched season to date, and *All Stars 3*, featuring queens from seasons 1–9 began screening in January 2018, followed immediately by season 10 in March 2018 to capitalize on this momentum. A more recent addition to the *RPDR* legacy is a fan convention—RuPaul's Drag Con. The convention is held in several US cities, featuring performances and meet-and-greets with contestants, with spin off events held in England and Australia. The exponential growth of the audience for *RPDR* provides winners with an international fan base that can be leveraged into support for causes specific to the local LGBTIQ community, as well as those facing LGBTIQ individuals worldwide.

Drag Activism, National Identity, and 100 Days of Trump

Before the glossy programming of *RPDR* made drag for mainstream consumption, drag, and drag activism had a lengthy history. While a review of the history of drag activism is beyond the scope of this chapter, it is important to note that many battles for LGBTIQ rights have been focused in and around New York City. In this context, place becomes symbolic to the connection between LGBTIQ identity, activism, and community formation, as projects such as the NYC LGBT Historic Sites Project have documented (Stack, 2017).

As one of the most liberal cities in the world, New York has long been a beacon for the LGBTIQ community. Events such as the Stonewall Riots in 1969 are often considered the starting point for the modern American LGBTIQ rights movement. After the riots, the Gay Liberation Front was formed, and in 1970 the first Gay Liberation Marches took place in New York City, later becoming known as Pride (Mathur, 2017). It was common for transgender women and drag queens to spend their first years in NYC living on the street.

The history of drag culture and its connection to New York City can be traced back to the emergence of ball culture in the 1920s. When they first began, balls "consisted mainly of white men putting on drag fashion shows. Fed up with the restrictive and racist ball culture, the queer black community established their own ball culture in the 1960s" (Haenfler, n.d., para. 2). Balls are elaborate: "judged competitions between 'houses' [family-like structures that are parallel to, but distinct from constructed 'gay families' of choice] in which participants are awarded prizes for displaying mastery of particular performative categories" (Arnold, Sterrett-Hong, Jonas, & Pollack, 2016, p. 144). As ball culture became more established, the number of participants increased alongside the number of categories in which they could compete. As documented in *Paris Is Burning* (1990), balls quickly grew from an underground culture of queer minorities, to an influential subculture. The spread of ball culture gained mainstream attention when Madonna featured the dance phenomenon of voguing in her hit song *Vogue* (1990). *RPDR* continues the traditions of ball culture in both language use and format of the show, which each week features different categories for the final catwalk presentation. Like many performers before her, RuPaul began her career on the underground ball circuit after moving to New York and living with other homeless drag queens. The legacy that RuPaul extends with the new drag superstars of *RPDR* immortalizes New York's underground ball scene and the legendary performers featured in *Paris Is Burning*. In 2018, Ryan Murphy's series *Pose* debuted, capitalizing on the growing mainstream awareness of ball culture. This series, set in New York against the backdrop of the AIDS crisis of the 1980s has been widely praised not only for Murphy's "assiduous casting of transgender actors and creative staff" (Poniewozik, 2018, para. 4) but also for the way "it spotlights its characters aspirations [and acts as] an attempt to better understand the present by reclaiming the 1980s as an origin story" (Poniewozik, 2018, para. 9). The parallels between the world of *Pose*, and the New York of 2018 are further underscored in the show by the character Stan (Evan Peters), whose career aspirations lead him to work in Trump Tower, with the spectre of Mr. Trump constantly invoked by his malevolent supervisor Matt (James Van Der Beek).

New York can be viewed as a city where outward facing cosmopolitism, and values of global citizenship are valued beyond those found elsewhere in the United States. It is this cosmopolitanism that has earned New York the disdain of "middle America"; as Senior (2004) argues, the divide between New York and America at large can be traced back to "the populist movements of the 1890s, when New Yorkers were regarded as twee, good-for-nothing parasites" (para. 12). The divide between New York and middle America now manifests in expressions of contempt for "the culture and intellectuals," echoing Nichols's (2017) work on the increasing mistrust of experts and campaigns against established knowledge. Nichols (2017) bemoans not only "that people dismiss expertise, but that they do so with such frequency, on so many issues, and with such anger" (p. 252). These tendencies are exemplified by the Trump administration's obsession with equating evidence-based reporting with "fake news," often broadcast via angry outbursts on Twitter.

The election of Donald Trump as president of the United States in November 2016 was a shock to many, as he was declared "unelectable" during the presidential campaign (Bryant, 2016). Trump's surprise appointment was set against a backdrop of fear-based rhetoric appealing to disenfranchised American voters, at the expense of minority groups. After Trump's election, Strausbaugh (2016) in particular noted the high levels of resistance to Trump in New York City, where votes against him tallied 4 to 1. Since the election, both California (#Calexit) and New York (#Nexit) have produced calls to secede from the Union. In a speech the day after the election, Mayor Bill de Blasio of New York City addressed the fears of his citizens, stating:

> It's not the first time we have felt a sense of foreboding. But we also have to remember in each and every one of those instances, people regrouped. This is a moment when New York City needs to stand tall . . . . we need to focus our energies, prepare to show this entire country what New York City is all about—what we believe and why it is a better way. . . . We have a special obligation to be an example. Now, it's our turn to build a movement—a movement of the majority that believes in respect and dignity for all.
>
> (De Blasio, 2016, para. 27)

De Blasio's identification of the fears held about Trump's impact on the rights of minorities have been well founded in the LGBTIQ community. In particular, transgender individuals have been targeted under Trump's reforms, and the rights gained for other minority groups under previous administrations have been lost or threatened. Gay and Lesbian Alliance Against Defamation (GLAAD) President Sarah Kate Ellis has noted of Trump's tenure:

> One hundred days of Trump translates into 100 days of erasure for the LGBTIQ community. . . . From the Census exclusion, to rescinding Obama's guidance for trans youth in schools, and the lack of any LGBTIQ mentions on the White House website, he has spent the early days of his administration trying to remove us from the very fabric of this country, and we must resist.
>
> (Ellis, in O'Hara, 2017, para. 3)

In addition to Ellis's summary of erasure, Trump has attempted to reinstate the ban on transgender individuals serving in the military. His disdain for the contribution of transgender individuals is such that his edict was issued via Twitter, stating: "Our military must be focused on decisive and overwhelming victory and cannot be burdened with the tremendous medical costs and disruption that transgender in the military would entail" (Remnick, 2017, para. 3). However, Trump's legislation was blocked in the US District Court for the District of Columbia on October 30, 2017, allowing transgender individuals to begin enlisting again from January 1, 2018 (Ring, 2017). This decision was overturned in January 2019. Trump's restrictions on transgender military service began in April 2019, although there are four lawsuits pending. The National Center for Lesbian Rights, one of the LGBTIQ advocacy groups fighting the policy, said the legal battle is "far from over. All four cases are proceeding. Just because an injunction is lifted, doesn't mean [the] case is over" (Jackson & Kube, 2019, para.12).

As the lack of protection afforded to minority groups by the Trump administration becomes clearer, a climate of fear has become entrenched in many segments of the community. This fear has only intensified. In October 2018, it was revealed that the Trump administration planned "to adopt an explicit and uniform definition of gender as determined on a biological basis that is clear, grounded in science, objective and administrable" (Green, Benner, & Pear, 2018, para. 4), resulting in the complete erasure of transgender people. In such desperate times, people need an escape and a feeling of community. While it exists a world away from reality, *RPDR* and its contestants have the power to hold space, and raise awareness of issues while "acting back" (Gonzalez & Cavazos, 2016, p. 666) to the LGBTIQ community. Greenhalgh (2018) has also argued that increased visibility of drag in mainstream popular culture offers "a defiant position from which to challenge Trump's toxic masculinity" (p. 299). It is within this political climate that any and all LGBTIQ visibility, and activism represents a powerful means to push back against inequality.

Bob the Drag Queen and Sasha Velour—Political Queens on *RuPaul's Drag Race*

As Godfrey (2015) observes, "Drag queens have been fighting on the front line since the dawn of the modern LGBT rights movement . . . . many have continued to do so, using their prominent community status to champion equality" (para. 2). At first glance, viewers may not associate *RPDR* with serious political commentary; indeed, earlier seasons of the show played down the connection between drag and activism. However, in the context of two distinct election campaigns (2012 and 2016), politics has crept into the content and challenges, as well as informal discussions between contestants. In season four, the top five queens were tasked with preparing for a mock political debate, campaigning to become the first drag queen president (S4, E9, "Frock the Vote"). This episode was notable for the way it divided the queens into two camps: those who campaigned seriously on issues affecting the LGBTIQ community (Latrice Royale; Sharon Needles); and those who felt uncomfortable engaging with political content for a challenge (Chad Michaels; Dida Ritz; Phi Phi O'Hara). Despite shying away from politics during the challenge, Chad Michaels later expressed his desire for marriage equality, citing his own long-term partnership. Michaels stated: "There's a lot of things I could have said about gay marriage at that point, but I wanted to hit a nerve" (quoted in Carey-Mahoney, 2016, para. 19). In speaking out on equality from a personal perspective, Michaels demonstrates how the program can initiate meaningful dialogue and awareness among viewers, particularly in online spaces; Lawson, quoted in Rogers (2014, para. 26) insists that for those struggling with their sexuality, "social media makes difference accessible and visible and vocal." Carey-Mahoney (2016) suggests discussions such as those initiated by Michaels demonstrate:

> an overarching authenticity that runs deeply through the show: over the course of the series, there have been over 100 contestants of all shapes, ages, and races, each able to speak to the portion of the queer community they represent. . . . Because *Drag Race* doesn't come off as heavy-handed or overtly political, it paints the most realistic depiction of the queer community currently on television.
>
> (para. 20)

In contrast to Michaels's revelation, the eliminated contestant in the "Frock the Vote" episode, Dida Ritz stated: "she doesn't want to bring up politics because it's a personal topic that can easily cause confrontation" (quoted in Sava, 2012, para. 5). In the current climate this message is difficult to justify; the very act of drag can be confrontational for some, as it sends a clear message against heteronormative society, and social expectations, making it political by nature.

The increased impact of politics on both the contestants and the content (in the form of politically themed challenges) was most notable in season 8 (2016, during the Trump campaign) and season 9 (2017, post Trump's election). The winners of these seasons, Bob the Drag Queen and Sasha Velour, declared their intent to use their increased public profiles to raise awareness of issues affecting the LGBTIQ community. As figures already working in the New York drag scene, both Bob the Drag Queen and Sasha Velour demonstrate awareness of how drag can effectively address serious issues in their advocacy work with groups such as marriage equality group Queer Rising and the Silvia Riviera Law Project. Irish drag activist Panti Bliss insists that "activism enhances the entertainment.

A good activist needs to have a stage presence . . . because that's why people listen to you. And drag queens are used to that" (quoted in Godfrey, 2015, para. 12). Social media is central to the activism of both queens as a tool to interact with fans. In this case, "Online celebrity activism can act as connective tissue, reinforcing an 'authentic' (cohesive) set of core values and disseminating them both via social media and through on-and-off-line ventures" (Ellcessor, 2018, p. 264). The popularity of Bob the Drag Queen and Sasha Velour, coupled with their performance of authentic activist values both online and offline, can thus inspire fans to join them in political activity.

From her introduction into the competition, Bob the Drag Queen was vocal about her politics and frequently angered the other queens with her blunt appraisal of their performances. Despite being relatively new to drag (having stated that S1 of *RPDR* was her impetus for starting drag), the Manhattan-based queen had a long history of comedy, performance, and activism prior to her appearance on the show. In 2010, Bob the Drag Queen was part of a group called Drag Queen Weddings for Equality, which would conduct drag queen weddings in Times Square each Saturday and distribute information about inequalities facing the LGBTIQ community. During another marriage equality protest with grassroots, nonviolent action group Queer Rising, Bob the Drag Queen was arrested in drag with other activists for disrupting traffic by holding a large sign "New York Demands Marriage Equality Now." Throughout the competition, Bob the Drag Queen was an astute commentator of contemporary politics, a skill that was highlighted during the challenge, titled "Shady Politics" (S8, E7). In pairs, the queens were tasked with making political campaign advertisements promoting themselves as America's First Drag President, including a smear campaign against their rivals. During the season, and after her finale win, Bob the Drag Queen promoted herself as a "Queen for the People" who was not afraid to stand up to injustice, as her actions since the program demonstrate.

Since winning her season, Bob the Drag Queen has continued to be an outspoken advocate for issues affecting the New York queer community, and the negative impact of Trump on America. In her last interview as reigning queen, Bob the Drag Queen stated:

> My pride has always been about not just living without fear, but activism and living out loud. I said last year that living without fear is a form of activism, and I still believe it. . . . Drag might be recognized as more political now, but drag has always been extremely political. Drag queens were at the Stonewall riots for crying out loud. . . . Drag is being recognized more, and there are more people doing drag. But the act of drag itself is still punk rock. It is still political. It is still what it's always been, which is breaking the rules.
>
> (Fallon, 2017, para. 15)

Ellcessor's (2018) observations about the complicated nature of online celebrity can also be applied to Bob the Drag Queen's online persona. Ellcessor speaks to the dual mode of address, as celebrities act both as "spokesperson, broadcasting an official message and leveraging [their] celebrity to draw attention to an issue" and someone who speaks on their "own behalf, using a more informal tone and making more forceful demands" (p. 256). The contrast between these online modes of address suggest "two changes social media have wrought in recent years, namely, the ability of celebrities to communicate directly with audiences and the diffusion of activism from formal organizations to loosely connected groups organizing through digital networks" (Ellcessor, 2018, p. 256). Since her appearance on *RPDR*, Bob the Drag Queen has focused on fundraising efforts, such as auctioning memorabilia featured on the show, which she promotes via her website Charity4thePeople.com (Winfred, 2016). As a case study, Bob the Drag Queen affirms the potential for reality television personalities to harness their public profile and direct fans towards causes with which they share a connection. Similar observations of effective celebrity activism, and the use of social media have been found in studies such as Bennett's (2014) study of Lady Gaga, a popular singer and actress. This research highlights Gaga's use of social media to form meaningful relationships with fans, whom she can then guide towards her philanthropic causes. Bennett notes:

> Celebrities can now speak directly, and immediately to their audience, without the filters of the news media . . . celebrities can instead now . . . post images and appeals on Twitter and Facebook that directly reach not only a worldwide mass audience, but, most crucially, within this, a worldwide *fan* audience.
>
> (p. 150)

Both Bob the Drag Queen and Sasha Velour demonstrate a keen awareness of the possibilities of social media, and position themselves as concerned citizens who will use their public profile to advocate for LGBTIQ causes alongside their fans. As Daggett (2017) suggests: "The queens demonstrate a hyperawareness of new media spaces, but at the same time, they discuss [and perform] their experiences in traditional drag spaces" (p. 282). When reflecting upon the best use of her profile to effect social change, Bob the Drag Queen asserts:

> I've always said that I will be where I'm needed most. There was a time when I was needed on the front line, yelling, getting arrested. I feel like now, now I'm needed more advocating from this side of the jail cell. But if there ever comes a time where I need to be on the front line, that's where I'll be.
>
> (Brooks, 2016, para. 20)

Anticipation was high among fans for the premiere of season 9 of *RuPaul's Drag Race*, and its debut on VH1 in 2017. Season 9 was not only the most viewed season, but regarded as possessing one of the strongest fields of contestants. Sasha Velour was crowned the winner of season 9 in an unprecedented four-way playoff finale, which saw the top four queens compete in elimination lip synch battles. In contrast to the brash persona of Bob the Drag Queen, Sasha Velour was initially portrayed as a humorless, intellectual art queen. As the season progressed Velour reflected upon issues such as the Pulse Nightclub massacre, eating disorders in the LGBTIQ community, and living as a gay man in Russia. Velour quickly became a fan favorite for her breathtaking runway fashions, and advocacy of a new style of inclusive drag.

Velour resides in Brooklyn and has an arts background; she is both a trained cartoonist and Fulbright scholar who studied queer activism in Russia. Prior to her appearance on season 9, she was already the organizer of Nightgowns. Nightgowns is a night of inclusive drag and live performance, which takes place in Manhattan on a monthly basis, with profits donated to local LGBTIQ charities. Velour also publishes her own art magazine called *Velour*—each issue has a focus on drag, gender, and art. As someone who identifies as gender fluid, Velour advocates for inclusivity for different styles of drag, and different gender identifications to coexist. Velour has spoken (both on and off screen) about the need to create a space for the trans community to be welcomed as drag performers. Reporting on her victory, *Advocate* asked Velour to reflect on her performance style:

> I believe drag is a form of activism. It centers queer people and queer ways of being beautiful, especially in a political context where beauty is narrowly defined or what's considered important or valuable is narrowly defined, and drag always offers a different option. I took for granted how much drag is still about play, and how playing and being light about your identity and yourself is actually a form of resistance, too.
>
> (Velour, cited in *Advocate*, 2017, para. 5)

Velour's combination of art and politics can be framed in terms of Duncombe's (2007) work, which suggests that the way forward for celebrity political interventions is via "ethical spectacle, public performances that are pleasurable, participatory, and playful, yet also confront reality" (in Jenkins, 2012, para. 4.4). Thus, celebrity politics such as Velour's can be framed as "a politics that employs symbols and associations; a politics that tells good stories" (Duncombe, 2007, p. 9). Andrew Slack (2010) of the Harry Potter Alliance has described this style of intervention as "cultural acupuncture": "[which] is finding where the psychological energy is in the culture, and moving that energy towards creating a healthier world" (para. 4). Velour has established a large fan base by positioning her drag as a bridge between the drag, art, and political worlds, and expressing a message of inclusivity which she shares online. Velour's enhanced profile as the winner of *RPDR* has enabled her artistic endeavors centered within Brooklyn to reach and create a global community via social media.

Velour has toured relentlessly since her victory in June 2017, and has received extensive press coverage in addition to direct communication with her fans via her magazine, website, and social media platforms. Velour has gained attention from mainstream media outlets with profiles in *The Guardian* (Bromwich, 2017), *Vogue* (Barsamian, 2017), and *Rolling Stone* (Spanos, 2018) discussing her style and fashion icons, and drag activism, illustrating the increasing reach of drag into mainstream channels. Velour has continued to support her community through large scale productions of Nightgowns in prominent New York venues such as Terminal 5, reflecting the growth in audience demand. Velour has also stated that a substantial portion of her prize money from *RPDR* will go towards touring Nightgowns and turning it into:

> something that unites queer people and drag artists across the country. . . . at the same time, we're transforming Nightgowns into a non-profit organization that can raise money for queer people in need around the country in terms of raising money to support housing and educational needs.
>
> (Reynolds, 2017, para. 12)

In this way, Velour is able to utilize her digital profile promoting the aforementioned events to encourage financial contributions from fans toward her artistic and philanthropic endeavors. As Bennett (2014) observed of Lady Gaga, Sasha Velour uses social media to share insight into her daily life, creating a relationship with fans that Beer (2008) has described as a "perception of proximity." The perception of proximity, and the connection which is formed with fans can then be used by celebrities to instigate direct action. Velour achieves direct action by promoting upcoming benefits on Instagram and Twitter, and encouraging fans to attend, donate, and share with their own followers. A selection of fundraisers documented on Velour's Instagram page (June–July 2017) have benefited the Ali Forney Centre NY (providers of shelter and healthcare for LGBTIQ youth); Princess Janae Palace in the Bronx (trans housing); and the Sylvia Riviera Law Project NY (legal advice/representation for the LGBTIQ community). Thus, Velour's activism resists the divisive politics espoused by the Trump administration by "telling good stories." Velour achieves political impact by cultivating a fan community around her art, and directing fans to support causes that advance her activist goals. In so doing, she is able to create change in her local community, and inspire action internationally by documenting these changes online, and encouraging fan involvement.

As this chapter has documented, both Bob the Drag Queen and Sasha Velour have a strong connection to their local community. However, they do not limit their activism to local issues (despite that being the focus of many of their charitable efforts). For Velour, her enhanced public profile is a means to inspire change for the LGBTIQ community on a larger scale:

> Originally Nightgowns was created as a celebration of Brooklyn drag, but now that I have an international audience, I think the scope of the show should expand as well. We plan to pack up our traveling circus and take the show on the road, connecting with drag talents and audiences all over the country. to raise funds for queer people in need of support. . . . That's the true spirit of drag. Not just fierce shows, but an activist spirit.
>
> (Velour, in Street, 2017, para. 6)

Both Bob the Drag Queen and Sasha Velour have spoken of the need to make a connection with the LGBTIQ community worldwide, inspire young people to be themselves, and have hope, despite political division. While some may dismiss the political impact of popular culture, as Dyer (1985) has observed, "Entertainment offers the image of 'something better' to escape into" a means by which alternatives to the everyday can be imagined (p. 222). Drag is able to do this via the ethical spectacle of performance. By using their connection with fans, Bob the Drag Queen and Sasha Velour are able to draw attention to the issues affecting the LGBTIQ community worldwide, which is at the heart of their work as drag artists. This connection is made possible by the use of social media, which enable fans to feel a connection with the celebrity personas of Bob the Drag Queen and Sasha Velour, despite their physical location. For O'Halloran:

> grass-roots conversation and debate [is] made possible by the affective network of social media that ties together fans of the show, its former contestants, and those with the power to make substantive changes. . . . The political proximity of *RPDR* may thus lie in its capacity to bring into contact and proximity—both *on* and *off* screen—those whom we are *unable* to understand or agree with.
>
> (2017, p. 225, original emphasis)

It is this connection which fosters imagined communities of like-minded individuals worldwide, and offers hope to those fighting repressive regimes which aim to erase the LGBTIQ community.

Conclusion

This chapter has assessed the impact of *RPDR* on the mainstreaming of drag and its potential as a transformative method to advocate for social change. Despite criticism leveled at the show regarding its representation of consumerism, transphobic language, and racial stereotypes, it is clear the program has vastly expanded the public profile of contestants. Winners such as Bob the Drag Queen and Sasha Velour have been able to convert their win into a channel to promote drag activism. The potential for modern drag as activism is grounded in the legacy of drag, combined with digital media innovation as a communication tool for mobilizing the public. Drag personas such as Bob the Drag Queen and Sasha Velour promote the work of local LGBTIQ advocacy groups and a broader message of inclusion, using digital media to routinely involve their fans in activism. This combination has the potential to become a powerful form of resistance. In the divisive era of Trump, the banding together of minority groups around celebrity figureheads like Bob the Drag Queen and Sasha Velour, who preach a message of love and inclusion, may be one of the most powerful tools that ordinary citizens have at their disposal.

Notes

1. A word on acronyms: I have used LGBTIQ throughout this paper, although I acknowledge the evolution/contention around labels.

References

Advocate. (2017, June 24). *RuPaul's Drag Race* finale crowns a new Queen who believes in drag as activism. Retrieved from www.advocate.com/arts-entertainment/2017/6/24/rupauls-drag-race-finale-crowns-new-queen-who-believes-drag-activism

Arnold, E. A., Sterrett-Hong, E., Jonas, A., & Pollack, L. M. (2018). Social networks and social support among ball-attending African American men who have sex with men and transgender women are associated with HIV-related outcomes. *Global Public Health*, 13(2), 144–158. doi:10/1080/17441692.2016.11880702

Bailey, F., & Barbato, R. (Producers). (2009). *RuPaul's Drag Race* [Television series]. U.S.A.: Logo TV, Viacom Media Networks.

Bailey, F., & Barbato, R. (Producers). (2010a). *RuPaul's Drag Race: Untucked!* [Television series]. U.S.A.: Logo TV, Viacom Media Networks.

Bailey, F., & Barbato, R. (Producers). (2010b). *RuPaul's Drag U* [Television series]. U.S.A.: Logo TV, Viacom Media Networks.

Bailey, F., & Barbato, R. (Producers). (2012). *RuPaul's Drag Race: All Stars* [Television series]. U.S.A.: Logo TV, Viacom Media Networks.

Barsamian, E. (2017, June 30). Sasha Velour from *RuPaul's Drag Race* on her style icons and how to be a Queen. *Vogue*. Retrieved from www.vogue.com/article/sasha-velour-rupaul-drag-race-karl-lagerfeld-celebrity-style

Beer, D. (2008). Making friends with Jarvis Cocker: Music culture in the context of web 2.0. *Cultural Sociology, 2*(2), 222–241.

Bennett, L. (2014). "If we stick together we can do anything": Lady Gaga fandom, philanthropy and activism through social media. *Celebrity Studies, 5*(1–2), 138–152.

Bromwich, K. (2017, October 29). Sasha Velour: "Drag is darkness turned into power." *The Guardian.* Retrieved from www.theguardian.com/tv-and-radio/2017/oct/29/sasha-velour-drag-is-darkness-turned-into-power-rupaul-drag-race-interview

Brooks, R. (2016, June 22). In Bob we trust: New York's newest reigning Drag Queen snatches America's wig. *The Village Voice.* Retrieved from www.villagevoice.com/2016/06/22/in-bob-we-trust-new-yorks-newest-reigning-drag-queen-snatches-americas-wig/

Bryant, N. (2016, August 19). US election: Has Donald Trump already blown it? *BBC World News.* Retrieved from www.bbc.com/news/world-us-canada-37102763

Carey-Mahoney, R. (2016, August 24). *RuPaul's Drag Race* is more than a TV show: It's a movement. *The Washington Post.* Retrieved October 29, 2017, from www.washingtonpost.com/news/arts-and-entertainment/wp/2016/08/24/rupauls-drag-race-is-more-than-a-tv-show-its-a-movement/?utm_term=.fac4dc53307b

Click, M., Lee, H., & Holladay, H. W. (2017). "You're born to be brave": Lady Gaga's use of social media to inspire fans' political awareness. *International Journal of Cultural Studies, 20*(6), 603–619.

Daggett, C. (2017). "If you can't love yourself, how in the hell you gonna love somebody else": Drag TV and self-love discourse. In N. Brennan & D. Gudelunas (eds.), *RuPaul's Drag Race and the shifting visibility of drag culture* (pp. 271–286). Cham, Switzerland: Palgrave Macmillan/Springer International Publishing.

De Blasio, B. (2016, November 21). *Transcript: Mayor de Blasio, first lady McCray deliver public address at Cooper Union.* Retrieved from www1.nyc.gov/office-of-the-mayor/news/899-16/transcript-mayor-de-blasio-first-lady-mccray-deliver-public-address-cooper-union#/0c

de Moraes, L. (2017, September 9). RuPaul repeats as reality host Emmy winner. *Deadline Hollywood.* Retrieved from http://deadline.com/2017/09/rupaul-repeats-reality-host-emmy-winner-1202165750/

Duncombe, S. (2007). *Dream: Re-imagining progressive politics in an Age of fantasy.* New York, USA: New Press.

Dyer, R. (1985). Entertainment and utopia. In R. Altman (Ed.), *Genre: The musical: A reader* (pp. 175–189). London, England: Routledge/BFI.

Ellcessor, E. (2018). "One tweet to make so much noise": Connected celebrity activism in the case of Marlee Matlin. *New Media and Society, 20*(1), 255–271.

Eyrich, L. (Producer). (2018). *Pose* [Television series]. Los Angeles, CA: FX Productions.

Fallon, K. (2017, June 19). Bob the Drag Queen on *RuPaul's Drag Race,* his new film, and drag in the age of Trump. *The Daily Beast.* Retrieved from www.thedailybeast.com/BobtheDragQueen-the-drag-queen-on-rupauls-drag-race-his-new-film-and-drag-in-the-age-of-trump

Fincher, D. (Director). (1990). *Vogue.* [Recorded by Madonna] on *I'm Breathless* [music video]. U.S.A.: Warner Brothers.

Fisher, K. (Producer). (2016). *Gay for Play Game Show starring RuPaul* [Television series]. U.S.A.: Logo TV, Viacom Media Networks.

Godfrey, C. (2015, November 4). When drag is activism. *Advocate*. Retrieved from www.advocate.com/current-issue/2015/11/04/when-drag-activism

Goldmark, M. (2015). National drag: The language of inclusion in *RuPaul's Drag Race*. *GLQ: A Journal of Lesbian and Gay Studies, 21*(4), 501–520.

Gonzalez, J. C., & Cavazos, K. C. (2016). Serving fishy realness: Representations of gender equity on *RuPaul's Drag Race*. *Continuum, 30*(6), 659–669. http://dx.doi.org/10.1080/10304312.2016.1231781

Green, E., Benner, K., & Pear, R. (2018, October 21). "Transgender" could be defined out of existence under Trump administration. *The New York Times*. Retrieved from www.nytimes.com/2018/10/21/us/politics/transgender-trump-administration-sex-definition.html

Greenhalgh, E. (2018). "Darkness turned into power": Drag as resistance in the era of Trumpian reversal. *Queer Studies in Media & Popular Culture, 3*(3), 299–319. http://dx.doi: 10.1386/qsmpc.3.3.299_1

Gudelunas, D. (2017). Digital extensions, experiential extensions and hair extensions: *RuPaul's Drag Race* and the new media environment. In N. Brennan & D. Gudelunas (eds.), *RuPaul's Drag Race and the shifting visibility of drag culture* (pp. 231–244). Cham, Switzerland: Palgrave Macmillan/Springer International Publishing.

Haenfler, R. (n.d.). *Underground ball culture: Subcultures and Sociology*. Retrieved from http://haenfler.sites.grinnell.edu/subcultures-and-scenes/underground-ball-culture/

Hargraves, H. (2011). You better work: The commodification of HIV in *RuPaul's Drag Race*. *Spectator, 31*(2), 24–34.

Hills, M. (2008). Cult film: A critical symposium. *Cineaste, 34*(1). Retrieved from www.cineaste.com/winter2008/cult-film-a-critical-symposium/

Jackson, H., & Kube, C. (2019, April 13). Trump's controversial transgender military policy goes into effect. *NBC News*. Retrieved from www.nbcnews.com/feature/nbc-out/trump-s-controversial-transgender-military-policy-goes-effect-n993826

Jenkins, H. (2012). "Cultural acupuncture": Fan activism and the Harry Potter Alliance. *Transformative Works and Cultures, 10*. Retrieved from http://journal.transformativeworks.org/index.php/twc/article/view/305/259

Kelly, C. (2017, June 23). 8 things *RuPaul's Drag Race* needs to stop doing. *Queerty**. Retrieved from www.queerty.com/8-things-rupauls-drag-race-needs-stop-20170623

Livingston, J. (Producer/Director). (1990). *Paris is burning* [DVD]. U.S.A.: Lions Gate Home Entertainment.

Marwick, A., & Boyd, D. (2011). To see and be seen: Celebrity practice on Twitter. *Convergence, 17*(2), 139–158. https://dx.doi.org/10.1177/1354856510394539

Mathur, I. (2017, March 14). Marsha P. Johnson. *Damsel*. Retrieved from www.uwastudentguild.com/damsel-marsha-p-johnson/

Nicols, T. (2017). *The death of expertise: The campaign against established knowledge and why it matters*. New York, USA: Oxford University Press.

O'Halloran, K. (2017). *RuPaul's Drag Race* and the reconceptualization of Queer communities and publics. In N. Brennan & D. Gudelunas (eds.), *RuPaul's Drag Race and the shifting visibility of drag culture* (pp. 213–228). Cham, Switzerland: Palgrave Macmillan/Springer International Publishing.

O'Hara, M. E. (2017, April 27). First 100 days: How president Trump has impacted LGBTQ rights. *NBC News*. Retrieved from www.nbcnews.com/feature/nbc-out/first-100-days-how-president-trump-has-impacted-lgbtq-rights-n750191

Poniewozik, J. (2018, June 1). Review: *Pose* demands to be seen. *The New York Times*. Retrieved from www.nytimes.com/2018/06/01/arts/television/pose-review-fx-ryan-murphy.html

Redmond, S. (2008). The star and celebrity confessional. *Social Semiotics*, *18*(2), 109–114. https://doi.org/10.1080/10350330802002077

Remnick, D. (2017, July 26). The cruelty and cynicism of Trump's transgender ban. *The New Yorker*. Retrieved from www.newyorker.com/news/news-desk/the-cruelty-and-cynicism-of-trumps-transgender-military-ban

Reynolds, D. (2017, June 26). Sasha Velour: Drag superstar today, POTUS tomorrow? *Advocate*. Retrieved from www.advocate.com/television/2017/6/26/sasha-velour-drag-superstar-today-potus-tomorrow

Ring, T. (2017, October 30). Court blocks trans military ban. *Advocate*. Retrieved from www.advocate.com/military/2017/10/30/court-blocks-trans-military-ban

Rogers, K. (2014, February 20). With *Looking*, RuPaul and *Modern Family*, is LGBT life now mainstream? *The Guardian*. Retrieved from www.theguardian.com/culture/2014/feb/19/looking-rupaul-modern-family-lgbt-gay-culture

Sava, O. (2012, March 27). *RuPaul's Drag Race*: "Frock the vote." *AV Club*. Retrieved from https://tv.avclub.com/rupauls-drag-race-frock-the-vote-1798172160

Selva, D. (2016). Social television: Audience and political engagement. *Television and New Media*, *17*(2), 159–173.

Senior, J. (2004, n.d.). The independent Republic of New York. *New York Magazine*. Retrieved from http://nymag.com/nymetro/news/rnc/9573/

Slack, A. (2010, July 2). Cultural acupuncture and a future for social change. *The Huffington Post: The Blog*. Retrieved from www.huffingtonpost.com/andrew-slack/cultural-acupuncture-and_b_633824.html

Spanos, B. (2018, October 23). Sasha Velour meets world: *Drag Race* winner talks life before and after Ru. *Rolling Stone*. Retrieved from www.rollingstone.com/culture/culture-features/rpdr-rupauls-drag-race-sasha-velour-drag-queen-nightgowns-744535/

Stack, L. (2017, June 19). New York's LGBTQ story began well before Stonewall. *The New York Times*. Retrieved from www.nytimes.com/2017/06/19/us/gay-pride-lgbtq-new-york-before-stonewall.html

Strausbaugh, J. (2016, November 30). Nexit: A call for New York City to secede from the Union. *Observer*. Retrieved from http://observer.com/2016/11/nexit-a-call-for-new-york-city-to-secede-from-the-union/

Street, M. (2017, July 6). A night of drag activism with Sasha Velour. *Paper*. Retrieved from www.papermag.com/sasha-velour-2454452819.html

Vesey, A. (2017). "A way to sell your records": Pop stardom and the politics of drag professionalization on *RuPaul's Drag Race*. *Television and New Media*, *18*(7), 589–604.

Winfred, T. (2016, April 18). Bob the Drag Queen recollects the time she was thrown in Jail in full drag. *Queerty**. Retrieved from www.queerty.com/Bob the Drag Queen-the-drag-queen-recollects-the-time-she-was-thrown-in-jail-in-full-drag-20160418

4 Brexit and EU Migration on the BBC and CNN
Britishness Versus EU Identity

Fathi Bourmeche

Background to the Study

Intercultural communication, identity, and social movements have generated a number of studies. Martin and Nakayama (2010), for example, devoted one section of their study on the changing immigration patterns in the United States highlighting their impact on the American social makeup.[1] Britain has also witnessed significant changes in immigration patterns in the sense that it has been the preferred destination of a large number of Eastern Europeans following the fifth EU enlargement. This enlargement, transforming the EU from a "Western European entity into a pan-European organization" (Barnes & Barnes, 2010, p. 418), resulted in a large influx of Eastern Europeans. Such an influx has generated a bulk of studies on the whole trend and its impact on Britain's social makeup. The influx has also been covered by British newspapers, emphasizing the nature of such a trend and its impact on British society, especially in relation to the British national identity. This coverage in turn increased readers' concern about the trend, reviving Britons' sense of belonging to an island race, distinct from their European counterparts in many respects, and increasing Euro-skepticism in Britain, thus putting Britain's position within the EU at stake.

What should be noted is that in the aftermath of World War II, Britain, though acknowledging the significance of Europe, prioritized the Empire and Commonwealth, along with the special Anglo-American relationship. This was reinforced by Churchill, who argued that Britain "stood at the point where three circles crossed—Europe, America, and the Empire," prioritizing the Empire and America over Europe (Stephen, 1998, p. 14).[2] Stephen (1998) argues that the British Department of State and the Treasury shared the view that Britain "was a global power, and only incidentally a European power," (p. 39) shaping policies in accordance with Britain's global responsibilities. Despite the recognition of decline on the international scene, Britain's position "was seen as being at the right hand of the new dominant power, the United States, acting as a sort of first lieutenant" (p. 39). It has been pointed out that British governments had no intention to play a leading role in Europe, assuming that Britain had a different role and status from the other European countries. The first application to the European Economic Community was vetoed by Charles de Gaulle, who believed that Britain was not "yet sufficiently European in its policy and outlook" (Gamble, 1998, p. 16).[3] But Stephen (1998) argues that the French veto could be explained by de Gaulle's awareness of Britain's intentions, namely dominating the EEC on behalf of the United States, bearing the fact that the latter was a strong advocate of Britain's membership (pp. 39–40).

Alistair Jones (2007) points out that the establishment of the European Free Trade Association (EFTA) in 1960 was an attempt by the British government to set up an alternative organization, enhanced by the initial success of the EEC, with different objectives, such as promoting free trade between member countries (Austria, Denmark, Finland, Norway, Portugal, Sweden, and Britain) rather than creating a supranational organization. Yet, EFTA proved to be less beneficial to Britain in the sense that economies of the member states were not comparable to that of Britain (pp. 14–15).

Though results of the 1975 referendum showed the endorsement of Britain's membership to the EEC, the European issue has long raised concern in British politics. Gamble (1998) recalls that both the Conservatives, traditionally seen as a party of Europe, and Labor, with a majority seen as strong opponents, have changed their stance on the EU as from the 1990s. Labor has become pro-European whereas proponents among the Conservatives have been struggling "to keep control of policy towards Europe against a background of a rising tide of anti-European feeling in the party" (p. 11). What is more, under Margaret Thatcher, the Conservatives were also seen as pro-European, possibly attributed to Labor's anti-European attitudes;[4] but David Cameron, who engineered the June 2016 referendum, has been regarded as the most Euro-skeptic leader in the Conservative party. Indeed, the Conservative party has appeared as a reluctant European, raising calls to withdraw from the EU (Jones, 2007, pp. 129–133).

It is noteworthy that the major issue around which Britain's relationship to Europe has been linked was the transfer of British national sovereignty to the European supranational institutions at Brussels in terms of decision-making (Jones, 2007, p. 25). In the same vein, Jones (2007) holds that Britain's reluctant-European label stems from the complexity of the relationship between Britain and the EU, emphasizing the "inconsistencies in the attitudes of the British government, the British media and the British people towards the European Union—and vice versa" (p. 1).

Such inconsistencies enhanced Euro-skepticism, raising concern about the terms and conditions under which Britain would remain part of the member states. Recently, Euro-skepticism has escalated, particularly in the aftermath of the fifth EU enlargement which resulted in an influx of

Eastern Europeans into Britain. Roar against the trend, this time involving EU nationals whose rights have been enshrined in EU laws, has had a major impact on Britain's socio-political landscape. In other words, the trend raised concern about the impact of the new arrivals on the British social composition and also on Britain's position within the EU, particularly during the campaign for the 2010 general election when Gordon Brown reacted to Gillian Duffy's query about Eastern Europeans by describing the lady as a bigoted woman. Gillian Duffy, a lifelong Labor supporter from Rochdale and a grandmother, stopped Brown during his electoral campaign in April 2010 to ask him a few questions, including one on Eastern European immigrants. Brown described her as a bigoted woman, which was broadcast live on ITV.

Such reaction seemed to have been fatal, putting Brown and Labor in a difficult situation, thus ending their 13-year period of rule and starting a historic coalition between the Conservatives under David Cameron and the Liberal Democrats under Nick Clegg. The coalition government and Cameron, in particular, promised to curb EU migration by working on reducing net migration to the tens of thousands. Such a promise, though proved later to be hard to achieve, was also reiterated during the campaign for the 2015 general election when EU migration appeared among the most important issues facing the country. The whole situation paved the way for another referendum in June 2016, resulting in Britons' decision to leave the EU, which put European integrity at stake.

This chapter is an attempt to gain a better understanding of the nature of Britain's relationship with Europe at a time when Euro-skepticism has peaked in British society, leading to the second referendum on the future of the country in Europe which has been fought with two main issues in focus, namely British sovereignty and immigration. This is carried out through a qualitative analysis of the BBC and CNN coverage of Brexit and EU migration into Britain prior to and in the aftermath of the June 2016 referendum. It is basically a thematic analysis of the content of the selected corpus, focused on the different frames and attributes used in relation to the two main issues, namely Brexit and EU migration, with particular attention to the notion of Britishness as well as EU identity. The intention is to gain a better understanding of the impact of media on public opinion, particularly in relation to Britishness, juxtaposing the different frames to opinion polls dealing with the same issues.

Linda Colley (1992) argues that Britishness was not the result of the integration and homogenization of three distinctive cultures (the Welsh, the Scottish, and the English) but was rather "superimposed over an array of internal differences in response to contact with the Other, and above all in response to conflict with the Other" (p. 6). Given the inflow of people from different parts of the world and their impact on British society as a whole, Britishness has also been dealt with in relation to immigration, rendering perceptions and reactions to immigrants a defining feature of

Britishness. In the same vein, Stuart Hall (1999) contends that migration is "changing the composition, diversifying the cultures and pluralizing the cultural identities of the older dominant nation states, the old imperial powers, and, indeed, of the globe itself" (p. 16). This chapter, therefore, seeks to shed more light on the nature of British society in terms of its relation to the EU, with particular attention to the impact of Brexit and EU migration on British national identity.

Objectives and Research Questions

The chapter aims to delve into the way the BBC and CNN have covered Brexit and EU migration, two topical issues which have raised major concerns among politicians and academic circles. Free mobility within the EU has raised controversy in Britain, particularly in the aftermath of the fifth EU enlargement resulting in the influx of Eastern Europeans which appeared as one of the most important issues facing the country. Such controversy seemed to have affected results of general elections, particularly that of 2010, ending Labor's 13-year rule and starting a historic coalition between the Conservatives and the Liberal Democrats.

One of the reasons behind Brown's inability to secure a fourth Labor term could possibly be explained by his reaction to Gillian Duffy's query about Eastern Europeans. Immigration as a whole, and that of Eastern Europeans, remained among the most important issues during the campaign for the 2015 general election, possibly because of Cameron's failure to keep his promises on reducing net migration to the tens of thousands, thus paving the way for the June 2016 referendum, with a campaign fought on, among other things, free mobility within the EU. Britons' decision to leave the EU has had enormous repercussions on the EU, as well as Britain, an argument confirmed by Lucy Hawking (2016), who stated that the result of the referendum "bitterly divided the entire nation [and] caused a downgrading of the U.K.'s credit rating," and thus bringing about "instability and Europe-wide insecurity for years" (para. 5). But Brexit is highly significant in relation to British sovereignty and European identity. The intention of this chapter is to examine the way the BBC and CNN have framed Brexit and EU migration through a qualitative analysis of the content of their coverage prior to the June 2016 referendum and in its aftermath, using Maxwell McCombs' (2004) model of media framing. In this chapter, I argue that media coverage of Brexit and EU migration has enhanced British national identity and put EU identity at stake. This will be demonstrated by juxtaposing media coverage of these issues to opinion polls conducted by Ipsos MORI dealing with related themes.

McCombs and Ghanem (2001) consider frames as "organizing principles incorporating and emphasizing certain lower level attributes to the exclusion of many others. Frames serve as efficient bundling devices of micro-attributes and, in turn, can be thought of as macro-attributes"

(p. 74). In McCombs's view, framing is "the selection of—and emphasis upon—particular attributes for the media agenda when talking about an object" (McCombs, 2004, p. 87). In this case study, focus is on the way two media outlets framed two major issues, namely Brexit and EU migration in order to see their impact on Britons' attitudes in relation to their national identity compared to EU identity.

Methodology

Corpus of the analysis consists of two items: articles from the BBC and CNN and opinion polls, selected prior to and in the aftermath of the June 2016 referendum. The keywords used in the selection are Brexit and EU migration in order to consider articles and opinions dealing with such topical issues. Articles were from BBC and CNN's official websites, whereas opinion polls were selected from the official website of Ipsos MORI. This choice is meant to shed more light on the effect of media framing, achieved, according to McCombs (2004), through a comparison of opinion polls with content analysis of news media. The selected articles have, therefore, been qualitatively analyzed in a thematic way, with particular attention to the different frames with regards to Brexit and EU migration and juxtaposed to the polls on the same themes for a close examination of media effects.

Major Findings and Discussion

Brexit and EU migration have been framed in relation to three major themes, all of which would threaten world order and put so many things at stake. The first one is the impact on Britain's position on the international scene and its relationship with Europe. The second theme is the impact on global economy and trade. The third theme is the impact on Britain's social makeup and national identities. Indeed, the two issues, namely Brexit and EU migration, have been covered by both CNN and BBC in relation to their repercussion on Britain both in terms of its relationship with EU member states and with other countries, particularly the United States, given the special relationship that has characterized the ties between the two countries. They have also been framed in relation to their impact on the global economy, threatening London's status as a hub for international businesses. Equally important, the two issues have been framed with respect to their impact on British national identity at a time when other regional identities are in the rise, particularly the case of Scotland after the emergence of Nicola Sturgeon as a prominent leader of the Scottish National Party (SNP). Such concerns have also been reflected in opinion polls dealing with the two issues and related themes, putting Brexit and EU migration as the most important issues facing the country.

The Impact on Britain's Position on the International Scene and on Its Relationship With Europe

The idea of the split between Britain and the EU raised a lot of concern about its impact on the country's position on the international scene as well as its relation to the EU. Brexit, seen by US officials as a terrible idea, was framed in the media as a major concern to the US government, leading Obama to join Cameron at a London News conference in a bid to save the Union and avoid the split, a mission he considered as part of the special Anglo-American relationship. Obama's intention was to address British voters to remain within the EU because Britain's leaving would represent a major threat to Western prosperity and security (Charles, 2016). It has been emphasized that the American government, as well as the whole world would need Britain's continued influence even within the EU. According to Obama's top aides, Brexit would downgrade Britain's valuable alliance with the United States; Heather Conley, of the Centre for Strategic and International Studies in Washington, argued that Americans would not be ready for any hazards at a time of global instability in different parts of the world, particularly in the Middle East, Europe, Asia, and Russia (Charles, 2016).

A study conducted by Ipsos MORI between March 25 and April 8, 2016, showed similar concerns on the effect of Brexit on Britain's role in the world, particularly in terms of the Anglo-American special relationship. What is significant is that the majority of interviewees, 60% of Americans and 58% of Britons, did not believe that Brexit would make any difference to the link between the two countries. However, Britons were more worried than Americans about the implications of Brexit, with 26% who believed that it would weaken the relationship between the two countries against 14% who believed that it would strengthen it, compared to 20% among the Americans on both sides (Mori, 2016).[5]

Britain is said to be a major contributor to the EU budget, which is meant to support farmers, deprived areas, or a number of businesses in the sense that it pays more than it receives from EU funded programs, a situation used by Leave campaigners to persuade voters to split from the Union (Kottasova, 2016c). The implication is that Britain has a considerable weight in the Union; yet EU leaders were criticized for their stubborn silence on Britain's referendum despite the fact that voters' decisions would be vital in shaping the future of the EU. One exception could possibly be Brussels reaction to Boris Johnson, the former Mayor of London and supporter of the Vote Leave campaign, who drew a parallel between the EU's ambition to unify member states to those of Mussolini and Hitler (Von Ondarza, 2016).

Silence among Europeans was further emphasized by Lister (2016) in another article, titled "Brexit: Europeans Hope Britain Will Stay, But They're Not Begging," posted on the CNN website on June 22, 2016, despite the fact that they would not be happy with Brexit, given the significance of Britain to Europe. Churchill's statue in Paris was highlighted as a reminder of his intention to establish a United States of Europe on his visit to Paris in the aftermath of World War II by re-creating the European family, at the heart of which lie Germany and France. The article mentioned the reaction of some European newspapers, all of which were begging Britain not to leave the EU. One example appeared in the front page of *El País*, a Spanish leading daily newspaper, showing a woman in front of the British Parliament with the banner "Together Stronger." Another one appeared in the front cover of *Marianne*, the French weekly, showing Elizabeth II and Mr. Bean, with a banner reading *"Ils sont fous, ces Anglais"* [The English are crazy].

An article posted on the BBC website one day after the referendum emphasized the wave of shock echoed all over Europe after British voters decided to leave the EU. It was argued that European leaders would like to keep relations with Britain by forging a good deal. However, given the rise of Euro-skepticism across Europe, European leaders were unwilling to show that exiting the Union would be an easy process. France and Germany, along with other countries within the EU, struggling "to digest the fact that Europe's political order has been overturned" ("Brexit: Europe stunned," 2016) by Brexit, would put forward further integration, as Britain would not block such process. But Marine Le Pen was said to have hailed Brexit and was calling for Frexit. Le Pen, the far-right National Front leader interpreted Brexit as "victory for freedom," calling for similar referenda in France and in other European countries; Marion Marechal-Le Pen, her niece and member of the National Front, claimed that Europe would be a focal theme in the coming French presidential elections. Geert Wilders, the Dutch far-right politician and leader of the anti-Islam, anti-immigration Freedom Party, congratulated Britain on its Independence Day and promised—if elected—to have a Nexit referendum ("Brexit: Europe stunned," 2016).

An article, titled "EU referendum: Is Brexit bad news for Poland?" posted on June 25, 2016, on the BBC website (i.e., two days after the referendum) showed Poles in Warsaw supporting the EU. Brexit was said to have had a major impact on Poland because Britain's decision to leave the EU would affect a large number of Poles, most of who are getting wages four times higher in Britain for the same jobs in their home country. An estimated 850,000 Poles make the largest non-British nationality, sending remittances, reaching more than £728 million a year, according to Poland's National Bank, enhancing consumption in many parts of their home country. Indeed, uncertainty overwhelmed the new arrivals who did not reach the five-year threshold to apply for permanent residency in Britain. In political terms, Brexit meant that Poland would lose a powerful ally in the EU, with similar views about the single market and sanctions against Russia (Easton, 2016).

In fact, triggering article 50 of the Treaty on European Union, following the letter sent by Theresa May, Cameron's successor as prime minister, to Donald Tusk, president of the European Council on March 29, 2017, was considered a seismic moment in Europe, implying the weight that Brexit may leave on the EU. Tim Barrow, the British ambassador, headed to Brussels to deliver the letter triggering the negotiations for Brexit. This was a historic moment for May on which Tusk tweeted: "After nine months the U.K. has delivered" (Johnson, 2017, para. 7). The event, which could mark the beginning of the end of Britain's global influence and usher in a new era for British power outside the EU, was celebrated by UKIP (UK Independence Party) Members of the European Parliament (MEPs) in a pub across the road, opposite the European Parliament.

Britain seemed unprepared for leaving the EU as two articles posted on the CNN website in January 2017 emphasized. One aspect of such unpreparedness could be felt in the resignation of Sir Ivan Rogers, UK's permanent representative to the EU, also known as the British Ambassador to the EU. Such resignation was seen by former Deputy Prime Minister Nick Clegg as a body blow to the government's plans (Roberts, 2017). Details on his resignation, published in British media outlets, revealed that the British government was not yet ready to have a sound negotiating stance on Brexit. Indeed, Rogers, known as a "sharp, witty, fast-thinking, intellectually challenging and hard-working" civil servant, had been Tony Blair's principal private secretary, "an ideal senior civil servant, and one with the rare gift of being able to move seamlessly between prime ministers" (McTernan, 2017, para. 4). He then became former Prime Minister Cameron's adviser on Europe in 10 Downing Street and later Cameron's nominee as ambassador to the EU, who excelled in his job, delivering almost all that Cameron wanted from a pre-referendum deal. Rogers was also the engineer of the Brexit agenda for May. In this sense, Rogers's resignation meant that the British government lost a person whose skills and deep relationships would have made Brexit negotiations successful (McTernan, 2017, paras. 6–7).

Yet May claimed that Brexit could change Britain for the better. Her intention was to keep Britain in the single market by building a new relationship with Europe, refusing the idea of hard and soft Brexit. A hard Brexit, favored by Brexiteers, implies that Britain would have full control of its borders after leaving the single market and the customs union, thus necessitating new trade deals with the EU. A soft Brexit, favored by Remainers, implies that Britain would leave the EU but would also keep access to the European single market, thus abiding by some EU laws and regulations. In the same vein, Angela Merkel insisted on limiting Britain's access to the single market if the British government does not abide by the principle of free movement of people. May argued that debate over immigration and trade was not a zero-sum game, emphasizing her intention to seize the opportunity offered by Brexit to carry out fundamental changes in Britain (May, 2017, paras. 58–59). Around the same period of time, the January 2017 Ipsos MORI Political Monitor conducted between January 13 and 16, 2017, revealed that Britons were divided on priorities for Brexit negotiations, with 44% for Britain's access to the single market and 42% for immigration control. Such division seemed to have affected May's popularity in that 45% of voters were satisfied with her job (down 5 points) and 39% were dissatisfied (up 4 points).[6]

May's view was to adopt effective state intervention to tackle issues such as educational underachievement and health disparities among certain people. Her belief is that the government should not be rooted in the laissez-faire liberalism that would hail individualism but rather engaged in tackling various problems:

> Not just in the traditional way of providing a welfare state to support the most vulnerable, as vital as that will always be. But actually in going further to help those who have been ignored by government for too long because they don't fall into the income bracket that makes them qualify for welfare support.
>
> (May, 2017, para. 27)

What is noteworthy is that attitudes towards the EU during that period of time were not very positive in the sense that 57% of EU nationals believed that the EU was on the wrong track as a study conducted by Ipsos MORI between February 17 and March 3, 2017, revealed.[7] In the same vein, the March 2017 Ipsos MORI/Economist Issues Index conducted between March 10 and 19, 2017, revealed that Brexit was the most important issue facing the country, with 51%, up 6 points from the February index of the same year and the highest since records began in September 1974.[8] In the August 2016 Ipsos MORI Issues Index, the EU was the second most important issue, with 31% after immigration/immigrants, with 34%,[9] though the July 2016 Index showed that it was the first issue, with 40%, followed by immigration/immigrants, with 38%.[10] Such fluctuations could be explained by the conflicting views on the way to find the best deal with the EU whether among members of May's government or among members of other political parties.

The Impact on Global Economy and Trade

Brexit and EU migration were also framed in relation to their impact on global economy and trade, affecting Britain and other countries whether in Europe or elsewhere. In January 2016, Mark Rutte, the Dutch prime minister, emphasized the importance of open borders within the EU secured by the Schengen treaty. Rutte expressed his worries about losing that privilege, particularly with the rise of the refugees' crisis and Brexit (Thompson, 2016a). In another article, titled "Why You Should

Care About the Brexit Vote" and posted on the CNN website in June 2016, Brexit, which was fought with two focal issues, namely immigration and the economy, was depicted as a worldwide concern in the sense that Britain represented the world's fifth biggest economy and, therefore, an imminent recession after Brexit would have serious effects on global growth. It was argued that businesses would have second thoughts about their investments in Britain and "a messy EU divorce would likely make that worse" (Thompson, 2016b).

The impact of Brexit on the economy was reinforced in another article reporting on worries of big banks, some of which spent a large amount of money to support the Remain campaigners (like Goldman Sachs), about a Britain-less Europe as it would have a considerable effect on the pound (Kottasova, 2016a). Kottasova (2016b) pointed out some figures showing the link between Britain and the EU in terms of investment and trade. It was reported that 45% of British exports (£230 billion) were directed to other member states and 53% of its imports (£289 billion) originated from EU members, making 3.4 million British jobs dependent on such a trade. As for immigration, Leave campaigners, who have been strong advocates of a curb on immigration to relieve housing, welfare, jobs, and wages, argued that such a curb would not be possible when Britain remains within the EU, basically because of free mobility. But Remain campaigners believed that EU migrants have been an asset to the labor market, contributing to the economy through taxes (Thompson, 2016b).

Another article, posted on the CNN website after the referendum (June 26, 2016) reported on the price that London banks would pay for Brexit. It was argued that London's status as the undisputed financial capital of Europe was put at stake after Brexit. It was pointed out that a large number of global banks would use Britain as a "springboard" for their business activities all over Europe, knowing that banks with premises in one EU country could spread their business across Europe without any further license. In addition, global trade carried out in London was mostly in euros, with transactions, including shares, bonds, and other financial contracts worth trillions of euros. Indeed, Britain had gone to court to stop the European Central Bank from forcing some of that business to take place in the Eurozone, which would likely be corrected by the bank and EU leaders for being considered as anomalous. Jeroen Dijsselbloem, the Dutch finance minister and key euro official, argued that Brexit would deprive Britain of full access to the rest of Europe, benefiting rival financial centers such as Amsterdam and Frankfurt (Kottasova, 2016d).

In November 2016, it was reported that Britain would be pushed to borrow an extra £58.7 billion over the next five years to meet the economic slowdown caused by Brexit according to the Office of Budget Responsibility. Philip Hammond, treasury chief, reckoned that growth would suffer because of growing uncertainty and high inflation as a result of a decline in the pound, slumped 17% against the dollar since

June 23, 2016, putting potential growth at 2.4% lower than that of a different referendum result i.e., victory of the Remain campaigners (Kottasova, 1016e).

The impact of Brexit on the economy was further reiterated in January 2017, highlighting the fact that British households started feeling the pain of the decision to leave the EU. For example, retail sales had a steeper drop than previously expected, both in conventional stores and online, reaching 2.1% according to the Office for National Statistics (ONS). The sharp decline of the pound after Brexit manifested itself in higher prices of imported goods, including food and electronics. After some resistance, consumer spending started to shrink because British consumers were "starting to buckle" under such high prices (Kottasova, 2017).

A number of polls revealed that such economic instability contributed to an increase in uncertainty among Britons. For example, an Ipsos MORI Political Monitor conducted between 14 and 16 May 2016 showed that 49% of voters believed that Britain's economy would get worse in the next five years because of Brexit. Equally important, 43% of voters believed that Brexit would have a major impact on Britain's influence in the world.[11] What is more, in November 2016, 63% of Britons thought that things were on the wrong track ("What Worries the World," 2016).

The Impact on Britain's Social Makeup and National Identities

CNN and BBC coverage emphasized the impact of the two issues on Britain's social makeup in relation to national identities, particularly Britishness versus EU identity in the sense that EU migration involved EU citizens who would theoretically enjoy the same rights as Britons within the EU. An article, titled "Net Migration at 323,000 Prompts EU Referendum Row" and posted in February 2016 on the BBC website, revealed that net migration was at high record, reaching 323,000 arrivals which had prompted the row over a referendum on the EU. This was possibly enhanced by Nigel Farage's view that controlled immigration would not be possible without leaving the EU, presumably because a large number of immigrants were EU nationals. Indeed, it was revealed that there were 165,000 EU citizens in Britain for job prospects, 58% of who had jobs to go to and 42% as job seekers, boosting their employment to two million, according to figures from the Labor Force Survey (October to December 2015). In the case of Bulgarians and Romanians, there were 45,000 new arrivals on the year up to September 2014 for job prospects, with two-thirds having definite jobs to go to ("Net Migration at 323,000," 2016).

The same article reported that Cameron was said to have been warned by the Work and Pensions Secretary against failure to curb immigration, as this would give rise to the far right, stating: "If you do not control your borders, my observation is that you get parties led by people like Marine

Le Pen and others who feed off the back of this, and ordinary decent people feel life is out of control," ("Net Migration at 323,000," 2016).

Madeleine Sumption, director of the Migration Observatory at the University of Oxford, admitted that free mobility within the EU had significantly contributed to high levels of net migration, though in her view other driving factors were behind such high levels. It was argued that EU migration was a "defining issue in the referendum debate" ("Net Migration at 323,000," 2016) despite the difficulty in predicting accurate levels of migration whether by the Remain or the Leave campaigners. Yet, Cameron was severely criticized even by ministers in his own government because immigration figures, after about two years in power, remained three times higher than Cameron's promise ("Net Migration at 323,000," 2016), reaching a second highest record, 333,000, as another article revealed ("Net Migration to UK Rises to 333,000," 2016).

Britons' decision to leave the EU seemed to have shocked not only many people around the world but also Britons themselves, thousands of whom sought to get EU passports to preserve their rights as EU citizens, putting Britishness at stake. It was reported that the German, Italian, Swedish, Polish, and Hungarian embassies and consulate offices registered an upsurge in applications in the wake of the referendum. For example, 200 calls and emails were received by the German embassy in London one day after the referendum had been held, though slowing later to 100 calls a day inquiring about the application process, compared to 500 calls for the Italian embassy to get citizenship applications (Petroff, 2016). However, a survey conducted between July 26 and 29, 2016, and published on September 9 of the same year revealed that 6 in 10 preferred to be British citizens rather than citizens of any other country, with 29% who tended to agree and 31% who strongly agreed on being a citizen of Britain.[12] Among the elderly, percentages were higher, with 71% of 55 to 75 years old who would rather be citizens of Britain. More importantly, in relation to British/European identity or English/Scottish/Welsh, most of the interviewees identified with Britishness or national identities rather than the European one, with an average of 4.6 points allocated for the home country, 4.5 points for Britishness and 0.9 points for the European identity. The implication is that feelings of Britishness have been rekindled at the expense of European identity, presumably as a result of Brexit. A more recent survey, titled "Britain Lags Behind Canada and the U.S. in New Inclusiveness Index" and posted on Ipsos MORI on June 25, 2018, is more illustrative of such feelings. It has been found out that Britain is the 10th country after Canada, the United States, South Africa, France, Australia, Chile, Argentina, Sweden, and Spain, in terms of acceptance of social and cultural diversity.[13]

Nevertheless, the trend of applying for other passports was reinforced in another article, posted on the CNN website in January 2017, revealing that there was a 41% increase in applications for Irish passports among Britons, with 65,000 applications in a bid to retain their EU travel documents, bearing the fact that the British passport was traditionally considered as a privilege, giving its holder global mobility (Petroff, 2017). The same theme was already covered in an article in the BBC, presenting the views of Sigmar Gabriel, German vice chancellor, who suggested that young Britons living in Germany, Italy, or France should get passports of their host countries to keep the privileges offered by EU citizenship (Allen, 2016).[14] Gabriel's suggestion was preceded by the statement of Matteo Renzi, the Italian prime minister, in which he suggested offering British students at European universities EU citizenship. Any Briton with one parent born in an EU country would have an easy process to get such a citizenship. In the case of Ireland, Britons with one Irish grandparent could claim Irish citizenship, knowing that it is possible to pass the Irish identity if a generation registers before the birth of the next without residency requirements. Great-grandchildren of a Lithuanian origin could be offered citizenship; a Maltese citizenship could be obtained by someone who would invest £965,000, adding the requirement of a one-year residency to meet EU pressure (Allen, 2016). Such applications would possibly contribute to the emergence of new Britons within the EU after Brexit.

Conclusion

It has been argued that Brexit and EU migration have been framed by the CNN and BBC in relation to their impact on Britain's position on the international scene, with particular attention to the special Anglo-American relationship and its relation to the EU. The two issues have also been framed in terms of their repercussion on the global economy as well as the British one. Equally important, particularly in relation to Brexit, attention has been paid to its impact on Britishness and EU identity, reiterating the nature of the partnership between Britain, traditionally known as reluctant European and awkward partner, and the EU. The idea of divorce, along with soft and hard Brexit, has been a recurrent theme in the selected articles, putting so many things at stake. Occasionally, Britain has been portrayed as a strong power which could be even better outside the EU, though Brexit and the way to choose the right deal with the EU have had major repercussions on British society, raising uncertainty and division which proved to be unredeemable without a snap election in June 2017. This implies that May, though coming to power without a general election, was unable to settle the issue without seeking to strengthen her position in Parliament. The outcome of the snap election, called by May, particularly because controversy over Brexit negotiations were intense, would be very significant, given the changing nature of the British political landscape, with many signs marking the end of the two-party system and the rise of third parties. Indeed, a divided Opposition, under Jeremy Corbyn, could possibly put the SNP under Nicola Sturgeon, who is gaining more popularity, particularly in Scotland, traditionally Labor's stronghold, in a better position, thus appealing to a large number of British voters. This situation seems to have been the result of media framing in relation to the two issues dealt with in this study, namely Brexit and EU migration, putting more pressure on politicians, May in particular, to respond to people's worries, mainly about the implication of Brexit on the future of the country. In this view, media seem to have raised more tension between Britons and their European counterparts, increasing Euro-skepticism considerably. This in turn seems to have had a major impact on intercultural communication, despite the fact that it has involved people of the same European stock (i.e., EU nationals).

Notes

1. For further details see Martin and Nakayama (2010, pp. 8–11).
2. "The idea of a special relationship with the United States was based on the belief that the Americans would need guidance in how to conduct themselves in international affairs, and would be prepared to accept such guidance from another English-speaking nation which had lately played the role of dominant power in the world" (Stephen, 1998, pp. 14–15). "The Commonwealth, then, had considerable economic and political importance for Britain, but it became a real barrier to co-operation with the six states that eventually came together to form the European Communities. As with the special relationship with the United States, the existence of the Commonwealth as a perceived British sphere of influence deterred British policy-makers from seeing any need to be part of a 'narrow' European grouping" (ibid., pp. 15–16).
3. For further details about Gaulle's veto, see Stephen (1998, pp. 37–38). It has been pointed out that from the end of the Napoleonic Wars to the outbreak of the First World War, Britain, largely because of its early industrialization, had been the dominant state in the international system. It had used this dominance 'to usher in the age of free trade', and had then acted to maintain the system against any threat to its stability" (ibid., p. 12).
4. Labor's stance, according to Stephen (1998), could be explained by their strong "attachment to the ideals of the Commonwealth and the special relationship with the United States" compared to the Conservatives (ibid., p. 35).
5. The survey was carried out among 1,000 online adults aged under 65 in each country. Ipsos MORI 2016, April 22.
6. Ipsos MORI interviewed a representative sample of 1,132 adults aged 18+ across Britain.
7. "60 Years of 'Europe'—A Success Story?" (2017, March 24) Ipsos MORI.
8. A representative quota sample of 1,020 adults aged 18+ across Great Britain was interviewed in a spontaneous manner and face-to-face at 236 sampling points across Britain.
9. A representative quota sample of 1,025 adults aged 18+ across Britain from 188 sampling points.
10. Ipsos MORI interviewed a representative quota sample of 1,025 adults aged 18+ across Great Britain at 188 sampling points.

11. Ipsos MORI interviewed a representative sample of 1,002 adults aged 18+ across Britain.
12. Ipsos MORI interviewed a representative sample of 1,099 adults aged 16–75 across Britain.
13. The Overall Inclusiveness Index is based on the findings of an Ipsos Global Advisor survey of over 20,700 men and women aged under 65 in 27 countries online. Respondents were asked about as many as 28 types of people and for each type, they were asked if they consider such a person to be a "real" national ("a real Briton" in Great Britain, "a real American" in the United States, etc.) or not.
14. It should be noted that under German laws, British citizens could hold on to their UK passport and get a new German one which could be kept even after Brexit. Allen, C. (2016, July 4) "Brexit: Dual Nationality on the Table for Britons?" *BBC*. Retrieved from www.bbc.co.uk.

References

Allen, C. (2016, July 4). Brexit: Dual nationality on the table for Britons? *BBC*. Retrieved from www.bbc.co.uk.
Barnes, I., & Barnes, P. (2010). Enlargement. In C. C. Michelle & N. P. Solórzano Borragán (Eds.), *European union politics* (3rd ed., pp. 418–435). Oxford: Oxford University Press.
Brexit: Europe stunned by UK Leave vote. (2016, June 24). *BBC*. Retrieved from www.bbc.co.uk
Charles, R. (2016, April 29). U.S. officials think Brexit is a terrible idea. *CNN*. Retrieved from www.cnn.com
Colley, L. (1992). *Britons: Forging the nations 1707–1837.* (Rev. ed.). Bath: The Bath Press.
Easton, A. (2016, June 25). EU referendum: Is Brexit bad news for Poland? *BBC*. Retrieved from www.bbc.co.uk
Gamble, A. (1998). The European issue in British politics. In D. Baker & D. Seawright (Eds.), *Britain for and against Europe: British politics and the question of European integration* (pp. 11–30). Oxford, UK: Clarendon Press.
Hall, S. (1999, September). Thinking the diaspora: Home-thoughts from abroad. *Small Axe, 6*, 1–18.
Hawking, L. (2016, June 30). *UK vote stuns the world.* Retrieved from http://amsterdamnews.com
Jones, A. (2007). *Britain and the European Union.* Edinburgh: EUP.
Johnson, D. (2017, March 29). Brexit: Seismic moments at the heart of the EU. *BBC*. Retrieved from www.bbc.co.uk.
Kottasova, I. (2016a, February 15). Why the big banks really hate Brexit. *CNN*. Retrieved from www.cnn.com
Kottasova, I. (2016b, February 21). Brexit: The big numbers you need to know. *CNN*. Retrieved from www.cnn.com
Kottasova, I. (2016c, June 2). How much does the EU really cost Britain? *CNN*. Retrieved from www.cnn.com
Kottasova, I. (2016d, June 26). London banks will pay the "price" of Brexit. *CNN*. Retrieved from www.cnn.com
Kottasova, I. (2016e, November 23). U.K. economy to grow at slowest pace since 2009. *CNN*. Retrieved from www.cnn.com

Kottasova, I. (2017, February 17). Brexit Britain: U.K. shoppers feel the sting of rising prices. *CNN*. Retrieved from www.cnn.com

Lister, T. (2016, June 22). Brexit: Europeans hope Britain will stay, but they' re not begging. *CNN*. Retrieved from www.cnn.com

Martin, J. N., & Nakayama, T. K. (2010). *Intercultural communication in contexts* (5th ed.). Boston, MA: McGraw-Hill.

May, T. (2017). *The shared society: Prime Minister's speech at the charity commission annual meeting.* Retrieved from www.gov.uk

McCombs, M. (2004). *Setting the agenda: The Mass media and public opinion.* Cambridge, UK: Polity Press.

McCombs, M., & Ghanem, S. (2001). The convergence of agenda setting and framing. In S. D. Reese, O. H. Gandy, Jr., & A. E. Grant (Eds.), *Framing public life* (pp. 67–81). London, UK: Lawrence Erlbaum Associates.

McTernan, J. (2017, January 4). How prepared is Britain for Brexit? *CNN*. Retrieved from www.cnn.com

Net migration at 323,000 prompts EU referendum row. (2016, February 25). *BBC*. Retrieved from www.bbc.co.uk

Net migration to UK rises to 333,000: Second highest on record. (2016, May 26). *BBC*. Retrieved from www.bbc.co.uk

Petroff, A. (2016, July 18). Thousands of Brits rush for EU passports after Brexit vote. *CNN*. Retrieved from www.cnn.com

Petroff, A. (2017, January 5). Brexit Britain: Applications for Irish passports surge 41%. *CNN*. Retrieved from www.cnn.com

Roberts, E. (2017, January 3). *UK ambassador to EU resigns months before Brexit negotiations. CNN*. Retrieved from www.cnn.com

Stephen, G. (1998). *An awkward partner: Britain in the European community* (3rd ed.). Oxford, UK: Oxford University Press.

Theresa May: Brexit can "change Britain for the better." (2017, January 9). *BBC*. Retrieved from www.bbc.co.uk

Thompson, M. (2016a, January 21). Two months to save Europe? Refugee crisis and Brexit risk break up. *CNN*. Retrieved from www.cnn.com

Thompson, M. (2016b, June 23). Why you should care about the Brexit vote. *CNN*. Retrieved from www.cnn.com

Von Ondarza, N. (2016, June 8). Europe's nervous silence on Brexit. *CNN*. Retrieved from www.cnn.com

What worries the world. (2016). *Ipsos Mori*. Retrieved from www.ipsos.com/ipsos-mori/en-uk

5 Who Am I? Who Are They?

Otherness in the Human Rights Discourse of the United Nations Facebook Pages

Monserrat Fernández-Vela

New technologies occupy almost every space in modern societies, from industrial development and public services to personal entertainment and leisure activities. Their fast advance is so exponential that the amount of technological inventions produced in one year in 2000 would take only 30 seconds to occur by 2020 (The Emerging Future, 2016). Therefore, human beings are pushed to adapt and change rapidly to keep up with the pace of innovation. New information and communications technologies (ICTs) are changing how people interact and acquire information. Furthermore, during this century in particular, those changes are quicker and deeper. Traditional social networks formed by close relatives and community members now tend to be created in technological spaces that are broader and more diverse because the physical limitations have been erased (Pew Research Center, 2017). The boundaries between the public and the private spheres, home and work, consumer and producer, are unclear (Pew Research Center, 2017).

The fast advance of ICTs pushed new forms of interaction through social networks in virtual spaces. Social network sites (SNS), also called social media (such as Facebook and Twitter), belong to the Web 2.0 characterized by its interactivity, interconnectivity, personalization, and cooperation. Even though the main use of SNS is for personal identity construction, social relationships, or entertainment, recent evidence shows a turn toward using SNS for public affairs like political debate, civic participation, and activism (Gil de Zúñiga, Jung, & Valenzuela, 2012; Harlow, 2011).

During the last decade, SNS have become the focus of research in topics such as the structure of networks (Castells, 2010), the organizational use of SNS in marketing, communication and advertisement (Kaplan & Haenlein, 2010; Thackeray, Neiger, Hanson, & McKenzie, 2008), and audience studies about reception, credibility, and access to SNS (Min Baek, Bae, & Jang, 2013; Westerman, Spence, & Van Der Heide, 2014). Therefore, the limited number of studies about the implications of the use of SNS in human rights activism opens possibilities for new areas of scholarly attention.

In this context, this chapter provides a critical analysis of the human rights discourse produced by three United Nations (UN) entities on the social network site Facebook (FB). The goal of this work is to discuss otherness, the construction of the subject of rights in relation to the positionality of the UN agency towards its audiences, and the production of the messages in this virtual setting, within the international discourse of human rights.

Social Network Sites and Human Rights

The original purpose of SNS was to create public and semi-public profiles for users, allowing them to participate in networks with other people with similar interests and backgrounds (boyd & Ellison, 2008). However, the consumption of SNS has transcended the private interpersonal sphere. In recent years, SNS have been employed by social movements and other public and private organizations to promote and encourage activism and political debate. Moreover, "According to a 2009 survey by DigiActive, social network sites (SNS) are the most common entrance to online activism, despite the fact that SNS were not created with activism in mind" (Brodock et al., 2009, cited in Harlow, 2011, p. 229). The Web 2.0 configuration makes it possible to encourage awareness/advocacy and organization/mobilization by overcoming time, space, and politics (Gil de Zúñiga et al., 2012).

Therefore, ICTs represent, for some scholars and activists, a universe of opportunities (Metzl, 1996). ICTs help attain the universal human right of accessing "as much accurate, complete, relevant, and up-to-date information as everyone needs for the free and full development of their personality" (Walters, 2001, p. 19). Using ICTs in human rights work is not only about free information gathering and dissemination for personal or institutional use, it also implies the possibility to expand the ability of human rights organizations to uncover and analyze patterns and trends in human rights violations (Keck & Sikkink, 1998; Walters, 2001).

In addition, the information revolution raises deep problems for democracy and human rights (Walters, 2001). For those who fear the possible implications of the information era, ICTs can be used as much to violate human rights as to promote them (e.g., the hate propaganda in SNS used by extreme right movements) (Metzl, 1996). The uneven distribution of power among peoples within nations and worldwide is also an important concern. For example, while almost 75% of Africans are non-Internet users, only 21% of Europeans are not (ITU, 2016). Moreover, as Foucault proposed, the gap in the access to knowledge reflects an exacerbation of the privileged position of the developed societies, states, and individuals (Foucault, 1980; Metzl, 1996). The gap reflects a deep power imbalance at the global level between Western developed countries and the nations of the Global South.

Finally, given the flexibility and creative thinking of activists and social movements, the use of technologies and innovations are not new to them. Nevertheless, some scholars suggest that ICTs can "undercut a movement's value, creating a half-hearted, meaningless activism, or 'slacktivism'" (Harlow, 2011, p. 230). The fact remains that ICTs play an increasingly important role in the international human rights community, and its effects are still not fully understood. The dangers and opportunities that they pose represent a prominent area of study for scholars and activists.

The Problematic Discourse About Human Rights in SNS

The transnational human rights discourse is a construction produced and distributed by formal human rights networks (like the UN and other nongovernmental organizations, or NGOs), and informal human rights advocates (grassroots activism and cultural productions) (Hesford, 2011). This discourse represents certain values as universal and uncontestable (Donnelly, 2013), which are disseminated by international networks as neutral and necessary (Keck & Sikkink, 1998). Nevertheless, for an increasing number of scholars around the world, the human rights discourse responds to power relations based on a privileged Western positionality, which legitimizes certain cultural subjectivities and identities over others (Chong, 2014; Coysh, 2014; Dutta & Acharya, 2014; Hesford, 2011; Hunt, 2007; Santos, 2014). In recent years, ICTs have played a central role in circulating a particularly Westernized perspective of international human rights advocacy and activism.

According to Hesford (2011), the media have transformed the human rights discourse into a *spectacular rhetoric* about the construction of the idea of rights directed to Western audiences. The spectacular rhetoric implies the construction of messages about violations against rights and vulnerable populations by appealing to the universal power of emotions (using shocking images and touching stories), and through that to generate public engagement towards human rights principles. However, it is not only the speed, coverage, and visual impact of media messages that make it spectacular, but also the discourse visions, the modes of visibility, and the politics involved. Some critical scholars argue that instead of discussing about vulnerable populations (without really doing anything about them), it is important to discuss which economic, political, social, and cultural circumstances, have created asymmetrical conditions, where some societies (generally Western) have become the bearers of "all" compassion while others (usually non-Western) are the receivers of pity. Therefore, because the spectacular media messages are built particularly to move and engage Western audiences according to their taste, the discourse of human rights presented in the media reveals more about the gaze of the viewer than about the subject of the human rights violations.

Hence, the construction of the subject of rights is related to the imaginary construction of otherness (Alvarez, 2000). On one side is the subject who identifies him/herself as part of the community and positions him/herself as part of the dominant discourse as *I/we*, and in opposition, there is the subject who is imaginary and is positioned outside the community, who becomes the *Other*, the different, the outsider (Alvarez, 2000; Anderson, 2006). Therefore, according to this perspective, talking about otherness in the human rights discourse is not about the Other (as a person bearer of rights); it is an imaginary construction of the Other and the I/we positionalities—who belongs or not in the dominant community, who has the right to speak, and who must be silenced.

Conversely, Levinas (1996) proposed that the Other is more than a concept imagined in oneself. It is a subject outside oneself, by himself worthy of all recognition, and even sympathy and love. The recognition of otherness is an active process which goes beyond mere contemplation. Levinas (1996) remarks that:

> Our relation with the other (*autri*) certainly consists of wanting to comprehend him, but this relation overflows comprehension. Not only because knowledge of the other (*autri*) requires, outside of all curiosity, also sympathy or love, ways of being distinct from impassible contemplation, but because in our relation with the other (*autri*), he does not affect us in terms of a concept. He is a being (*étant*) and counts as such.
>
> (p. 6)

In summary, the (re)creation and (re)production of otherness in SNS reflect complex and intertwined relations between organizations, SNS specificities, and the transnational discourse of human rights. First, the UN entities position themselves in relation to their conception of human rights and towards their audiences. They also answer to the specific characteristics of SNS's messages (such as personalization, interdiscursivity, and intertextuality). Finally, they (re)create and (re)produce those conceptions of human rights and subjects of rights within the international system of human rights. In that context, this research tries to identify some of those relations and positionalities of UN entities in the particular setting of Facebook.

The Context of the United Nation's System of Human Rights

Human rights organizations compete with other agencies for public attention. They attempt to promote the perception of their issues as salient and worthy of attention over other organizations or topics (Tolbert, McNeal, & Smith, 2003), increase public awareness and understanding of issues, invite the public to debate or participate, have an impact on polit-ical agendas, and influence decision makers (Merilainen & Vos, 2011). ICTs and SNS are new spaces to develop communication strategies which bring attention to and promote human rights activism.

Therefore, the UN as the largest human rights organization in the world, is not the exception. The UN communication strategies match the tech-nological advances and innovations of the new era, yet they vary greatly among entities inside the UN. Due to its size and the diverse scope of action of its six core organs and its many organizations, the United Nations is a complex system. Even though all the UN agencies follow the same objectives stated in the UN Charter and coordinate efforts to maximize their effectiveness in action, the autonomy in decision-making and the managerial settings produce unclear roles, redundancies, duplications, high-level fragmentation, and lack of harmonization. For this reason, several reforms were enacted from 1997 to 2006 to fortify and unify the operations within the UN system. However, criticism towards the perceived incoherence and lack of coordination of UN entities' work remains strong (Missoni & Alesani, 2014).

Despite their critics and possible limitations, "the UN has been the cen-tral institution where international human-rights law and politics have met, and often clashed, and where the gap between human rights ideals and realities is especially apparent" (Freeman, 2011, p. 11). Moreover, the international human rights system based on the UN Charter and the Bill of Rights tends to be one of the most common sources of informa-tion about rights worldwide. Therefore, due to the importance of the UN as a producer of a considerable part of the international human rights discourse, studying the communication strategies in SNS of this orga-nization represents a contribution in the analysis of the communication strategies through which the discourse of human rights is constructed and reproduced at the international level.

Human Rights Discourse Analysis of UN Facebook Pages

Founded in 2004, Facebook is the most popular and broadly spread social network site. With around 1.2 billion daily active accounts world-wide, its mission is to "give people the power to share and make the world more open and connected [. . .] to stay connected with friends and family, to discover what's going on in the world and to share and express what matters to them" (Facebook, 2017). It has been increasingly used by INGOs (international nongovernmental organizations) like Human Rights Watch and Amnesty International, and countless human rights and grass roots movements to promote and expand their messages about rights.

In that context, in this chapter, I compare the discourse about human rights on the Facebook pages of three UN entities, selected as an example of the intricacy of the UN system and the variety of its communication strategies. First, UN Women is the FB page of the United Nations Entity for Gender Equality and the Empowerment of Women, an organization dedicated to gender equality and the empowerment of women (UN Women, 2016). Second, UN Refugee Agency is the FB page of the United Nations High Commissioner for the Refugees (UNHCR), dedicated to the rights of refugees, and displaced and stateless people. Third, United Nations Human Rights is the FB page of the Office of the High Commissioner for Human Rights, whose mandate is to promote and protect all human rights (OHCHR, 2016).

The analysis is centered on the idea that the diversity in form and content of the three UN Facebook pages was not arbitrary or a result of organizational inefficiency, but the result of each entity's particular discourse about human rights, actors, voices, roles, and audiences. Having followed these pages for a long time, I decided to retrieve all the posts uploaded during a period of 15 days. All the entries posted between May 15 and 31, 2016, were included (144 in total). Although it is admittedly a small portion of all the posts produced by the organizations, this exploratory piece focuses on multiple perspectives such as the voices and positionality of the actors and agents (who speaks), the formats and representations of those voices (how they speak), and the rationale for the agenda of topics (what is said), within the context of the discourse about human rights of each organization and the UN system as a whole. In this chapter, I propose a multimethod analysis which follows the theorization of Foucault (1980), about power and discourse, Levinas's ideas of otherness (1996), and critical discourse analysis (CDA) theories of Jorgensen and Phillips (2002), and Fairclough (2014).

The first factor analyzed is the agenda of the FB pages and its relation to otherness (Levinas, 1996), and the subject within the discourse (Foucault, 1980). Based on Levinas and Foucault's philosophical proposal, I argue that the positionality of the UN agency (I/We) and its audience in relation to the Other is represented not only by the topics in the agenda, but by the selection of voices and the speaker's status.

Second, I focus on the discursive practices, interdiscursivity, and intertextuality (Fairclough, 2014; Jorgensen & Phillips, 2002) of the UN agencies Facebook pages. Based on Jorgensen and Phillips (2002), I argue that the way in which a text is displayed in a post is, at the same time, structure and practice, and that it shapes language instances. On the one hand, as Merilainene and Vos (2011) noted, the discursive practice is determined by the organization's position about rights, and this delimits what can be said. It demonstrates the complexity of the UN system, the diversity of goals of the agencies (to raise awareness, mobilize, or position itself), and their particular zeitgeist about human rights. On the other hand, it reflects a practice in which the production of the posts is (relatively) determined by the particularities of the SNS, which force the interdiscursivity and intertextuality of the text as proposed by Fairclough (2014).

The Agenda of Human Rights and the Alterity

The selections from the human rights agenda in online communication are used to generate attention to human rights violations, to promote mobilization, to increase public awareness and understanding of issues, or to discuss salient topics (Merilainen & Vos, 2011). In the cases studied, the diversity of the UN organizations was tangible in the agenda proposed in the Facebook pages of UN Women, UNHCR, and OHCHR. Each entity used a different style, and even though some trending topics were common (such as the World Humanitarian Summit—#ShareHumanity, and the refugee crisis especially in relation to the Syrian refugees fleeing to European and Asian countries), the way the information was presented followed unique guidelines appropriate to each one.

According to Indra et al. (2018), trending topics, emerging topics or emerging trends are based on events that produce growing interest in the posts of SNS over time. Those events can be disruptive or political, or daily routines. The study of trending topics is a research area of rising interest in computer sciences and communication scholars. The trending topics of the UN entities followed the specific interest of each organization.

It is also important to highlight the focus of the agenda and the discourse in each agency. According to UN Women, gender is the center of their interest. This follows some feminist authors that propose that every aspect of life (such as health, education, conflict and peace, disabilities) is affected by gender and should be read from that point of view (Jaggar, 1983). Conversely, for the UN Refugee Agency, the macro socioeconomic factors of refuge and displacement, the rights of refugees, and the humanitarian crisis worldwide, are the center of its concern rather than the everyday life issues of refugees. A broader agenda is proposed on the FB page of the High Commissioner of Human Rights. It aims to protect all the rights, and denounce violations at state level. Certainly, the agendas of the three UN entities reflected their special lens about rights.

The first entity analyzed was UN Women. Its page articulated its agenda through topics about gender equality selected by the entity to become a trend (#HeForShe, #FromWhereWeStand, and #DayInTheLife), or topics that answered to the current women rights issues (#Planet5050, and #WomenForSyria). With more than 709,000 likes by June 2016, it was the most prolific FB page of the three organizations analyzed (82 posts in 15 days, and an average of 5.4 per day). Its varied agenda was associated to conferences (organized or not by UN Women), other conflict areas (e.g., Niger, Liberia, Burundi, Congo), commemorative dates (e.g., Parent's Day, Peacekeeper's Day), and diverse topics (e.g., LGBTQ, disabilities, climate change, reproductive health, decision-making, education, sports).

On the UN Women FB page, women were active participants, speakers, and actors in the campaigns. Their voices were heard in the posts through testimonies, stories, and quotes from professionals, advocates, activists, and UN-representatives (almost only female). Examples of posts at UN Women FB page said: "We, as military," "When I joined the Indian police force," "I'm ready to start a monitoring mission," "The project has given me hope and helped me save my children" (UN Women, 2016). It also implied a vision of women as decision-makers in charge of their future in which empowerment is basic to achieve equality goals (e.g., "Women are important actors in the aftermath of natural disasters," "Women are the most active in calling for the need to adapt to #climatechange") (UN Women, 2016). Its position about gender implied that all women must be united as one with common objectives (e.g., "Women need to be one. Our tribe, our party, should be called women," "We are from all around the world, but we have a common objective"), and also, united with men in common goals because "[b]oth men and women are considered human, so they are both part of Human Rights, and Human Rights are for every gender" (UN Women, 2016). The audience's sense of belonging was diluted because the I/We included the producer and the receiver of the message.

In summary, the zeitgeist represented on UN Women Facebook referred to the liberal reading of human rights as self-evident, universal, and individual. Additionally, it followed the mandate of the Convention on the Elimination of All Forms of Discrimination against Women (CEDAW) and the Beijing Declaration and Platform for Action (PFA), which include values such as the empowerment of women and the achievement of equality for both sexes as partners of development. The posts rarely addressed macro issues such as policy changes in states or at the international level, which is, according to Parisi (2013) one of the main criticisms of UN Women. There was no mention of the cases where decision-making is not possible, or in which the constraining of personal liberties does not allow change (at least in the near future). The FB page showed part of the complexity in the women's rights ontological debate, mentioned by authors like Parisi (2013) and Zalewski (2013), about the recognition of women's rights as human rights, women/men rights, gender mainstreaming, and the praxis of these conceptions in the transformation of the reality of women around the world.

The second entity analyzed was the UNHCR. Its Facebook profile is named UN Refugee Agency. This page had 1.18 million likes in June 2016 and it published an average of 2.5 posts per day (38 posts in 15 days). In addition to the trending topic of the World Humanitarian Summit, the focal point of this FB page agenda was the refugee crises (mainly regarding Syrian refugees and the repercussions of their presence in Greece, Iraq, Lebanon, and Germany). However, the UNHCR FB page included other refugees and people displaced by conflicts in Yemen, Libya, Burundi,

China, Niger, Tanzania, and East Harasta (Syria). Unlike UN Women, where women's rights appear in every aspect of life, few topics presented by UNHCR (about one-third of the posts) diverge to other aspects of refugee life, like education, gender, and climate change. Therefore, the agenda was more focused on the macro socioeconomic and political factors of the crisis, and less on the micro aspects of the daily life of the refugees.

The posts analyzed showed that the UNHCR Facebook page talked about refugees, yet the voices of the refugees were almost absent (3 of 36 posts). Conversely, the dominant voice heard in the first person is that of the agency. For example: "Our assistance to refugees and migrants," "We are witnessing the highest level of human suffering," "This week we helped get the first aid since 2013 to this besieged Syrian farm town," "As we tackle the greatest humanitarian crisis since World War II" (UNHCR, 2016b). Also, UN representatives, volunteers, or staff spoke directly to the audience in one of every three posts (e.g., "You can help shelter them," "UNHCR is speaking to you live") (UNHCR, 2016b).

According to Arendt (1958), rights are connected to being a member of a community (mainly referred to a state). Through their displacement, refugees lost their belonging to a community and therefore, their citizenship and their rights. It does not matter "who" they are but "what" they are. They are no longer recognized as speakers and have no voice to demand protection (Benhabib, 2004; Fiske, 2016). Hence, they lost their condition as humans (Arendt, 1958). In the study, even in the few cases where some speakers managed to present their claims at the international level, they seemed to represent the exception rather than the rule. For example, the coverage and stories told by the Team Refugees, formed by ten elite athletes under the auspices of the UN who competed at the Olympic Games 2016 in Rio de Janeiro (Brazil), were not enough voices compared to the 65 million refugees worldwide. Moreover, after their participation in Rio, their ephemeral belonging to a team or the Olympic community disappeared, and they returned to being "refugees."

Additionally, in the case of the refugees worldwide, Western nations perceive that they have no obligation to grant protection and aid to non-Western refugees, and push the non-Western nations to host their neighbor nations' refugees (Betts, 2009). The statistics showed that from the 65.3 million forcibly displaced people (among whom were 21.2 million refugees and 10 million stateless persons), only 6% were hosted by European nations, and 12% by American nations. Asian and African nations hosted the rest of them, mainly neighbors of the conflict (Jordan, Ethiopia, Islamic Republic of Iran, Lebanon, Pakistan, and Turkey) (UNHCR, 2016a).

Following Arendt's argument, if refugees have no voice, then the dominant speaker represented by the *We* (of the UN agency), must speak for the refugees. For example, "Our assistance to refugees," "How can we prevent conflict," "A young sister and brother from Syria," "We are seriously concerned about." In the UNHCR page, there was a complete separation between the speaker (represented by the I/We of the UNHCR), the audience (not included in the I/We), and the refugee as the subject of the message (Other). Its treatment of the information was opposite to the UN Women's FB page, where the We of the UN agency identified the audience as part of the speaker.

The third entity analyzed was the OHCHR, whose Facebook page is called UN Human Rights. With 1.5 million likes by June 2016, it was the most visited of the three pages, yet it had the smallest number of posts (26 in 15 days, an average of 1.7 per day). Due to its nature, in addition to the World Humanitarian Summit and the refugee's crisis in Syria, this FB page covered a variety of topics such as LGBTQ advocacy, death penalty and torture, international system concerns, and the crises in Palestine, Congo, Kenya, Mexico, and Chad. The main voice heard belonged to the UN organization (OHCHR), and it spoke for those whose rights were jeopardized. Nevertheless, the difference from the UNHCR position is that the tone of the OHCHR is demanding (e.g., "We condemn," "We are disturbed," "We are deeply concerned," "We welcome the verdict") (OHCHR, 2016). The OHCHR strongly defended the universal ideal of human rights. As an example, the UN-representative stated his position in the following post.

> Homophobia & Transphobia are no different from sexism, misogyny, racism or xenophobia. Yet we've seen many comments claiming that #humanrights do not apply to all, or downplaying the violence & discrimination that LGBT faces globally. We must meet the challenge that humanity still faces today—the task of learning to live together, as equals, in dignity, and with respect. In the words of our Deputy High Commissioner, "You don't have to like me to respect my rights."
> (OHCHR, 2016)

Another difference with the other two FB pages is that the OHCHR imputed accountability to the states responsible for human rights violations. It did not empower the community (as in the case of UN Women) (Parisi, 2013), or search for cooperation by persuasion (as in the case of UNHCR) (Betts, 2009). It also did not address the audience as insiders (UN Women) or as witnesses (UNHCR). The OHCHR exercised a tone of authority appropriate to the rank of the spokesperson of the entire UN organization in topics related to human rights.

The Discursive Practice of UN Organizations in SNS

Language "as a form of social practice" is a "socially conditioned process, conditioned, that is, by other (non-linguistic) parts of society" (Fairclough,

2014, p. 56). The particular language used by SNS (such as FB) crosses
the boundaries of traditional discourses. The innovative nature of SNS
requires creative discursive practices which challenge and combine different discourses. Also, SNS texts produce intertextual chains, which
incorporate elements from different types of texts (media text, scientific
reports, audience's text and talk). At the same time, the "new 'interdiscursive mixes' are both a sign of, and a driving force in, discursive and
thereby socio-cultural change" (Jorgensen & Phillips, 2002, p. 73). Therefore, the posts analyzed included certain intertextual and interdiscursive
practices produced by editorial decisions shaped by the type of media
and organization, the kind of texts produced, and the context in which
they were generated. The research suggests that the use of interdiscursive
and intertextual practices is specific to the range of actions and topics of
interest of each UN entity.

The UN Women Facebook posts were highly intertextual. First, every
post included a link to an enhanced text at UN Women websites (e.g., UN
Women Asia and the Pacific, or UN Women Africa), and other UN websites
or related human rights' organizations. Most of them had hashtags (e.g.,
#Together4Peace, #Planet5050, #WomenForSyria, #FromWhereIStand,
#HeForShe, #WhyWeFight, #globalgoals, #WorldEnvironmentalDay,
#ParentsDay, #WomenRefugee), which allowed a quick follow-up of the
topics. The length of the text was short (approx. 100 characters), concise, and linked to further information. Every post also had audiovisual
materials (photos, videos, or infographics), including visual keys such as
headings, quotes, or photo captions. One salient characteristic was that
some women (professionals, activist, UN representatives, volunteers)
were usually represented in an empowered position (crossed arms, facing
and looking directly at the camera), and a small text about topics of their
concern accompanied each photo inside the image. In other cases, adult
women were presented in active roles, sometimes giving testimony about
their struggles. This characteristic of the UN Women page ratified three
aspects mentioned above: the ontological conception of women as actors
and agents of change, the interconnection of women's rights intertwined
with other (human) rights and aspects of life, and the direct engagement
with the audience as part of the message (speaker and audience had the
same I/We positionality).

The interdiscursive practices in the UN Women page were also related
to its goal and philosophy. It incorporated texts by UN representatives
(like the Head of Arab States Section of UN Women, or the Executive
Director of UN Women), activists and practitioners (like the Vice President of the Executive Council at Kobani Canton), professionals (e.g.,
a psycho-social therapist, a lawyer, and a journalist). Mainly, the post
depicted the voices of experts and authorities, using a more technical
language. However, UN Women also incorporated several voices of
women, through testimonies and stories, which provided an alternative

perspective closer to the common reader of the audience. The post about the story of a refugee in the Central Africa Republic, or the testimony of an LGBTQ couple of Cambodia, were examples of alternative voices presented by UN Women. Additionally, one salient aspect of this FB page was the connection between educational and informational content. On the one hand, there were texts produced by an SNS journalist, which followed the concise informational style of an SNS text (small and clear texts supported by different images, videos, and infographics); on the other hand, there was educational material, such as the Compendium of Good Practices on Training for Gender Equality. The variety of languages reflected the goals of educating and disseminating women's rights, including a variety of voices and empowering women in all positions.

In the case of the UN Refugees Facebook page, this organization had a different editorial policy. Its posts were longer (between 100 and 500 characters) and had fewer external links. Two-thirds of the photographs included midground shots of children looking at the camera in passive roles without adding phrases or quotes as part of the photos. The other third of the photographs showed diverse aspects of the refugees, yet the positionality of the refugees was passive. The Facebook page used only a few hashtags, yet had more videos (approx. 50 seconds long). One salient characteristic of this FB page was that one-third of its posts advertised the organization (e.g., "We have a new webpage," "Our assistance to refugees," "Melissa Fleming—UNHCR is speaking to you live, " "Coming up shortly—Facebook Live tour of our refugee registration simulation," "From our archives") (UNHCR, 2016b). Moreover, the speaker of some of the videos was the UN-representative of the High Commissioner for Refugees. This narrative portrayed the UNHCR as the center of the action, as saviors, a common positionality of Western human rights discourse (Barranquero, 2011; Dutta & Acharya, 2014; Griffin, 2015). It also demonstrated the agency's need to show its work, call for witnesses, prove its value and make its voice be heard among its Western audience (Benhabib, 2004). In contrast, the discourse ratified the construction of the Other (refugees) as passive subjects, as victims in need of help (Hesford, 2011).

The UN Refugees Agency interdiscursive practices were limited. As explained above, the language was dominated by the expert voice of the Agency as an entity. The otherness was portrayed through a few testimonies of refugees from Uganda, Syria, and Niger (mainly on the videos posted). However, the notable aspect of UNHCR Facebook page was the higher number of videos (eight videos of approximately 50 seconds each). The audiovisual language by itself was a different mode of presentation for the information. According to Gubern (2000), and Wodak and Meyer (2016), the strength of the audiovisual materials is the strong and immediate emotional response generated by images over textual messages. Also, the tone of the FB posts was mainly informative and did not add explicit educational content, address the refugees, or educate the audience about refugee rights. Moreover, the UN Refugee Agency pushed a self-promotional discourse through the posts (e.g., several posts where the organization promotes itself, its work, its web page, and Facebook page). Therefore, the discursive practice of this FB page seemed to follow the UNHCR's goal of protecting through persuasion (Betts, 2009), with very few interdiscursive practices.

The Facebook page of the OHCHR, called United Nations Human Rights, incorporated characteristics of the other two FB pages. It had even longer texts, multiple links, and hashtags (e.g., #ShareHumanity, #WhyWeFight, #Kenya, #Syria). Its audiovisual resources included longer videos (from two to ten min.), produced photographs (with captions or headings), and some infographics. The portrait of the Other switched from the active roles of activists to passive victims of human rights violations. In this case, the UN agency also had a dominant central role as the speaker (dominant I/we). Nevertheless, its texts were not intended to promote itself, but to state its position toward human rights violations.

The interdiscursivity of the OHCHR Facebook page was more related to its political discourse than to the genre of the text. The highly demanding and denouncing tone of the posts implied a positionality articulated within the political scenario of the international human rights system. Its positionality departed from the modern and liberal idea of universalism as a moral standpoint. Therefore, from this perspective, all human rights violations are proscribed, and all subjects are accountable for their acts (Benhabib, 2004). Consequently, its audience is also universal, because every state and individual are equally entitled to human rights and accountable for their violations. This position uncovers the fact that universalism maintains a particular cultural articulation of the Westernized zeitgeist about human rights (Hesford, 2011).

Conclusions

In this chapter, I argue that the differentiated communicative strategies of the UN agencies' FB pages were not arbitrary, but the result of the particular construction of human rights discourse emanated by the UN Women, the UNHCR, and the OHCHR. As we have reviewed, multiple dimensions play a role to link the notion of otherness, the relationship of power and knowledge, the discursive practices in social media, NTIC's and SNS language and production specificities, with the strongly debated discourse about human rights and the role of the media in the construction of the human rights discourse. Hence, the value of this research is the interdisciplinary and multifocal perspective that made possible a critical discourse analysis of the three FB pages, centered on the construction of the otherness (through the agenda of Facebook), the positionality of the organization (zeitgeist about human rights), and its articulation on the discursive practices (intertextuality and interdiscursivity) within the contextual framework of the international human rights discourse.

Additionally, the analysis shows that each agency proposed a specific construction of the I/we and the Other. Following Jorgensen's (2002) premise, a starting point for discourse analysis is to understand the characterization of the subject. According to Foucault (1980), subjects are created in discourse, yet the representation of the I and the Other is not only enacted within the consciousness through language, but they have concrete repercussions on the reality (Levinas, 1996). The position of the agencies represented the implicit ontological conception of rights (women's rights, refugees' rights, and human rights), the constitutive principles and policies of each organization (UN Charter, bodies, and agencies), which are not explicit.

Also, the use of the SNS of these three UN entities as sources of information about human rights impacts the way in which audiences understand and construct their notions of human rights. Depending on the agenda of each FB page, the readers can identify certain topics as more prominent and worthy of attention than others. The agenda, which is not arbitrary but the result of the zeitgeist of the agency, can also affect the proximity and identification with the topics, the actors, the expected role and answers to those problems, and the possible outcomes of their actions. The positionality of each agency also influences the way human rights are constructed and perceived. However, it is necessary to acknowledge that those perceptions are intertwined with the reader's own ontological position towards rights. Hegemony is not only a process of dominance but a negotiation of meanings and stages of resistance (Fairclough, 1992, p. 91, cited by Jorgensen & Phillips, 2002, p. 76)

In contrast, according to Jorgensen and Phillips (2002), "by analyzing intertextuality and interdiscursivity it is possible to gain insight into the role of discourse in processes of social change" (p. 139). The evidence of the three FB pages suggested abundant intertextuality. In the three pages, it was common to use hashtags to direct the attention of the reader, audiovisual materials (images, videos, and infographics) to create impact and emotional identification, and links to other websites of the entities and other organizations. However, each entity's editorial decisions about the resources followed a specific conception of human rights, and it was reinforced by the selection of the types of texts, and the voices included in that text. Moreover, the editorial decisions about the texts reflected the way in which otherness was constructed. Therefore, the intertextuality analyzed showed a high inter-referentiality among UN entities within the UN system, a predominance of the UN voice (as a whole organization), its dominant zeitgeist over Others (regional or local standpoints), and a contextualization of human rights within the international liberal Westernized discourse of rights.

Moreover, the three FB pages introduced interdiscursive practices, in which different types of discourses were articulated within the same post. Mainly, the core discourse was about human rights, but it was intertwined with discourses about poverty, health, conflict, education, and gender. There was also a predominant expert language based on authority, such as UN representatives, heads of states, renowned advocates and organizations, whose value rested on the voices they represented. It also referred, in some cases, to the voices of different Others, presented through testimonies, stories, and quotes. Similarly, it included the language of the media, dictated by the laws of text production in journalism (concision, precision, accuracy, clarity, and intelligibility) and of the audiovisual language (rules, frames, shots). Additionally, it introduced components of the edu-communicational discourse, in the UN Women FB page, the promotional discourse in the Refugee Agency page, and the political discourse of the OHCHR page. The interdiscursivity and intertextuality of the three FB pages reinforced the idea that the production of the discourse of each entity reflects its positionality within the human rights international discourse of the UN system which is produced for and through Western audiences, silencing divergent worldviews.

More research is needed in relation to the possible use of SNS to encourage awareness/advocacy and organization/mobilization, by overcoming time, space, and politics (Gil de Zúñiga et al., 2012; Harlow, 2011), or to undercut a movement's value by creating a half-hearted, meaningless activism, or "slacktivism" (Morozov, 2009; Van de Donk et al., 2004, cited in Harlow, 2011, p. 230). It is important to develop studies that analyze the articulation between the production of human rights discourse in SNS and the mobilization of their audiences in real life. More research will also be needed to link this study to other aspects of the production and consumption of SNS related to human rights, such as studies about the audiences or the communicational strategies of other human rights organizations.

Finally, I argue that without ignoring the enormous advances of human rights, generated by the UN system and other activists and advocates around the world, now more than ever, it is necessary to question the dynamics operating behind the apparent neutrality and universality of the human rights discourse, and to problematize the cultural assumptions, the voices silenced, the otherness ignored, the over-institutionalization of UN agencies and the strong Westernized zeitgeist imposed through the international discourse of human rights. From that perspective, non-Western nations can consolidate the democratization of the discourse about human rights in virtual networks incorporating diverse voices and articulating them with their macro-sociological realities.

References

Alvarez, F. (2000). *Las derivas de la alteridad*. Quito, Ecuador: Abya-Yala.
Anderson, B. (2006). *Imagined communities*. London, UK: Verso Books.

Arendt, H. (1958). *The human condition*. Chicago, IL: University of Chicago.

Barranquero, A. (2011). Rediscovering the Latin American roots of participatory communication for social change. *Westminster Papers in Communication and Culture, 8*(1), 154–177.

Benhabib, S. (2004). The right to have rights: Hannah Arendt on the contradictions of the nation-state. In S. Benhabib, *The rights of others: Aliens, residents, and citizens* (pp. 49–69). Cambridge, UK: Cambridge University Press.

Betts, A. (2009). *Protection by persuasion: International cooperation in the refugee regime*. Ithaca, NY: Cornell University Press.

boyd, d., & Ellison, N. (2008). Social network sites: Definition, history, and scholarship. *Journal of Computer-Mediated Communication, 13*, 210–230.

Brodock K., Joyce, M., & Zaeck, T. (2009). Digital activism survey report 2009. *DigiActive*. Retrieved from http://www.digiactive.org/wpcontent/uploads/Research4_SurveyReport2009.pdf

Castells, M. (2010). *The information age*. Chichester, UK: Wiley-Blackwell.

Chong, D. (2014). *Debating human rights*. London, UK: Lynne Rienner Publishers.

Coysh, J. (2014). The dominant discourse of human rights. *Journal of Human Rights Practice, 6*(1), 89–114.

Donnelly, J. (2013). *Universal human rights in theory and practice*. Ithaca, NY: Cornell University Press.

Dutta, M., & Acharya, L. (2014). Power, control, and the margins in an HIV/AIDS intervention: A culture-centered interrogation of the "Avahan" campaign targeting Indian truckers. *Communication, Culture & Critique, 8*, 254–272.

The Emerging Future. (2016). *Disruptive technology*. Retrieved from http://theemergingfuture.com/disruptive-technology.htm

Facebook. (2017). *Newsroom*. Retrieved from Company Info: http://newsroom.fb.com/company-info/

Fairclough, N. (2014). *Language and power*. London, UK: Routledge.

Fairclough, N. (1992). *Discourse and social change*. Cambridge: Polity Press.

Fiske, L. (2016). Human rights and refugee protest against immigration detention: Refugee's struggles for recognition as human. *Refuge, 32*(1), 18–27.

Foucault, M. (1980). *Power/knowledge*. New York, NY: Routledge.

Freeman, M. (2011). *Human rights*. Cambridge, UK: Polity Press.

Gil de Zúñiga, H., Jung, N., & Valenzuela, S. (2012). Social media use for news and individuals' social capital, civic engagement and political participation. *Journal of Computer-Mediated Communication, 17*, 319–336.

Griffin, R. (2015). Problematic representations of strategic whiteness and "post-racial" pedagogy: A critical intercultural reading of the help. *Journal of International and Intercultural Communication, 8*(2), 147–166.

Gubern, R. (2000). *El eros electrónico*. Madrid, Spain: Santillana.

Harlow, S. (2011). Social media and social movements: Facebook and an online Guatemalan justice movement that moved offline. *New Media & Society, 14*(2), 225–243.

Hesford, W. (2011). *Spectacular rhetorics*. Durham, NY: Duke University Press.

Hunt, L. (2007). *Inventing human rights*. New York, NY: W. W. Norton & Company.

Indra, Winarko, E., & Pulungan, R. (2018). Trending topics detection of Indonesian tweets using BN-grams and Doc-p. *Journal of King Saud University: Computer and Information Sciences, 31*, 266–274.

ITU. (2016). *Development*. Retrieved from ICT Facts and Figures 2016 www.itu.int/en/ITU-D/Statistics/Documents/facts/ICTFactsFigures2016.pdf

Jaggar, A. (1983). *Feminist politics & human nature*. Lahman, MD: Rowman & Littlefield.

Jorgensen, M., & Phillips, L. (2002). *Discourse analysis as theory and method.* London, UK: Sage Publications.

Kaplan, A., & Haenlein, M. (2010). Users of the world, unite! The challenges and opportunities of social media. *Business Horizons, 53*(1), 59–68.

Keck, E., & Sikkink, K. (1998). *Activists beyond borders: Advocacy networks in international politics.* Ithaca, NY: Cornell University Press.

Levinas, E. (1996). *Emmanuel Levinas: Basic philosophical writings* (A. Peperzak, S. Critchley, & R. Bernasconi, Eds.) Bloomington, IN: Indiana University Press.

Merilainen, N., & Vos, M. (2011). Human rights organizations and online agenda setting. *Corporate Communications: An International Journal, 16*(4), 293–310.

Metzl, J. (1996). Information technology and human rights. *Human Rights Quarterly, 18*(4), 1–30.

Min Baek, Y., Bae, Y., & Jang, H. (2013). Social and parasocial relationships on social network sites and their differential relationships with users' psychological well-being. *Cyberpsychology, Behavior, and Social Networking, 16*(7), 512–517.

Missoni, E., & Alesani, D. (2014). *Management of international institutions and NGOs: Frameworks, practices and challenges.* Abingdon, UK: Routledge.

Morozov, E. (2009). Iran: Downside to the 'Twitter Revolution'. *Dissent, 56*(4), 10–14.

OHCHR. (2016). *United Nations human rights*. Retrieved from www.facebook.com/unitednationshumanrights/info/?entry_point=page_nav_about_item

Parisi, L. (2013). Gender mainstreaming human rights: A progressive path for gender equality? In C. Holder & D. Reidy (Eds.), *Human rights: The hard questions* (pp. 436–157). Cambridge, UK: Cambridge University Press.

Pew Research Center. (2017). *Internet & Tec.* Retrieved from Three Technology Revolutions www.pewinternet.org/fact-sheet/social-media/

Santos, B. S. (2014). *Derechos humanos, democracia y desarrollo*. Bogotá, Colombia: Dejusticia.

Thackeray, R., Neiger, B., Hanson, C., & McKenzie, J. (2008). Enhancing promotional strategies within social marketing programs: Use of Web 2.0 social media. *Health Promotion Practice, 9*(4), 338–343.

Tolbert, T., McNeal, R., & Smith, D. (2003). Enhancing civic engagement: The effect of direct democracy on political participation and knowledge. *State Politics and Policy Quarterly, 3*(1), 23–41.

UNHCR. (2016a). *Global trends 2015.* Retrieved from Statistical Yearbooks www.unhcr.org/figures-at-a-glance.html

UNHCR. (2016b). *UNHCR, UN refugee agency*. Retrieved June 2016, from www.facebook.com/UNHCR/

UN Women. (2016). Retrieved June 2016, from www.facebook.com/unwomen/

Van de Donk, W., Loader, B. D., Nixon, P. G., & Rucht, D. (2004). *Cyberprotest: New media, citizens and social movements.* London: Routledge.

Walters, G. (2001). *Human rights in an information age: A philosophical analysis.* Toronto, Canada: University of Toronto.

Westerman, D., Spence, P., & Van Der Heide, B. (2014). Social media as information source: Recency of updates and credibility of information. *Journal of Computer-Mediated Communication, 19*, 171–183.

Wodak, R., & Meyer, M. (2016). *Methods of critical discourse studies.* London, UK: Sage Publications.

Zalewski, M. (2013). Hard questions about women's human rights. In C. Holder & D. Reidy (Eds.), *Human rights: The hard questions* (pp. 362–381). Cambridge, UK: Cambridge University Press.

Part II

Intercultural Communication and Online Social Movements

6   Tents, Tweets, and Television

Communicative Ecologies and the *No to Military Trials for Civilians* Grassroots Campaign in Revolutionary Egypt

Nina Grønlykke Mollerup

A 19-year-old boy was subjected to military trial and was beaten absolutely horribly [in prison]. Beaten horribly. We managed to get the mother on TV and discuss everything and to say everything that happened to her son, including the violence inside the prison. As soon as she came off the air someone from the Ministry of Interior called her and said, "I'm at your command."

Activist from *No to Military Trials for Civilians*[1]

On February 11, 2011, the Supreme Council of the Armed Forces (SCAF) deposed Egyptian president for 30 years, Hosni Mubarak, after 18 days of mass protests and strikes across Egypt. SCAF took over presidential powers of the country in what it, pressured by the masses in the street, professed as a transitional phase to elections. Army tanks first moved into the epicentre of the protests, Tahrir Square, on January 28, 2011. They were welcomed as heroes. People clapped, shook hands with and kissed the soldiers, climbed triumphantly on the tanks and armed personnel carriers (APCs) and chanted, "*al gīsh wa al sha'b yid waḥda*" ("the army and the people are one hand").[2] Though some were confused about the role of the army, particularly as it stood by and watched as protesters in Tahrir Square were attacked on several occasions (Batty & Olorenshaw, 2011; Weaver, Siddique, Owen, & Adams, 2011), the army generally maintained a reputation as the saviours of the revolution at this time. On the night of February 25, 2011, two weeks after Mubarak was deposed, the army violently cleared Tahrir Square of protesters. Some protesters had remained there and some had come back to mark the two weeks since the overthrow. Many of these protesters were beaten and arrested. Several activists told me that it was at this point, they started realizing the extent to which the army, notwithstanding their popularity, had been arresting and torturing protesters and subjecting them to quick and unjust military trials. That is, trials in which lawyers were not allowed to represent the accused and in which uniformed judges, subject to orders from their military superiors, presided (Human Rights Watch,

2011a). Activists told me they had realized that large numbers of people had been sent to military courts since the army entered the streets on January 28, 2011. They also told me that even death sentences were handed out in such trials. A small group of activists met and discussed the issue of military trials for civilians. This was the beginning of one of the most significant human rights grass roots campaigns in Egypt after the revolution was popularized on January 25, 2011. The campaign, which came to be pertinently named *No to Military Trials for Civilians*, aimed at ending the practice of military trials for civilians. They started working to do so by trying to give legal support to victims of military trials, lobbying for changing the practices and laws regarding military trials, and spreading awareness of the trials and related issues such as torture and violence, which many victims of military trials were subjected to. Despite the power and popularity of the army, the history of lack of freedom of expression in Egypt, and the mainly upheld red line of critique of the army, *No to Military Trials for Civilians* managed to get broad attention to army abuses of civilians. They did so in many ways, including getting victims and family members of victims of military trials on major political talk shows and other institutional media, getting candidates of the 2012 presidential elections to speak up against military trials, and influencing street mobilization both by calling for demonstrations and encouraging participation in demonstrations. I use the term "institutional media" to designate state media outlets, corporate media outlets, and other more established media outlets. In contrast, I use the term "cheap media" to designate media, which—mainly due to its cost—is more accessible than for instance a satellite television station. The cheap media I particularly have in mind includes phones, graffiti, placards, banners, computers, projectors, and walls, as well as digital platforms such as Twitter, Facebook, YouTube, Vimeo, Flickr, and much more. However, it is important to point out that I do not wish to impose any rigid distinctions between the categories.

This chapter describes how this campaign despite the odds succeeded in gaining a significant amount of public recognition and attention, including from regime-friendly institutional media. With the analytical lens of communicative ecologies, I describe in empirical detail how the vast array of communicative practices involved in the campaign played a role in enabling *No to Military Trials for Civilians* to get criticism of the army out in institutional media and thus cross red lines of censorship. I argue that the campaign's success must be understood in the context of these practices, which include people directly and indirectly involved with the campaign exchanging phone numbers in lines in the desert, producing video testimonies, embedding such a video in a Human Rights Watch statement, occupying Tahrir Square, setting up a campaign tent during sit-ins, organizing press conferences, tweeting from battles, and much more.

The chapter is based on seven months of ethnographic fieldwork carried out in Egypt in 2012 and 2013, previous fieldworks and stays in Egypt, and an extended period of fieldwork at a distance (Peterson, 2015). When in Cairo, I have interviewed activists and journalists and carried out participant observation at the office of video activist collective, Mosireen, which included several members of *No to Military Trials for Civilians*. I also participated in a demonstration outside the military facility, C28, during the last session in the case of Samira Ibrahim against the military doctor who subjected her to a so-called virginity test.[3] I have followed institutional and cheap media as events unfolded, whether in Egypt or not. I have stayed in contact and kept up to date with activists and journalists since my last fieldwork in 2013 through continuous visits to Egypt and through cheap media, including follow up interviews carried out with phones, Skype, emails, and Facebook.

Communicative Ecologies: Media, Entanglements, and the Environment

Understanding *No to Military Trials for Civilians*' ability to reach institutional media entails looking beyond specific media types and beyond media itself. With a point of departure in media as emplaced, that is, as part of a corporeal and moving environment, I investigate the communicative practices related to the campaign using the analytical lens of communicative ecologies. Jo Tacchi (2005) describes communicative ecologies as "the complete range of communication media and information flows in a community" (p. 343) and emphasizes that technologies emerge in already existing and continuously changing communicative ecologies (pp. 343–344). Taking this approach is useful because it allows me to (1) pay attention to media as part of an environment, (2) emphasize media as emerging, and (3) maintain that while relations are organic and unpredictable, they are informed by affordances. Let me elaborate on each point. First, the ecologies approach entails seeing media as part of an environment, or in Tim Ingold's (2006) words, what might be envisaged as "a domain of entanglements" (p. 14). That is, seeing media as part of an environment entails an awareness of the entanglements of media in their environment. It avoids the unconstructive focus on one particular media or focusing solely on media and instead focuses on the entanglements between media and other things. That is, nothing in an ecology exists on its own; it exists as part of and in continuous engagement with a larger whole. Thus, this approach helps me overcome some of the misconceptions, which has haunted many studies of media and the Arab Uprisings, For instance, as Zeynep Tufekci (2012) has argued, too often debates about events such as the Arab uprisings have unconstructively focused on whether technology or people were the deciding factor, as if the two were independent of each other. Other similarly unproductive debates have focused on which medium was decisive in sparking uprisings (see for instance Alterman, 2011; Eltantawy & Wiest, 2011; Howard et al., 2011; Khamis & Vaughn, 2011), deemphasizing the interdependence between different types of media. Second, with the focus on media as part of an environment comes an understanding of media as emerging, because focusing on media as part of the environment brings entanglements and therefore movement to the forefront. That is, this approach prioritizes becoming over being (Goddard, 2015) and understands media as part of a world of things that continually comes into being as they are brought into correspondence, rather than a world of ready-made objects to which meaning has already been attached (Ingold, 2008; 2013). As things move and are moved, they merge and move on in a different state. As a video of military violence against protesters is moved from a computer through a projector, it becomes light in the air, which merges with the huge makeshift screen of the state TV building and becomes images, showing screening participants new ways of countering state television (Mollerup & Gaber, 2015). Focusing on media as emerging encourages attention to history and the processes that have brought about the current environment. Peter Dahlgren (2011) has argued, social media platforms like Twitter and Facebook do not create new networks or new practices in a social vacuum. Rather, he contends, new media tap into old networks and alter these in a way that is dependent on historical, political, and social contexts as well as on technology. The ecologies approach allows a focus on the relations between what uses of particular media means for the organization of dissent and what the organization of dissent means for uses of particular media. That is, it does not favour a unidirectional cause and effect logic, but rather prioritizes interdependence in all its complexity. Third, the ecologies approach to media allows attention to affordances of an environment. Vaike Fors, Åsa Bäckström, and Sarah Pink (2013) explain that

> [affordances] are relative to an organism; it is not an objective property of the environment (e.g., water affords breathing for the fish but not for the human). Thus, the term affordance refers to whatever it is about the environment that contributes to the kind of interaction that occurs with a strong emphasis on movement as the constituent of perceptual activity.
>
> (pp. 172–173)

The concept of affordances is particularly crucial for the ecologies approach to media as it sees qualities as relational and not as objective properties and thus it avoids the technological determinism, which has haunted so many recent studies of particularly new media in Egypt and elsewhere (Armbrust, 2012).

No to Military Trials for Civilians

In the following section, I describe parts of the communicative ecologies of *No to Military Trials for Civilians* focusing particularly on the period from the campaign's creation in February and March, 2011, and until July 3, 2013, when a new military coup deposed Muslim Brotherhood President Mohammed Morsi after widespread protests (Kingsley & Chulov, 2013). During this period, many media corporations, which for different reasons had been supportive of the Mubarak regime, changed their course and became critical of authorities, thus functioning more as a watchdog than a mouthpiece of the regime as they had done previously. Other media corporations, which had provided critical journalism of the Mubarak regime to the extent it was possible, as for instance Aljazeera Mubasher Misr, became less critical when Mohammed Morsi became the president, changing from a role as a watchdog to more of a mouthpiece. The shifting alliances and styles of journalism were influenced by financial models, political alliances, and editors, who were strategically placed by different power holders (Reporters Without Borders, 2014). In other words, as media corporations were entangled with their intensely moving environments, they were moved, some becoming more critical of authorities and other losing their critical approach. Their criticism or lack thereof was not an objective property of the corporations, rather it was relational to their environment. After the overthrow of Mubarak, freedom of speech and institutional media's interests in critiquing those in power reached unprecedented heights in Egypt, yet the army remained a red line, which was very difficult to cross (Sakr, 2013). Criticism of the army at this time in Egypt was unpopular and dangerous. Blogger Maikel Nabil experienced this, when he was given a three year jail sentence after posting a blog entry on March 7, 2011, named "The army and the people were never one hand" (Human Rights Watch, 2011a).[4] The blogpost drew on the popular chant, "the army and the people are one hand" while providing critique and video evidence of military violence against protesters. In this environment, the people behind the *No to Military Trials for Civilians* campaign had a very difficult challenge in gaining any kind of support or attention for their plight. An activist described to me some of the challenges they were facing at the time:

> People in Egypt back then were supportive of the military and they refused to criticize what was going on and they believed that the military trials were better for society and were controlling the amount of crimes in the street. So we were really on our own in the beginning. In the beginning we were always attacked by people.

Yet the lack of support did not stop the people involved with *No to Military Trials for Civilians* from their work. Let me now turn to particular aspects of the communicative ecologies of the *No to Military Trials for Civilians* campaign.

Torture and Testimonies

After Mubarak was deposed on February 11, 2011, most protesters left Tahrir Square and the world's attention shifted from the square. The round the clock live camera Aljazeera had had on Tahrir Square was removed and journalists went on to new assignments. However, a group of protesters continued the sit-in in the square to keep pressure on the SCAF, which was now leading the country. When the army violently cleared Tahrir Square of protesters on the night of February 25, 2011, many protesters were arrested as were people who by chance were in the area. Little attention was given to the clearing beyond the people who were present. A group of around ten people who had been part of the protests in the square met and discussed the problem of military trials and the need to organize around this issue. This was the start of the *No to Military Trials for Civilians* campaign. A group of protesters went back to the square after the February 25 clearing. On March 9, 2011, the military once again cleared the square violently. The arrested were taken to the Egyptian Museum where they were beaten and tortured (see Human Rights Watch, 2012). An activist I spoke with, whose friends were tortured at the museum on this day, described it as some of the most vicious violence he had heard of at the time. This time, many of the people who were arrested were well-connected activists. Several of them had even been part of the many small regime-critical demonstrations in the decade leading up to 2011. At least one journalist was among the arrested, but she was released before the others. Many of the people who were arrested on March 9, 2011, already knew each other from the 18 days of protest in Tahrir Square or from the protest movement leading up to January 25, 2011. These relations grew stronger with the events. When a group of people met after the first clearing of the square on February 25, they did so in response to the clearing. The meeting was influenced by their relations, which were dependent on previous events, just like their relations was influenced by the meeting; that is, the events afforded the activists an opportunity to come together and organize. Thus, they were able to develop new ways of organizing, including hosting a press conference with testimonies from torture victims.

The group of activists, lawyers, and others, who had met and discussed military trials after the first clearing of Tahrir Square, arranged a press conference on March 16, 2011, under the name *No to Military Trials for Civilians*. The press conference was held in collaboration with the Liberties Committee at the Press Syndicate. Victims from the torture of March 9, 2011, who had been released by the military, gave their testimonies. A man described, "I had long hair then. They dragged me by the hair. As they dragged me, they started beating me in every possible way.

They began giving me electric shocks in sensitive areas" (tahrirDiaries 2011a). Salwa El-Hosseini Gouda also spoke at this press conference. She was the first woman to publicly testify to being submitted to so-called virginity testing:

> We were put in a room with two doors and a window. [. . .] Every girl had to take off all her clothes to be searched while cameras were filming from outside to help them make prostitution cases against us [. . .] and any girl who said she was a virgin was subjected to a check-up by a man (tahrirDiaries 2011a).

Family members of victims of military trials, who had not been released, also testified. A father said:

> For a month I didn't see my son or hear anything about him. I got a phone call from Al Wadi Al Gedid [Prison], "your son, Ahmed, is in Al Wadi Al Gedid." I went to Al Wadi Al Gedid, a 10 hour journey, to see my son. Until now, I don't know what my son was sentenced with. One said "five years," I don't know. Another said "one year," I don't know. I went to the military court, but I couldn't get any statement about my son. I want to know on what charges my son is imprisoned and why he was arrested (tahrirDiaries 2011a).

Many activists later told me that the most important aspect of *No to Military Trials for Civilians* was the courage of the victims to come forward, something which was unusual even though Egyptian authorities had a long history of torturing citizens. A journalist, who attended the press conference told me:

> This was the first time that the people have been really severely tortured by the military. [. . .] People that were arrested spoke about what happened to them and the torture and they told the stories. It really was one of the most powerful press conferences of the last year because the stories were really very shocking at the time. It was the first time that we hear about such very hard abuse.

With the relative freedom allowed to her from writing for a mainly English language newspaper, she was one of the few to write about the torture described at the press conference, including the sexual assaults of the so-called virginity tests. Some journalists, who went to the press conference, covered parts of the torture but left out particularly troublesome parts such as the so-called virginity tests.[5] A human rights worker involved with the *No to Military Trials for Civilians* campaign told me:

> Some of the reporters working for some of the bigger Egyptian newspapers, especially Al Masry Al Youm and Al Shorouq, would then

contact the group afterwards and say, "look, we're really sorry, you know, our editors wouldn't let us publish anything about this."

While torture at the hands of the Egyptian military had gotten some attention in international media even before this, the Egyptian institutional media were very reluctant to mention the torture, especially the so-called virginity tests. An activist told me regarding the press conference, "the media weren't very . . . they weren't there. I remember that a lot of bloggers were there, some private media was there, but the conference wasn't full of media and we even actually had to harass people like Yosri Fouda and ask him to talk about it." However, while the press conference did not get much institutional media attention, the activists from *No to Military Trials for Civilians* met a number of journalists who were interested in making stories about military trials. Contact information was exchanged. Thus the press conference helped shape communicative infrastructures enabling and facilitating contact at later times. The press conference also gave *No to Military Trials for Civilians* a platform to carry out their activism from, as the campaign with the press conference and other events was becoming a significant movement regarding military trials.

Tents and Trials

At the time of the press conference, the *No to Military Trials for Civilians* campaign started becoming known in activist circles with discussions on Twitter and Facebook, face-to-face interaction, phone calls, and the sharing of videos, including some related to the press conference. More people joined the campaign. That is, while institutional media was reluctant to deal with the issue of military trials, the campaign started getting attention and momentum through cheap media and face-to-face meetings, including through continued street mobilization. Calls for ending military trials for civilians also started appearing on banners at demonstrations and marches. After 18 days of sit-in in Tahrir Square in January and February, 2011, the small group of activists, who had worked for change in Egypt for years, had become well connected with a larger group of newfound activists. After they had lost their collective space in Tahrir Square, they maintained easy access to each other through continuous street mobilization, new collective work spaces, such as the Mosireen Collective's office, and cheap media. The tents in Tahrir Square, which had given them a collective workspace for a while, had been burned down, but the tents had already grown into the communicative ecologies. People knew each other and had ways of contacting each other, which were not dependent on the shared physical space of the square. Thus, when the tents were burned down in the violent clearings of the square, what had been created in the tents had already moved way beyond the physical confines of the tents.

Another crucial part of the work of *No to Military Trials for Civilians* was the work carried out by lawyers in the campaign, mostly pro-bono or at very low costs. Apart from the direct help provided by the lawyers, getting people out of jail and more, the lawyers also supported the substantial grassroots work done by *No to Military Trials for Civilians*, collecting information about civilians who were subjected to military trials. The collection of information about those detained happened both as people were getting arrested and afterwards. Apart from the information collected by *No to Military Trials for* Civilians, there was very little information about the amount of civilians subjected to military trials or their conditions. Many times, people got arrested during demonstrations or sit-ins, which *No to Military Trials for Civilians* activists would either take part in or at least have knowledge about through a variety of communication practices. These included tweets, phone calls, YouTube videos, Facebook posts, graffiti, television and other forms of institutional media, as well as talking face-to-face with other activists, protesters, cab drivers, and others with knowledge. When people got arrested, information about the arrests would be shared on Twitter and through phone calls, often particularly directed at getting lawyers to go to the military court or other places it was expected the arrested could be taken. Twitter and phone calls were used to organize the effort of the lawyers, manifested in tweets such as "We have lawyers @ C28, but they r not sufficient. If ur a lawyer, pls go. #NoMilTrials or call 01007821006 for more info."[6] This tweet was particularly directed at lawyers following the hashtag #NoMilTrials, that is, mainly lawyers who were already engaged with the campaign. One of the founders of the campaign explained to me that it was not enough to be a lawyer to help; it had to be a lawyer who knew the tricks the military used. The lawyers tried to provide legal assistance to people subjected to military trials though civilian lawyers are not allowed to represent defendants in military trials. There were also many people who were arrested before *No to Military Trials for Civilians* was started, and after it was started, many were arrested without people involved in the campaign knowing. This made documenting the cases more difficult. Often, even the families of the victims did not know what had happened to their loved ones. An activist told me:

> So at the beginning, as I said, it was a mystery. People didn't know what these procedures were and lots of people thought their kids were dead for two weeks until they got a phone call, "your kid is being transferred to the Al Wadi Al Gedid Prison" [. . .] and "he's being sentenced to five years in prison, go visit him!" But this would happen way after the legal procedures. [. . .] It's not even an official phone call. Lots of the time, it's soldiers who are doing a favour for the prisoners.

No to Military Trials for Civilians managed to reach many families of victims of military trial enabling the campaign to provide them with support.

The substantial number of cases documented by *No to Military Trials for Civilians* were collectively significant. With this documentation, *No to Military Trials for Civilians* succeeded in maintaining a detailed and usually fairly updated database of victims of military trials. The database was created in a Google spreadsheet and was accessible to the people involved with *No to Military Trials for Civilians*. At times it was also shared with journalists. In the first seven and a half months after the mass protests broke out on January 25, 2011, *No to Military Trials for Civilians* recorded about 12,000 cases of military trials. As official numbers on detainees were known to be unreliable, many journalists used *No to Military Trials for Civilians'* numbers in contrast to official numbers when covering stories related to military trials. The comprehensiveness of this database enabled *No to Military Trials for Civilians* to provide journalists and others with concrete and extensive documentation. This facilitated the campaign's access to institutional media, initially mainly international media, English language Egyptian media, and a few of the more critical private, Egyptian media corporations, but eventually around the summer of 2011 a much broader array of Egyptian media, including television. This access was also facilitated by the substantial attention the campaign was getting through street mobilization and cheap media. While journalists would contact *No to Military Trials for Civilians* when wanting information about a certain case or about numbers in general, activists from *No to Military Trials for Civilians* would also contact journalists when they wanted institutional media attention to a certain case. Sometimes they got institutional media attention to specific stories when television channels showed the video testimonies from the YouTube channel. At other times, as in the initial quote of this chapter, activists called employees at talk shows and convinced them to bring a family member of a detainee on the talk show, sometimes leading to immediate response from authorities.

In early summer, 2011, *No to Military Trials for Civilians* started a hotline, which people could call in order to get help for friends and relatives subjected to military trials. The number was shared on leaflets handed out at sit-ins and demonstrations. Yet even before the designated hotline, the phones of several of the founders of the campaign effectively functioned as hotlines and were spread to people needing help for detained family members. Shortly after the March 16 press conference, *No to Military Trials for Civilians* started a YouTube channel, tahrirDiaries. Here they posted edited videos with testimonies from victims and families of victims of military trials. Many testimonies included stories of violence and torture. In the beginning, they wrote their blog at the end of the video, but after the hotline was started they began including the number at the end of the videos. On July 8, 2011, Tahrir Square was occupied by a large number of protesters once again, this time with demands that Mubarak be put to justice. *No to Military Trials for Civilians* set up a tent in Tahrir Square, where people could get in contact with the campaign. An activist from the campaign told me:

> In the July sit-in for example, we had a tent with the No Military for Civilians banner on it. Lots of people who were subjected to injustice in 2011, when they had nothing else to do, or when they had nowhere else to go, they would just go to Tahrir Square and look for someone that listened to them. If someone, who were from the people sitting in, found someone who was crying, someone who had a problem, someone like that, they referred them to our camp and then in turn we did their cases. Mothers as well, networks of mothers of detainees, they're a great source for [finding out about cases] because for example, they would go there, they would visit their kids at the prison, they would see other women, who had gone through the same with their children, and they take their numbers and they make a database and they bring it to us. [. . .] So the mothers of victims of military trials were an extremely important, *extremely* important factor in helping us get information on detainees.

The "networks of mothers" were also important in terms of sharing the number for the *No to Military Trials for Civilians* hotline. When mothers and other relatives met, in lines outside military prisons in the desert as in other places, they shared the number of the hotline. That is, the lines in the desert were significant for the communicative practices related to the hotline.

Television and Trust

Institutional media channels also played a role in enabling the grassroots work of *No to Military Trials for Civilians*. During the July sit-in, one of the founders and key people in *No to Military Trials for Civilians*, Mona Seif, was interviewed on a talk show on a private television station. She mentioned that they had a tent in Tahrir Square. Activists were later told by people who came to Tahrir Square that they had travelled all the way from Upper Egypt to Tahrir Square after seeing Mona on TV, because they did not know where else to turn to in order to get help for imprisoned family members. Thus while the comprehensiveness of the *No to Military Trials for Civilians* database at times helped the campaign get institutional media attention, institutional media attention enabled the campaign to get in touch with families of victims of military trials, which in turn allowed them to elaborate on the database. That is, talks in tents were enabled by talks on television. But talks on television were concurrently enabled by talks in tents and other places. When Mona got access to television, it was in relation to the substantial amount of grass roots and documentation work done by *No to Military Trials for Civilians*. When Mona was able to speak on television during the July, 2011, sit-in, it was also because the red line of army critique was being moved. Within 6 months of being founded, *No to Military Trials for Civilians* had started getting sympathetic institutional media attention to the issue of military trials. Major talk shows on private television stations, including Reem Maged's, Beladna bil Masry on ONTV and Mahmoud Saad's, Akher Al Nahar on Al Nahar started showing *No to Military Trials for Civilians'* video testimonies. By the beginning of 2012, all the journalists and human rights workers I spoke with agreed that *No to Military Trials for Civilians* were the most reliable source on the topic of military trials. As one journalist said to me, "If we ever want to know anything about detainees or military trials, Mona Seif is the person that we contact."

In November, 2011, 8 months after the torture in the Egyptian Museum and the so-called virginity tests, the military had made no signs they would follow up on their initial promises of investigating the events. Omar Kamel, a video producer and activist in *No to Military Trials for Civilians* made a video with a 23-minute interview with Samira Ibrahim in which she told her story about being subjected to so-called virginity tests and other abuses by the army (tahrirDiaries 2011c). This was one of many testimonies he recorded that were put on the *No to Military Trials for Civilians* YouTube channel, tahrirDiaries. It was arranged by another activist in the campaign who knew Samira. Omar had not met Samira before making the video. He explained to me that he believed he had been able to get Samira's trust to do the video because of the credibility of *No to Military Trials for Civilians*. That is, the video was not just made in a meeting between Omar and Samira, but also depended on their trust in the campaign and their relations to other people involved in it. Once on YouTube, the video was spread through Twitter and other platforms. Human Rights Watch, having followed the campaign closely from the initial meetings, embedded the video in a statement about the military investigations of the so-called virginity tests (Human Rights Watch 2011b). Over 600,000 people watched the video on YouTube. With the red line of army critique having been at least partially broken over the summer, the Human Rights Watch statement with the video embedded and the many views on YouTube, journalists, who initially had been unable to write about the so-called virginity tests, were able to convince editors that it was an important story and that it would not be dangerous to cover it.

Having succeeded in bringing the issue of military trials for civilians to public attention, activists in *No to Military Trials for Civilians* felt a momentum for the campaign at this time, which was also sparked by the thousands of people who responded to the campaign's call for a demonstration, which gathered thousands in Tahrir Square in November, 2011, demanding the end of military trials for civilians. An activist involved in the campaign explained to me that this sense of momentum made them think in new ways about how they could continue the campaign. With presidential elections approaching, they came up with the idea to make a video with statements against military trials for civilians from the presidential candidates. In this way, thousands of protesters in Tahrir Square were part of the making of presidential candidates' video statements. *No to Military Trials for Civilians* managed to get 7 out of 12 candidates to make statements against military trials for civilians in the video (tahrir-Diaries 2011b) after an effort to get in contact with the candidates. Two of the members of *No to Military Trials for Civilians* were children of politicians, one of them being Noor who is the son of then presidential candidate, Ayman Noor. They used their contacts to get through to some of the candidates. Other candidates were contacted by calling people who might know someone who might know someone. At this point, *No to Military Trials for Civilians* was well-known, which made it easier for them to get responses. The video was put on the campaign's YouTube account and sent to a number of television stations. Several television stations showed the video including some that picked it up on their own from the YouTube channel and some that would not usually show things critical of the army. After about a year of campaigning and documenting cases, *No to Military Trials for Civilians* had grown from being a small group of about ten people without much support to becoming influential enough to get presidential candidates to speak up about military trials and to get dominant, institutional media to cover it.

Pushing the Limits of Journalism

> Sometimes our sources are victims of the state. If someone was tortured, for example Samira Ibrahim; she is supposedly a victim, who was subjected to virginity testing by a state entity. Before, I would have dealt with a hospital report, something like that, but not anymore. Now I deal directly with the victim.[7]

No to Military Trials for Civilians' ability to reach institutional media is significant not least because it shows that the campaign helped push the limits of journalism in a country, which has experienced and continues to experience severe repression of free speech. In the following, I elaborate on how *No to Military Trials for Civilians* helped push the borders of journalism particularly by enabling victims of army violence and military trials to come forward. *No to Military Trials for Civilians* enabled victims to come forward in two ways: by influencing the communicative infrastructures, which enabled victims and journalists to get in contact with each other and by supporting those who came forward, which in turn helped others get the courage to come forward. Showing how *No to Military Trials for Civilians* enabled victims to come forward, I focus particularly on the story of Samira Ibrahim.

Samira Ibrahim was among the women who were subjected to so-called virginity tests on March 9. She famously pressed charges against the military for the assaults she was subjected to. Samira won a court case banning the practice of so-called virginity tests in Egypt, but the case against her offender was transferred to a military court. Originally, Samira had pressed the charges against the military generals of SCAF as she argued they were the ones giving orders, but she had only been able to press charges against the doctor carrying out the assaults (Human Rights Watch, 2012). However, an activist from *No to Military Trials for Civilians* told me that the man standing trial was not the actual man who had committed the assaults, but just someone the military had put forward for the trial. Since it was not possible to get the actual offender to stand trial, one of the activists told me, they figured any man was better than none for the sake of having a trial. That is, seeking legal justice was not the main goal of the trial. And while the justice admitted to Samira Ibrahim through the court system was extremely limited, there were other implications of the trial. The court cases enabled journalists to cover her story in detail since stating that there was a trial was easier to get past editors than stating that Samira said the army had committed sexual assaults against her. Thus the assaults in an indirect way made it into a broader range of institutional media. Samira's story is especially telling, because she was one of the first victims of military assaults to get significant institutional media exposure and because *No to Military Trials for Civilians* in many ways was influenced by her story.

The initial press conference was important both to Samira Ibrahim's ability to get in contact with journalists and for her courage to do so. A journalist, who participated in the press conference, told me:

> Afterwards, one of the people that were arrested with Samira called me and told me, "one of the girls is ready to speak up about the virginity test." So I met with her—that was before she became famous—and she told me the whole story and we did [a story] about that. And after a while she called me and told me "I'm going to press charges" and we covered that also.

The journalist had exchanged phone numbers with activists at the press conference. While Samira Ibrahim had not been at the press conference, she was able to get in contact with the journalist. This was so because the journalist, through the press conference, was in contact with an activist, who had been arrested with Samira and whom Samira had exchanged contact information with. That is, both the March 9, 2011, arrests and the following March 16 press conference influenced the communicative infrastructure, which enabled the contact. But the press conference facilitated the encounter between Samira Ibrahim and the journalist beyond the more logistical challenge of exchanged phone numbers and agreements on meeting points. That is, from the testimonies at the press conference, the journalist had an idea what to expect she would be told. Samira on her part had an expectation of how she would be met when she told her story to a journalist as she had seen how other victims who came forward had been received. John Postill (2010) has argued that "there is ample ethnographic evidence to suggest that ritual and other performative practices around the world are being influenced by practices seen on television and other media" (p. 17). In a similar fashion, the press conference influenced the communicative practices of victims of military violence and trials, activists, and journalists by providing a shared point of reference.

Samira Ibrahim's story eventually got a lot of institutional media exposure both in Egypt and internationally. While Samira Ibrahim was moved and enabled to come forward by the campaign, she also in many ways moved the campaign as the attention to Samira Ibrahim often included attention to *No to Military Trials for Civilians*. Samira inspired many other victims when she came forward. An activist involved in both *No to Military Trials for Civilians* and *Operation Anti Sexual Harassment and Assault* (*OpAntiSH*), a group that helped victims of severe mass sexual assaults, told me of a victim of sexual assault who came forward. "She said that without the support that she saw that Samira is receiving and the love and everything, she would have never thought of [telling her story publicly]." Seeing a victim being well received when coming forward left other victims encouraged to come forward and thus enabled journalists to interview people who would earlier have been too scared of repercussions. That is, seeing others come forward influenced how victims engaged with their environments. It influenced the paths they moved along and took part in shaping a symbiotic relationship between journalists, activists, and victims (including activists and journalists), allowing all parts to benefit from each other.

Conclusion

No to Military Trials for Civilians has been an influential campaign even though they have not succeeded in ending the practice of military trials for civilians. *No to Military Trials for Civilians* got many people out of military jails. The campaign also helped enable victims of military violence and trials and their families to come forward to tell their stories. It particularly did so in two ways: by providing people with someone to speak to and by giving them courage to do so. By enabling these victims to come forward, by providing specific events to cover and by meticulously documenting cases of military trials, *No to Military Trials for Civilians* has been influential in pushing the limits of journalism and at least to an extent and for a time, moving the red line of critique of the military. I have described a vast array of communicative practices, which were significant in this process and shown how none of these practices can be understood on their own, detached from their environment. I have shown how each communicative practice was dependent on other communicative practices and the communicative infrastructures, which they were enabling. That is, the communicative practices of *No to Military Trials for Civilians* were an organic, closely interrelated, and continually evolving mix of tweeting, talking on phones, talking in tents, recording and uploading videos to YouTube, and much more. One form of communication influenced and facilitated others. The campaign's work to get in contact with victims and families of victims involved many different media, which could not be understood individually. The *No to Military Trials for Civilians'* tent in Tahrir Square during the July, 2011, sit-in is co-constitutive of Mona Seif's appearance on a talk show, tweets to lawyers during battles, presidential candidates' statements, and more and concurrently the tent is co-constituted by such and other communicative practices. The communicative process of a mother of a detainee calling a *No to Military Trials for Civilians* activist, whom she already knows and whose number she already has and the activist, in turn, calling a known contact from a talk show, who knows the campaign and accepts the mother of the detainee on the talk show is relatively uncomplicated. Yet communicative processes such as this were facilitated by a complex and comprehensive range of processes that by no means can be reduced to media. The shared places of people involved with *No to Military Trials for Civilians*—in tents, in lines in the desert, at press conferences, and more—were absolutely crucial to the campaign. Digital media did not weaken the importance of shared places, but they did play a role in making and expanding such places.

Notes

1. Interview with author.
2. See www.youtube.com/watch?v=gr2iSo082o0 for an example of a video of tanks moving into Tahrir Square, while protesters standing on the tanks chant, "the army and the people are one hand."
3. See more information about the case at Human Rights Watch (2012).
4. See the original blogpost at www.maikelnabil.com/2011/03/blog-post_07.html.
5. See for instance this video from Al Masry Al Youm: www.youtube.com/watch?t=1&v=W1K2cWCHSPk.
6. Tweeted by Shahira Abouellail during the Abbassiya clashes in early May 2012 on the Twitter account @fazerofzanight, which is no longer active.
7. Egyptian journalist, interview with author.

References

Alterman, J. B. (2011). The revolution will not be tweeted. *The Washington Quarterly, 34*(4), 103–116.

Armbrust, W. (2012). A history of new media in the Arab Middle East. *Journal for Cultural Research, 16*(2–3), 155–174.

Batty, D., & Olorenshaw, A. (2011, January 28, updated 2014, May 20). *News blog: Egypt protests: As they happened.* [Live blog]. Retrieved from www.theguardian.com/world/2011/jan/29/egypt-protests-government-live-blog

Dahlgren, P. (2011, June 30). *Keynote address on democracy and engaged citizens: What digital media can and can't do.* From Pop Culture to Popular Media, Netherlands-Flemish Institute, Cairo, Egypt.

Eltantawy, N., & Wiest, J. B. (2011). Social media in the Egyptian revolution: Reconsidering resource mobilization theory. *International Journal of Communication, 5,* 1207–1024.

Fors, V., Bäckström, Å., & Pink, S. (2013). Multisensory emplaced learning: Resituating situated learning in a moving world. *Mind, Culture, and Activity, 20*(2), 170–183.

Goddard, M. (2015, August 3). Paper presentation: Ontogenesis before ontology: Media ecologies, materialisms, and objects. *The Secret Life of Objects: Media Ecologies conference, Rio de Janeiro, Brazil.* Retrieved from www.academia.edu/14766299/Ontogenesis_before_Ontology_Media_Ecologies_Materialisms_and_Objects

Howard, P. N., Duffy, A., Freelon, D., Hussain, M., Mari, W., & Mazaid, M. (2011). Opening closed regimes: What was the role of social media during the Arab Spring? *Project on Information Technology & Political Islam.* Retrieved from http://papers.ssrn.com/sol3/papers.cfm?abstract_id=2595096

Human Rights Watch. (2011a, September 10). *Egypt: Retry or free 12,000 after unfair military trials.* [Press release]. Retrieved from www.hrw.org/news/2011/09/10/egypt-retry-or-free-12000-after-unfair-military-trials

Human Rights Watch. (2011b, November 9). *Egypt: Military 'Virginity Test' investigation a Sham.* [Press release]. Retrieved from www.hrw.org/news/2011/11/09/egypt-military-virginity-test-investigation-sham

Human Rights Watch. (2012, April 7). *Egypt: Military impunity for violence against women.* [Press release]. Retrieved from www.hrw.org/news/2012/04/07/egypt-military-impunity-violence-against-women

Ingold, T. (2006). Rethinking the animate, re-animating thought. *Ethnos, 71*(1), 9–20.

Ingold, T. (2008). Bindings against boundaries: Entanglements of life in an open world. *Environment and Planning A, 40,* 1796–1811.

Ingold, T. (2013). *Making: Anthropology, archaeology, art and architecture.* New York, NY: Routledge.

Khamis, S., & Vaughn, K. (2011). Cyberactivism in the Egyptian revolution: How civic engagement and citizen journalism tilted the balance. *Arab Media & Society,* (13). Retrieved from www.arabmediasociety.com/?article=769

Kingsley, P., & Chulov, M. (2013, July 4). Mohamed Morsi ousted in Egypt's second revolution in two years. *The Guardian.* Retrieved from www.theguardian.com/world/2013/jul/03/mohamed-morsi-egypt-second-revolution

Mollerup, N. G., & Gaber, S. (2015). Making media public: On revolutionary street screenings in Egypt. *International Journal of Communication, 9,* 2903–2921.

Peterson, M. A. (2015). In search of antistructure: The meaning of Tahrir Square in Egypt's ongoing social drama. In A. Horvath, B. Thomassen, & H. Wydra (Eds.), *Breaking boundaries: Varieties of liminality* (pp. 164–82). New York, NY: Berghahn.

Postill, J. (2010). Introduction: Theorising media and practice. In B. Bräuchler & J. Postill (Eds.), *Theorising media and practice* (pp. 1–32). Oxford, UK: Berghahn.

Reporters Without Borders. (2014). *Country file: Egypt.* Retrieved from http://en.rsf.org/report-egypt,149.html

Sakr, N. (2013). *Transformations in Egyptian journalism: Media and the Arab uprisings.* London, UK: I.B. Tauris.

Tacchi, J. A. (2005). Radio and new media technologies: Making technological change socially effective and culturally empowering. In S. Healy, B. Berryman, & D. Goodman (Eds.), *Radio in the world: Radio conference 2005* (pp. 342–353). Retrieved from http://eprints.qut.edu.au/00004397

tahrirDiaries. (2011a, April 6). *Witnesses of torture – shahūd ʿala taʿdhib elgesh elmaṣry lilmaʿataqalīn [Witnesses of torture – Witnesses to the Egyptian army's torture of the detainees].* Retrieved from https://www.youtube.com/watch?v=W1K2cWCHSPk

tahrirDiaries. (2011b, September 2). *morashaḥī elriasah el maṣrīyīn ḍid elmaḥākamāt elʿaskarīyah lilmaʿataqalīn [Egyptian presidential candidates against military trials for civilians].* Retrieved from www.youtube.com/watch?v=gs_5FljIDnU

tahrirDiaries. (2011c, November 16). *samīra wa elgesh: qissat fatāh maṣrīyah [Samira and the army: a story of an Egyptian woman].* Retrieved from https://www.youtube.com/watch?v=c29CAXR141s

Tufekci, Z. (2012, March 5). What does Twitter have to do with revolution? *Brite '12 Conference,* Columbia University, New York, USA. Retrieved from http://technosociology.org/?p=1021

Weaver, M., Siddique, H., Owen, P., & Adams, R. (2011, February 2). News blog: Egypt protests: Wednesday 2 February. *The Guardian.* Retrieved from www.theguardian.com/news/blog/2011/feb/02/egypt-protests-live-updates

7 "Unfriending" Is Easy

Intercultural Miscommunication on Social Networks

Olga Baysha

Since the 1990s, academic research has paid significant attention to the possibility of the emergence of transnational and transcultural public spheres through Internet communication. Scholars believed that digital exchanges among people of different cultural backgrounds could lead to global "consciousness raising" and the increasing influence of transnational public opinion on politics and international relations. New media were also celebrated because of their assumed ability to represent culturally marginalized voices and create opportunities for them to be incorporated into public deliberation on the most important social and political issues.

However, it has been increasingly recognized that Internet-based communication, rather than ushering in unity, may instead cause new tensions between culturally diverse publics. Researchers found that some groups of people introduced through the Internet to radically different ideas, images, or views on the self, had felt disillusionment, indignation, and estrangement (Karatzogianni, 2009). As a result, these groups retreated or lashed out, demonstrating what political theorists call "non-deliberative," "closed," or "unreflexive" discourse (Dahlberg, 2007, p. 139).

Communication scholars are now paying attention not only to the ability of Internet technologies to unite, but also to their potential to disconnect, deepen old social splits, and draw new boundaries. Because social networking services make it easier than ever to filter out dissonant voices, social media users tend to form homogeneous rather than heterogeneous social networks by disconnecting others whose views challenge their own (Noel & Nyhan, 2011; Pariser, 2011). Such acts of disconnectivity create more culturally homogeneous (homophilic) public spaces (Himelboim, McCreery, & Smith, 2013) and lead to a deterioration of intercultural discourse and civil deliberation (Stroud, 2010). Instead of creating all-inclusive communication spaces, as early theorists of globalization expected, social media often facilitate the exclusion of dissonant voices and discourage dialogue between the representatives of different cultural groups (Garrett, Dvir-Gvirsman, Jognson, Tsfati, Neo, & Dal, 2014; Himelboim et al., 2013; Noel & Nyhan, 2011; Stroud, 2010).

Of the respondents in a Pew Research Center (2014), 44% sharing liberal values and up to 31% of those holding conservative views reported they had "unfriended" other Facebook users because they disagreed with their values or beliefs. Overall, 26% of respondents said they had unfriended at least one person for reasons related to politics (Pew Research Center, 2014). This unwillingness to hear from the other side, in Pew Research Center's view, reflects the vast and growing gap between liberal and conservative cultures, which is a defining feature of American society today.

With their research on unfriending during the Israel-Gaza conflict of 2014, Nicholas A. John and Shira Dvir-Gvirsman provide further evidence in this respect. They found that a total of 16% of their survey respondents—Israeli residents—unfriended or unfollowed a Facebook friend during the conflict. The authors reported that the highest level of unfriending occurred among "people who were more ideologically extreme" (John & Dvir-Gvirsman, 2015, p. 963)—that is, hardliners who never questioned the normality of their beliefs.

Analyzing survey data from Hong Kong students at eight public universities during the height of the Hong Kong Umbrella movement, Qinfeng Zhu, Skoric, and Shen (2017) found that 15.6% of respondents engaged in "selective avoidance"—removing content and unfriending on Facebook. The confrontation here was among those sharing traditional Chinese cultural values and younger people adhering to the global culture of progressivism and advocating political modernization.

Several major factors influence the decision to withdraw from communication with cultural "others." The highest rate of selective avoidance is demonstrated by people who are ideologically extreme, politically active (involved in political struggle and street protests), and emotionally involved (Bode, 2016; John & Dvir-Gvirsman, 2015; Pew Research Center, 2014; Zhu et al., 2017). The number of online friends has been found to be another strong predictor for online disconnections: "People who had more friends were more likely to disconnect, and the people whom they unfriended did not play a significant role in their life" (John & Dvir-Gvirsman, 2015, p. 966). If one online friend does not play a significant role in the life of another one (and vice versa), this type of friendship is considered weak, and it can be sacrificed more easily than a strong relationship.

Several researchers argue that social networking services (SNS), which encourage users to unite in groups with similar interests, facilitate the creation of homophilic networks, the exclusion of dissonant voices, and the discouragement of dialogue between those with different political views (Garrett et al., 2014; Himelboim et al., 2013; Noel & Nyhan, 2011; Stroud, 2010). The exclusion of "others" through unfriending results in more homogeneous lists of Facebook friends and more homogeneous Facebook news feeds.

It is difficult, however, to discuss empirical findings from the United States, Israel, and Hong Kong in terms of their relevance to other cultural, social, and political contexts because of the specificity of each case, and because there is only scant literature examining trends, tendencies, and implications regarding unfollowing and unfriending in other cultural milieus (Bode, 2016). In John and Dvir-Gvirsman's (2015) view, "Only further studies of unfriending in relation to clearly demarcated events in other areas of the world will allow us to state whether the unfriending documented here constitutes a large amount" (p. 967). Taking up this invitation, this chapter discusses a survey of Russian-speaking Facebook users regarding the Ukrainian Maidan Revolution of 2013–2014 that ended in a civil confrontation within Ukraine and the deterioration of inter-state relationship between Ukraine and Russia.

Research Context: Between Civilizations and Cultural Zones

The Maidan Revolution started in Kyiv on November 21, 2013, when protesters expressed their disapproval of President Victor Yanukovich and the government of Ukraine for refusing to sign an Association Agreement with the European Union (EU) in favor of the Eurasian Custom Union (ECU) led by Russia. The events that followed are well documented: the dispersal of demonstrators by governmental special forces, the escalation of the confrontation, violent clashes between police and protesters, the first human casualties, the dismissal of the acting president, the annexation of Crimea by Russia, an insurgency in Donbas, and the fight of the Ukrainian Army against "terrorism" (Sakwa, 2015; Wilson, 2014).

The civil confrontation caused by the controversy around the Association Agreement reflected a deep, centuries-old cultural split within Ukrainian society. As Serhii Plokhy (2008) maintains, "Ukraine has been a borderland not only of different state formations but, much more importantly, of different civilizational and cultural zones" (p. 293), a border zone between the Great Eurasian Steppe, the Mediterranean world, Eastern and Western Christendom, and Islam. This borderland history explains its rich ethnic and cultural diversity.

Russians are the second biggest ethnic group of the Ukrainian population. Ethnically, Russians and Ukrainians are very close: originally, both nations descend from Eastern Slavs, as Kievan Rus, an ancient Eurasian state, was a forebear of both nations. It was the Mongolian invasion in the 13th century that separated the Russian and Ukrainian histories: "Russia remained under Mongol rule for another 150 years, whereas Ukraine gradually became part of the Polish-Lithuania medieval state" (Bukkvoll, 1997, p. 61). In the 17th century, the historical paths of Ukraine and Russia converged again. From the middle of the 17th century until the end of the 20th century, major parts of southeastern Ukraine were under Moscow's control; western Ukraine, however, remained under the Austrian Empire and Polish-Lithuanian Commonwealth. The unification of Ukraine was accomplished only in the 20th century under Soviet rule. However, centuries of living under different civilizations had left its mark. Northwestern Ukrainians predominantly speak Russian and attend the Russian Orthodox Church (Kovalova, 2007).

Since the declaration of Ukraine's independence in 1991, two ideas of national identity have been competing in Ukraine: the "Ethnic Ukrainian National" and the "Eastern Slavic" (Shulman, 2004, p. 38). The ethnic Ukrainian national idea is based on the notion that Ukrainian culture, language, and ethnicity-centered history should be the dominant integrating forces in the Ukrainian nation-state. This perspective presents the historical Ukrainian-Russian relationship as one of the colonized and the colonizer. The presence of Russians in Ukraine is explained as the result of imperial Russian policy, with the spread of the Russian language seen as the fruit of forced Russification.

In contrast, the Eastern Slavic idea of identity "envisages the Ukrainian nation as founded on two primary ethnic groups, languages, and cultures—Ukrainian and Russian—that are unified by their being embedded in a common historical and cultural space" (Shulman, 2004, p. 39). Its adherents strongly support imperial Russian and Soviet historiography's interpretation of the common historical and cultural paths of Russian, Ukrainian, and Belorussian peoples, who form "brotherly relations" or "Slavic unity" among the three Slavic groups.

The split in visions of Ukraine's cultural identity within its own society was reflected in the divergence of attitudes toward the Association Agreement with the European Union that became a pretext for the Maidan (Plokhy, 2015). Regional differences were very sharp: "Eighty-two percent in the West and 57% in Northern Ukraine preferred the EU. In the East, 63% preferred the ECU" (Kull et al., 2015, p. 7). The farther East one looked, the stronger and more unified a rejection of the Maidan with its European agenda one would find (KIIS, 2014). More than 75% of those living in Donetsk and Luhansk oblasts (two eastern regions of Ukraine predominantly populated by ethnic Russians and Russian speakers) rejected the agreement with the EU, suggesting that "Ukraine and Russia should be independent but friendly states with open borders and without visas" (ZNUA, 2014). Many ethnic Russians living in the Ukrainian East believed that the Maidan was an "armed coup-d'etat organized by the opposition with the help of the West" and did not approve of Maidan revolutionaries using weapons against police forces (ZNUA, 2014).

In early March 2014, Russian military forces took control of Crimea, a peninsula in the southern part of Ukraine populated predominantly by ethnic Russians. This only fueled the anti-Maidan movement in other southeastern regions, where many of anti-Maidan demonstrations were held under Russian state banners. In April 2014, protests in the Donetsk and Luhansk oblasts escalated into an armed insurgency, backed by Russia. Russia provided the rebels with weapons and supported them with regular Russian troops when the rebels appeared to be facing defeat in August 2014 (Sutyagin, 2015).

The new Ukrainian authorities declared anti-Maidan combatants "terrorists," while Maidan armed revolutionaries were considered heroes. In mid-April 2014, an "anti-terrorist" military operation (ATO) was launched. From its onset until February 20, 2019, a total of 13,000 combatants and civilians were killed, while 28,000 were wounded (UN, 2019). Hundreds of thousands have been internally displaced or have fled the country.

Surveying the Confrontation

Sample

This survey was launched in January 2017, almost three years after the victory of the Maidan and the announcement of the anti-terrorist operation. I conducted the survey using a two-step process. First, interviews with opinion leaders (13 journalists and political analysts) were conducted by Skype. Of the participants in these 20–30 minute conversations, seven lived in Ukraine and six in Russia (they immigrated there from Ukraine after the Maidan revolution won). One of those living in Ukraine opposed the Maidan and six supported it; all of those living in Russia opposed the Maidan. Thus, in total, six of my interviewees supported the Maidan and seven opposed it.

Based on the material gathered through these interviews, a survey with 30 closed-ended questions was prepared. It was disseminated among Facebook users between January 10 and January 31, 2017. The data were collected using SurveyMonkey.com, an online survey platform. To recruit respondents on Facebook, I used a snowball technique by asking the opinion leaders I had interviewed to share the survey link with their Facebook networks.

Relevant to the topic of my investigation—the narrowing of the possibilities of intercultural understanding in the age of digital media—it is pertinent to note, that many of those who supported the Maidan refused to participate in the survey because it was conducted in the Russian language. Despite an introduction explaining the academic purpose of the survey, some Maidan supporters suspected that the Russian Intelligence Service would somehow use its findings. Such sentiments were openly expressed in comments under the posts linking to the survey. "Why should I believe that this research is not for political purposes to be used in information wars?"—as one Facebook user put it.

The demographics of the respondents who participated in the survey reflect this mistrust.

Out of all 494 citizens of Ukraine participating in the research, 45.6% identified their ethnicity as Russian, 39.5% as Ukrainian, 6.3%

as Ukrainian and Russian, and 8.6% as neither Ukrainian nor Russian. However, as the language of everyday use, Russian was indicated by 78.1%, while 16.6% said they speak both Russian and Ukrainian, and only 4.9% said they use only Ukrainian in daily life. The majority of the Ukrainian citizens who took part in the survey (71.7%) identified their native regions to be that of Southeastern Ukraine: the population of these regions, as I have already mentioned, were skeptical about the Maidan and its European agenda. The survey results only confirmed these anti-Maidan sentiments: 67.7% opposed the Maidan, while only 30.4% supported it; 1.9% had difficulty answering this question.

Due to these demographic characteristics of the respondents and their attitudes toward the Maidan, it is not possible to take the sample under study as representative of the population of Ukraine. However, they do represent, albeit in an unbalanced proportion, two cultural groups: those who support the pro-European revolution (predominantly, but not exclusively, ethnic Ukrainians and Ukrainian speakers from western and central parts of Ukraine) and those who reject it in favor of the Union with Russia (mainly, but not entirely, ethnic Russians and Russian speakers from southeastern regions or Russia). Therefore, this research can provide a glimpse of how individuals in these two large groups of people used Facebook to communicate on the Maidan and other events related to it.

Survey Questions

The principal part of the survey asked the respondents to answer the following questions:

> "Have you ever unfriended anybody while discussing the Maidan and its outcomes?" and "Have you ever unfriended anyone on non-Maidan topics?" The respondents had to choose between the following answers: "Yes," "No," and "Difficult to say."

To illuminate the reasons for unfriending others, the respondents were asked to choose among several options describing the unfriended party: "They propagated *dissonant* views aggressively, using offensive language;" "Albeit in a non-aggressive manner, they propagated *dissonant* views;" "They propagated *non-dissonant* views but aggressively, using offensive language;" "They were trolls or bots;" and "Other." The option "Other" invited respondents to suggest an alternative explanation in their own words. The respondents were asked to select among the reasons for unfriending twice—first to identify the primary reason, then the secondary one.

To measure the level of participation in the revolution and the developments related to it, the respondents were asked to answer the following questions: "Did you support the Maidan?"; "Did you participate in peaceful pro-Maidan manifestations?"; "Did you participate in peaceful anti-Maidan manifestations?"; "Did you participate in street clashes on the Maidan side?"; "Did you participate in street clashes on the anti-Maidan side?" The respondents had to choose between the following answers: "Yes," "No," and "Difficult to say."

The level of intolerance to "cultural others" was measured by the question, "Have you ever quarreled and cut ties with close friends and relatives over the Maidan and related events?" The answers offered were: "Yes, I stopped communicating with one friend;" "Yes, I stopped communicating with several friends;" "Yes, I stopped communicating with one or more relatives;" "I have quarrels with friends and relatives but have never cut ties;" and "I have never quarreled with friends or relatives over the Maidan."

To measure the level of homogeneity of their Facebook networks, the respondents were asked, "How would you characterize your network of Facebook friends?" They were invited to choose among the following answers: "All my Facebook friends share my views;" "The majority of my Facebook friends share my views;" "The number of opponents and proponents of my views among my Facebook friends is approximately equal;" and "The majority of my Facebook friends do not share my views."

Each respondent was also asked to report his/her age, gender, educational level, ethnic origin, language of everyday use, country of residence, region of residence in Ukraine, and the number of Facebook friends in their networks. The numbers and percentages were cross-tabulated using SPSS; comments were analyzed qualitatively. Drawing on Ernesto Laclau's theory of articulation (2005), according to which all social identities and relations between them are discursively constructed, I analyzed how the supporters of the Maidan and their opponents used specific signifiers to construct the imagined communities of each other.

Findings: The More Extreme, the Less Friendly

Unfriending "Aggressive Others" But Keeping "Aggressive Us"

Overall, 699 respondents participated in the survey; 70.7% of them were citizens of Ukraine, 20.6% of Russia, and 8.7% had citizenship from other countries. Since I was interested in how the citizens of Ukraine communicated about the conflict, I eliminated all the participants with non-Ukrainian citizenship. Of the remaining 494 respondents with Ukrainian citizenship (hereafter, I will refer to them as "all respondents" and count 494 as 100%), 51.1% reported they had unfriended people while discussing the Maidan and its outcomes. For those respondents who had higher levels of involvement in the Maidan confrontation (street clashes), the rate of unfriending turned out to be even higher.

Of all Maidan supporters, 61.3% reported having unfriended some-one, as compared to 46.1% in the group of Maidan opponents. Of those who participated in peaceful protests on the Maidan side (24.3% of all respondents), 62.5% had engaged in unfriending; among anti-Maidan peaceful protesters (21.7% of all respondents), 57.0% had dropped an online friend. Participants in street clashes on the pro-Maidan side (5.7% of all respondents) had unfriended at a 64.3% rate, while the fig-ure for anti-Maidan combatants (4.1% of all respondents) was 60.0%. What these figures show is that the higher the level of involvement in the struggle (from simply supporting/rejecting the Maidan to participating in peaceful protests to fighting in the streets), the higher the proportion of respondents who had unfriended at least one person over ideological differences.

As previously mentioned, intolerance to cultural others was measured by the question about severing ties with friends and relatives offline. Out of all 494 respondents, 6.5% reported that, because of Maidan-related disputes, they cut contact with one offline friend; among this group of respondents, 53.1% had unfriended someone on Facebook. Another 29.2% of all respondents reported they had cut ties with several offline friends; 59.1% of these users had also unfriended someone online. Those who had stopped communicating with one or more relatives comprised 5.5% of all respondents; among this group, 77.8% had engaged in unfriending. As is evident from these figures, the greater the readiness to sacrifice relationships in real life (from breaking off with one friend to several friends to one or more relatives), the higher the likelihood of severing ties on Facebook. This finding came as no surprise given that Facebook disconnecting options make it much easier for people to shield from one another online than offline.

The number of online friends has turned out to be another strong pre-dictor of the greater likelihood of breaking off Facebook friendships. Peo-ple with more online friends showed a higher likelihood to have engaged in selective avoidance. Of the respondents with number of Facebook friends less than 200, 43.5% had engaged in online unfriending; among those who had more than 200 but fewer than 1,000 Facebook friends, 59.3% had unfriended someone online. For those who had more than 1,000 Facebook friends, the rate of unfriending was 79.1%.

The propagation of dissonant views "aggressively, using offensive lan-guage" was indicated as a primary reason for "selective avoidance" by 75.3% of the respondents who had a history of unfriending; 14.6% said that their primary reason for unfriending was the expression of disso-nant views, even if they were not presented aggressively; and only 0.4% reported that they unfriended people primarily because of online aggres-siveness, even though it was displayed by people sharing similar values.

The most important secondary reason for unfriending was the sus-picion that the "friend" was a troll or bot (42.1%); the next important secondary reason (27.2%) was the aggressive propagation of dissonant views; 22.5% said their secondary reason was the propagation of dissonant views, even if they were expressed politely; and finally, 8.2% reported their secondary reason as the aggressive propagation of similar views.

After combining all the answers for the primary and secondary reasons and taking the total as 100%, I found that the dominant reason for unfriending turned out to be the aggressive (impolite) propagation of dissonant views (51.3%). This was followed by the suspicion that the unfriended person was a troll or bot (25.8%), the propagation of dissonant views no matter how politely they were presented (18.6%), and, finally, the least common cause of unfriending was the expression of similar views in an aggressive (impolite) manner (4.3%).

If, based on these results, we would assume that the main reason for the lack of communication among different cultural groups was aggressiveness and rudeness, it would be difficult to interpret why only 4.3% of the respondents reported unfriending aggressive and rude people with whom they shared political views. Given that aggression from "cultural others" was identified as the dominant reason for unfriending by each of the conflicting sides, it is logical to assume that the real cause for "selective avoidance" was nothing but unwillingness to hear opposing views. My analysis of the comments of those respondents who had a history of unfriending "others" supports this proposition.

"There Are No Crazy People Among My Friends"

What unites the majority of the comments made by the Maidan opponents who had a history of Maidan-related unfriending is their vision of Maidan supporters ("maidauni," as they derogatively called them) as "stupid," "brainless," "crazy," "idiotic" or "out of touch"—not quite "normal," in other words. "There are no crazy people among my friends," one of the anti-Maidan activists boasted, equating "normality" with opposing the Maidan and suggesting that there is nothing to discuss with "mentally sick" people.

But why did opponents of the Maidan see their counterparts as crazed idiots? Because, in their view, the Maidan supporters fell victim to "satanic manipulations," as one of the respondents put it, perpetrated by "scoundrels" working to grasp political power through the "mass psychosis" of a staged revolution. According to some respondents, "Oligarchs fight to snatch the fattest pieces from each other and pay uneducated crowds for protests." Many opponents of the Maidan believed that only "idiots" can support such "mass chaos." Many opponents of the Maidan saw it this way. "A couple of times, I visited the Maidan—a pitiful picture of silly and naïve people. And the full podium of scoundrels," this comment is one of the best representatives of the general attitude of Maidan opponents toward those who "brainlessly jumped on the Maidan."

Another line of reasoning employed by many of the Maidan opponents was their presentation of the revolution as a coup d'etat—a "wide-scale provocation by Western secret services in Ukraine." This narrative also suggests it was "abnormal" to support the "orgy": "Nobody with a solid mind can support the coup d'etat." Answering the question regarding participation in peaceful pro-Maidan demonstrations, some anti-Maidan respondents asserted that "there were no peaceful pro-Maidan protests—everything was perpetrated by armed militants, who had been paid and trained." For some of the Maidan opponents, the revolution was not only illegal but "bestial": "To throw Molotov cocktails at militia? This is not human!!" In this view, it was a matter of public safety to isolate "maidauni" (a derogatory term to denote Maidan supporters) from the rest of society: "I wrote to the public prosecutor, demanding to imprison the scumbags!" According to the commentator, the prosecutor turned out to be a "scumbag" himself.

The third line of argument used to justify the lack of communication with pro-Maidan "others" was their support of the "fascist junta that had grasped power in Ukraine." Because ultra-radical, nationalistic forces in Ukraine were among the most vocal advocates of the Maidan, all Maidan protesters were often depicted by their opponents as "fascists" or "banderovets"—the followers of Stepan Bandera, an ideologue of Ukrainian nationalism known for collaboration with Nazis and complicity in genocide (Rossolinski, 2014). "My Mom and three of her sisters survived the fascist occupation and Bandera's slaughter on the borderland of Poland and Ukraine. I only hope Ukraine will survive this current occupation as well," one respondent said. The historical parallel suggested by this comment did not leave space for communication. Rather than compromise with "banderovets" and "fascists," the only possibility is a struggle to the victorious end.

As stated previously, the highest level of online intolerance was demonstrated by the groups of people who had broken relationships with friends and relatives offline. What is interesting, however, is that many of them argued it was not their fault: "It was not me who initiated the break with several friends—they did it," "Some relatives and friends cut ties with me; I did not try to make them change their minds," "I did not quarrel with anybody, but many 'maidanovtsi' [Maidan supporters] were astonished by my position and cut all contact," "I only tried to persuade them, but what I heard in response was 'pack your bags and go out to Russia,'" and so forth.

"I only tried to persuade them" is an important remark to understand the dynamics of miscommunication. Because many Maidan opponents imagined Maidan supporters as "stupid," "duped," and "manipulated," they considered it their mission to enlighten them, imposing their vision of the conflict as the only possible interpretation of it—the *truth*, as they understood it. Since Maidan proponents also saw their anti-Maidan opponents as "stupid idiots" and "serfs" unable to understand progressive aspirations (Baysha, 2019), the outcome of such "communication" was predictable: the retreat (unfriending) of each side of the conflict and the closure of discourse. This is evident from the following comments by anti-Maidan hardliners: "It is difficult to explain anything at all to them: their brains are stuffed with slogans"; "They are incorrigible; one cannot *correct* them"; "my attempts *to bring them to reason* failed." These commenters saw communication not as a two-way flow of opinions, but as a unilateral imposition of their "truth" on others, who were imagined simply as objects of persuasion and correction.

As I mentioned earlier in this chapter, fewer Maidan supporters than opponents were willing to participate in this research. The reluctance among Maidan supporters to communicate about the Maidan even for the sake of academic research was especially evident in comments: only one hardliner shared his reflections. In his view, the whole anti-Maidan movement was fake because "it was paid for by the Kremlin." Empirical evidence from other research on the Maidan confrontation suggests that this point of view was not atypical among Maidan supporters (Baysha, 2018; Korostelina, 2014; Onuch, 2015; Sakwa, 2015).

Given the dynamics of unfriending, as discussed above, it was not surprising to discover that 59.3% of all the respondents reported the majority of their Facebook friends share their views and 5.3% said that all their friends are like-minded people—taken together, these two groups comprised 64.6% of all respondents. For the group of those who had a history of unfriending others, the level of network homogeneity is even higher: 73.4% reported that the majority of their friends are of similar views, and 6.0% said the views of all their friends are identical.

What is also interesting, however, is that only 18.0% of survey participants responded in the affirmative when asked: "Have you ever unfriended anybody on non-Maidan topics?" This result is almost three times lower than the average rate of unfriending for all respondents discussing the Maidan.

Dividing Networks

The results of my research show a high rate of unfriending among Ukrainian Facebook users as compared to all the empirical findings discussed above: The US-based study by the Pew Research Center (2014), the Israel-based research by John and Dvir-Gvirsman (2015), and the Taiwan-based investigation by Zhu and colleagues (2017). The differences with the US and Taiwan cases are quite understandable given the lack of a devastating military conflict in these two cases, whereas in Ukraine thousands of citizens on both sides of the conflict have been killed or injured. It is well known that in times of war, communities intensify their moral and political boundary works for the sake of mobilization (Brubaker, Feischmidt, & Grancea, 2006).

It is surprising, however, that the level of intolerance among Ukrainian citizens, as measured by the rate of unfriending, has turned out to be much higher than that of Israeli Facebook users who dealt with a no-less-heated intercultural conflict (John & Dvir-Gvirsman, 2015). Was this attributable to the snowballing technique of collecting responses, which could have attracted the most active and, therefore, intolerant (as the results of my study suggests) Facebook users? It is unclear whether the average rate of selective avoidance would have been lower if the sampling were statistically representative of all the cultural groups and regions of Ukraine—this question needs to be clarified. What is already clear, however, is that the opportunities of networking offered by SNS were not utilized to make cultural bridges. On the contrary, they were used to get rid of opponents at a much higher rate than offline and thus created a much more homogeneous online environment—a finding that has already been proved by other researchers (Scwartz & Shani, 2016).

The results of my investigation are in line with the "digital skeptics" arguing that new SNS, instead of networking, can disconnect people by allowing them to create a digital environment that is much more homogeneous than the non-digital social world (Dahlberg, 2007; Karatzogianni, 2009; Light, 2014: Noel & Nyhan, 2011; Pariser, 2011). As my research shows, in the case of the Ukrainian Maidan, social media did not facilitate intercultural communication; rather, through the function of "unfriending," they allowed the deepening of already existing cleavages and enabled the creation of new splits.

The polarization of the Facebook users I observed within the Ukrainian context can hardly lead to the emergence of a vibrant intercultural public sphere, as early optimistic theories of new communication technologies suggested (Lull, 2007; Scott & Street, 2001; Touri, 2009; Volkmer, 2003). Technologically speaking, new media, including SNS, provide all the necessary resources for the inclusion of everybody with Internet access to participate in a respectful conversation on the most important societal matters. What we see in practice, however, is the mobilization of these technological opportunities to exclude cultural others and close discourse, which may only deepen cultural divides. Instead of opening discursive space for communication and dialogue, the options "unfriending," "unfollowing," and "blocking" make the splits fixed and insurmountable. If all possible divisions are established, no space exists for the creation of relationships that are not adversarial (Laclau, 2005).

To be sure, this is not a unique Ukrainian situation. We live in a world of complex, culturally differentiated societies where traditional bonds of ethical life have been lost and lifeworld certainties have become differentiated and pluralized to such an extent that different segments of society have created their own languages, meanings, and ways of reasoning. Under conditions of such profound complexity and heterogeneity, the attaining of societal solidarity, traditionally achieved and sustained by means of common values, beliefs, and norms, no longer looks like an easy enterprise (Habermas, 1984).

Reflecting on this complexity, Nicholas Garnham (1992) argues that a multicultural (global) public sphere should be characterized by the "duty to listen to the views of others and to alternative versions of events" (p. 368). James Bohman (1997) agrees. International peace, he claims, can be achieved only by means of such a public sphere, in which opinions are "multi-dimensional" and "many-sided" (p. 185). In Ulrich Beck's (2003) view, the whole meaning of learning in our complex globalized age should be reoriented toward "understanding of other cultures," "dialogical attentiveness," and "integrative thinking" (p. 138). In view of these and numerous other thinkers, such attention to other people's cultural values would pave the way to the formation of an inclusive political culture that would foster global peace.

It is a widely shared understanding that paying attention to the opinions of "cultural others" and engaging with them in a multicultural dialogue is critical not only for democracy but also for maintaining peace, both within national borders and globally. Without communication among all cultural groups within society, the latter has a potential to disintegrate into alienated cultural islands in a state of permanent war. This is what we observe in the case of Ukraine, where polarization between two cultural groups—those supporting and those rejecting the Maidan—has been radicalized to the extent of breaking out in civil conflict.

One may object that the case of the Maidan and its Facebook discussions is not a good example given the extremely heated character of the Ukrainian confrontation. Indeed, a majority of the participants of the survey were three times less likely to have unfriended others over non-Maidan topics than over Maidan-related ones. We should not forget, however, that the public sphere, as a "fundamental concept of a theory of democracy whose attempt is normative" (Habermas, 1992, p. 446), is not about discussing minor issues that have nothing to do with major societal splits. On the contrary, the public sphere is a realm where the most important societal problems are publicly evaluated to be further translated into legitimate political action. From this perspective, if Ukrainian citizens avoid discussing the most crucial aspect of their societal life with their own compatriots, who also have stakes in the conflict, they deprive themselves of an important cultural resource to negotiate contested meanings and work out peaceful solutions. To start a peaceful dialogue, one needs to assume the potential presence of alternative definitions, and thus the possibility of overcoming deadlocks and finding fresh outlooks.

Encouraging radicalization through the possibility of creating homogeneous networks is an option that may be heavily exploited in times of conflict. As my research suggests, SNS can create dangerous preconditions for totalitarianism springing from the terrain of democratic revolution (Baysha, 2017). The failure to see opponents as people worthy of fair consideration may become so widespread that the point of no return is reached, as in the case of the Ukrainian situation, where, instead of negotiations, an "anti-terrorist operation" was launched. This military operation only exacerbated the social contradictions that the Maidan had brought to life. Social media may have contributed to these tragic developments by encouraging the Jacobin practice of silencing opponents in the name of a one-sided "truth."

References

Baysha, O. (2017). In the name of national security: Articulating ethno-political struggles as terrorism. *Journal of Multicultural Discourses, 14*(4), 332–348. doi:10.1080/17447143.2017.136321

Baysha, O. (2018). *Miscommunicating social change: Lessons from Russia and Ukraine.* Lanham, MD: Lexington.

Baysha, O. (2019). Dehumanizing political others: A discursive-material perspective. *Critical Discourse Studies.* Online Before Print. doi:10.1080/17405904.2019.1567364

Beck, U. (2003). *What is globalization?* Malden, MA: Blackwell.

Bode, L. (2016). Pruning the news feed: Unfriending and unfollowing political content on social media. *Research and Politics, 3*(3), 1–8. doi:10.1177/2053168016661873

Bohman, J. (1997). The public spheres of the world citizens. In J. Bohman & M. Lutz-Bachmann (Eds.), *Perpetual peace: Essays on Kant's cosmopolitan ideas* (pp. 179–200). Cambridge, MA: MIT Press.

Brubaker, R., Feischmidt, M., & Grancea, L. (2006). *Nationalist politics and everyday ethnicity in a Transylvanian town.* Princeton, NJ: Princeton University Press.

Bukkvoll, T. (1997). *Ukraine and European security.* London, UK: Royal Institute of International Affairs.

Dahlberg, L. (2007). The Internet and discursive exclusion: From deliberative to agonistic public sphere theory. In L. Dahlberg & E. Siapera (Eds.), *Radical democracy and the Internet: Interrogating theory and practice* (pp. 128–147). New York, NY: Palgrave Macmillan.

Garnham, N. (1992). The media and the public sphere. In C. Calhoun (Ed.), *Habermas and the public sphere* (pp. 358–377). Cambridge, MA: MIT Press.

Garrett, R. K., Dvir-Gvirsman, S., Jognson, B. K., Tsfati, Y., Neo, R., & Dal, A. (2014). Implications of pro-and counterattitudinal information exposure for affective polarization. *Human Communication Research, 40*(3), 309–332. doi:10.1111/hcre.12028

Habermas, J. (1984). *The theory of communicative action.* Boston, MA: Beacon Press.

Habermas, J. (1992). Further reflections on the public sphere. In G. J. Calhound (Ed.), *Habermas and the public sphere* (pp. 421–462). Cambridge, MA: MIT Press.

Himelboim, I., McCreery, S., & Smith, M. (2013). Birds of a feature tweet together: Integrating network and content analysis to examine cross' ideology exposure on Twitter. *Journal of Computer-Mediated Communication, 18*(2), 40–60. doi:10.1111/jcc4.12001

John, N. A., & Dvir-Gvirsman, S. (2015). "I don't like you any more": Facebook unfriending by Israeli during the Israel-Gaza conflict of 2014. *Journal of Communication, 65*(6), 953–974.

Karatzogianni, A. (2009). New media and the reconfiguration of power in global politics. In A. Karatzogianni (Ed.), *Cyber conflict and global politics* (pp. 1–10). New York, NY: Routledge.

KIIS. (2014, April 20). The views and opinions of south-eastern regions residents of Ukraine: April 2014. *Kiev International Institute of Sociology*. Retrieved from www.kiis.com.ua/?lang=eng&cat=reports&id=302&y=2014&page=9

Korostelina, K. (2014). Conflict of national narratives of Ukraine: Euromaidan and beyond. *Die Friedens-Warte: Journal of International Peace and Organization, 89*(1/2), 269–290.

Kovalova, E. (2007). Ukraine's role in changing Europe. In D. Hamilton & G. Mangott (Eds.), *The new Eastern Europe: Ukraine, Belarus & Moldova* (pp. 171–194). Washington, DC: Center for Transatlantic Relations.

Kull, S., Kelleher, M. C., Ramsay, C., Lewis, E., & Pierce, E. (2015, March 9). The Ukrainian people on the current crisis. *Program for Public Consultation Affiliated with the School of Public Policy*. Retrieved from www.public-consultation.org/studies/Ukraine_0315.pdf

Laclau, E. (2005). *On populist reason*. New York, NY: Verso.

Light, B. (2014). *Disconnecting with social networking sites*. Basingstoke, UK: Palgrave Macmillan.

Lull, J. (2007). *Culture-on-demand: Communication in a crisis world*. Malden, MA: Blackwell.

Noel, H., & Nyhan, B. (2011). The "unfriending" problem: The consequences of homophily in friendship retention for causal estimates of social influence. *Social Networks, 33*(3), 211–218. doi:10.1016/j.socnet.2011.05.003

Onuch, O. (2015). EuroMaidan protests in Ukraine: Social media versus social networks. *Problems of Post-Communism, 62*, 217–235.

Pariser, E. (2011). *The filter bubble: What the internet is hiding from you*. New York, NY: Penguin Press.

Pew Research Center (2014, June 12). *Political polarization in the American public*. Retrieved from www.people-press.org/2014/06/12/appendix-a-the-ideological-consistency-scale/

Plokhy, S. (2008). *Ukraine and Russia: Representations of the past*. Toronto, Canada: University of Toronto Press.

Plokhy, S. (2015). *The gates of Europe: A history of Ukraine*. New York, NY: Basic Books.

Rossolinski, L. G. (2014). *Stepan Bandera: The life and afterlife of a Ukrainian nationalist: Fascism, genocide, and cult*. Stuttgart: Germany Germanyibidem Press.

Sakwa, R. (2015). *Frontline Ukraine: Crisis in borderlands*. London, UK: I. B. Tauris.

Scott, A. & Street, J. (2001). From media politics to e-protest? The use of popular culture and new media in parties and social movements. In F. Webster (Ed.),

Culture and politics in the information age: A new politics (pp. 32–51). New York: Routledge.

Scwartz, O., & Shani, G. (2016). Culture in mediated interaction: Political defriending on Facebook and the limits of networked individualism. *American Journal of Cultural Sociology, 4*(3), 385–421.

Shulman, S. (2004). The contours of civic and ethnic national identification in Ukraine. *Europe-Asia Studies, 56*(1), 35–56. doi:10.1080/0966813032000161437

Stroud, N. J. (2010). Polarization and partisan selective exposure. *Journal of Communication, 60*(3), 536–576.

Sutyagin, I. (2015, March). Russian forces in Ukraine. *Royal United Services Institute.* Retrieved from https://rusi.org/sites/default/files/201503_bp_russian_forces_in_ukraine.pdf

Touri, M. (2009). Transparency and accountability in the age of cyberpolitics: The role of blogs in framing conflict. In A. Karatzogiani (Ed.), *Cyber conflict and global politics* (pp. 48–58). New York: Routledge.

UN. (2019, February 20). Speakers urge peaceful settlement to conflict in Ukraine. *UN News Center.* Retrieved from https://www.un.org/press/en/2019/ga12122.doc.htm

Volkmer, I. (2003). The global network society and the global public sphere. *Development, 46*(1), 9–16. doi:10.1177/1011637003046001566

Wilson, A. (2014). *Ukraine crisis: What it means for the West.* New Haven, CT: Yale University Press.

Zhu, Q., Skoric, M., & Shen, F. (2017). I shield myself from Thee: Selective avoidance on social Media during political protests. *Political Communication, 34*(1), 112–131. doi:10.1080/10584609.2016.1222471

ZNUA. (2014, April 18). *Мнение и взгляды жителей Юго-Востока Украины: Апрель 2014* [Opinions and views of the citizens of the southeastern regions of Ukraine: April 2014]. Retrieved from http://zn.ua/UKRAINE/mneniya-i-vzglyady-zhiteley-yugo-vostoka-ukrainy-aprel-2014-143598_.html

8 Analyzing the Women to Drive Campaign on Facebook

Huda Mohsin Alsahi

Introduction

The main aim of this chapter is to examine the ways in which Facebook has served as a means for feminist expression, claim making, coordination, and mobilization in the complex and multifaceted context of the Women2Drive campaign in Saudi Arabia. Consequently, analyzing the dynamics of the campaign and the way it unfolded over Facebook was pursued for the sake of providing valuable insights into the arrays of meanings and discursive practices that emerged and manifested themselves online. By doing so, my intention is to shed some light on the local appropriations and online practices that occurred through Facebook in relation to the campaign, and examine the role of Facebook in affecting how Saudi Arabia's contemporary feminist movement is being portrayed transnationally, nationally, and locally.

Examining the origins of the Women2Drive movement is essential to understand, especially within a wider historical and analytical perspective, because t the highly mediatized Women2Drive campaign back in 2011 was not the first organized act of civil disobedience. Overall, the movement can be divided into three major phases: the 1990 Gulf War driving campaign, the 2011 Women2Drive drive campaign, and the 26th of October driving campaign in 2013.

The 1990 Gulf War Driving Campaign

The origin of the Women2Drive can be traced back to November 6, 1990, where in a daring defiance of the Saudi tradition against women driving, around 47 Saudi women gathered on the Al Tamimi Safeway supermarket parking lot. They dismissed their drivers and took the wheel in the first known open protest by Saudi women and a rare manifestation of public sentiment.

This was a response to the call for action that was directed towards women who had foreign driving licenses they had obtained abroad, primarily while studying. Thus, among the protesters, many were highly educated professionals. Many agree that the leading figure behind the protest was Aisha al-Maneh, a sociology professor who received her PhD degree from the University of Colorado in Boulder, and a well-known advocate for women's rights in Saudi Arabia (Ibrahim, 1990).

The demonstration came at a time when the Gulf region was witnessing the first Gulf War, where the presence of American and other Western forces, especially the American women military personnel to defend the country after the Iraqi invasion of Kuwait, was stirring considerable debate about whether to bring Saudi Arabia more in tune with the modern world (Doumato, 1992).

Nevertheless, the women who started driving were soon stopped by the religious police who were angered that the women refused to acknowledge their jurisdiction. Women insisted on being taken to the police headquarters instead, where they were released only after their male guardians signed pledges that confirmed that they would never drive again. Most of the women were fired from their jobs and were banned from traveling outside the country. Some were subsequently harassed by phone callers accusing the women of sexual immorality and of being agents for Western vices (Doumato, 1999).

Additionally, the Ministry of Interior issued a ban on all future political activity by women. The state-funded Directorate of Islamic Research, Ruling, and Guidance, headed by Shaykh 'Abd Allah ibn 'Abd al-'AzTz ibn Baz, sanctioned the ministry's ruling by issuing a religious edict which stated that "women should not be allowed to drive motor vehicles, as the Shari'a instructs that the things that degrade or harm the dignity of women must be prevented" thereby making official, the previously unofficial ban on women's driving (Doumato, 1992, p. 32).

The Revival of the Driving Campaign in the Aftermath of the Arab Spring

This earlier attempt to protest, as well as other scattered efforts to institutionalize the "Association for the Protection and Defense of Women's Rights in Saudi Arabia" which later became the driving force behind Saudi women's campaign to lift the driving ban during 2007–2008, did not manage to attract as much media attention as the Women2Drive grassroots campaign in 2011. A group of Saudi women, inspired in part by uprisings across the Arab world, decided to initiate a nationwide campaign to encourage women with international driver's licenses to drive on June 17, 2011.

The activists sought to leverage social media in their pursuit, as they created the Women2Drive campaign page on Facebook under the slogan, "Teach me how to drive so I can protect myself," which managed to attract thousands of supporters (HRW, 2013). Thus, the campaign was launched at the right time, in a country where there was no significant public protest during the Arab Spring to overshadow the women's protests; it was also well managed on the Internet, making it easy for protesters and the media to follow the strategic tactics of the movement.

As part of the campaign, Manal al-Sharif, an Internet security consultant for the Saudi Arabian national oil company, and one of the Women-2Drive organizers, decided to drive and post videos of herself driving on May 19, 2011 in the Eastern Province city of al-Dammam to encourage a higher turnout for the national protest that was scheduled to be on June 17, 2011. The eight-minute video of her, in which she urges women to learn how to drive in Arabic states: "We are ignorant when it comes to driving. You'll see a woman with a PhD and she doesn't know how to drive. We want to impose change in the country" (Medeiros, 2013).

The video went viral with over 600,000 views within two days. She was later arrested on May 21 for 9 days on charges of disturbing public order and inciting public disorder, only to be released afterwards as a result of outside pressure from an online petition requesting her immediate release that had organized more than 4,500 Saudi's signatories (Mac-Farquhar & Amer, 2011).

Consequently, several Saudi women got behind the wheel on June 17, 2011, in major cities across the kingdom, while documenting their driving experience. Some women who drove were stopped and arrested, only to be freed after being admonished not to drive again. On the other hand, encouragement poured in via the Internet, where Saudi newspapers were filled with testimonies of women who drove their children to school, a father to the airport, or themselves on errands.

In general, the June 17th drive-in was a success, as it highlighted one specific injustice—the ban on driving—and used it to illuminate the other social and political injustices inextricably linked to this ban. It also managed to point out the practical necessity of driving and the danger of being prevented to do so in emergency situations. Moreover, the campaign under the umbrella of the broader "Right2Dignity" movement made an attempt to politicize the issue, filing a lawsuit against the Saudi Traffic Department for denying Manal al-Sharif her driver's license despite there being no written law against issuing one to a woman, and called on those who are interested, in cyberspace, to file a similar lawsuit (Doaiji, 2012).

The campaign triggered a variety of responses on domestic and international levels, as it resonated globally, increased the media attention to this cause, and sparked an outcry from international rights groups where some protests were scheduled abroad in solidarity with the campaign (NBC Washington, 2011). The reaction domestically ranged from praise to vilification; the movement was not without its critics, as many religious clerics objected to the very idea of women being exposed to strangers outside their homes by driving (Shmuluvitz, 2011). Local politicians, on the other hand, tended to distance themselves from the issue by saying that the Saudi society is simply not ready for women to gain the right to drive.

The efforts of the campaign continued into 2012, where in June, to celebrate the anniversary of the June 2011 protest, the driving initiative was renewed once again to urge the authorities to look into this demand. Moreover, there were some attempts made by the citizens to sue the traffic department in Saudi Arabia's Eastern Province for the right to drive (Abu-Nasr, 2011).

Along with this, Saudi women's efforts continued through 2013 when activists arranged another grassroots campaign by announcing October 26th, 2013, as a day for defying the state ban on women driving and launched a website (www.oct26driving.com), calling for women to get behind the steering wheel and drive individually. Nevertheless, Saudi Arabia's passage of the anti-terrorism law as well as the modification of the anti-cybercrime legislation, combined with the month-long arrest of activists for attempting to drive in the same year, has suppressed the campaign's momentum. This continued into 2015, reflecting domestic uncertainties, such as the death of King Abdullah bin Abdulaziz and the Saudi military intervention in Yemen (Doaiji, 2017).

Analyzing the Saudi Women to Drive Facebook Page

The Facebook page "Women2DriveKSA" soon emerged in the context of the 2011 driving campaign to encourage Saudi women to post pictures and videos of themselves behind the wheel. It quickly managed to distinguish itself as one of the most active English-speaking pages in the driving campaign with more than 37,000 users.

Consequently, analyzing the dynamics of the campaign and the way it unfolded over this Facebook page was pursued to provide valuable insights into the arrays of meanings and discursive practices that emerged and manifested themselves online.

The different stages of analysis of the Facebook page include (a) examining the attributes of users' engagement, (b) identifying the various usage types, type of content and the size and composition of the participating audience, and (c) conducting a qualitative content analysis of the posts made by page administrators.

The data were acquired using the Netvizz application v1.44 for Facebook (Rieder, 2013), which is a data collection and extraction application that allows researchers to export data in standard file formats from different sections of the specified Facebook pages, including the complete list of posts, number of likes, shares and comments during a specific time period.

Accordingly, the collection of the data took place covering the full period of posting activity from the day of the creation of the Facebook page on May 22, 2011, until December 31, 2013, which marked the second round of the driving campaign which started in October 2013. The data comprised a total of 2,069 posts by the page administrators and page users and 8,489 comments and replies.

Examination of the Posts

When tracing the sources of the posted content, we found that a total of 449 posts were published by the page administrator(s), which comprised 22% of the overall sample, while page users posted 1,620 posts which constituted 78% of the gathered posts. A further in-depth examination of the administrators' posts and users' reactions towards them was made possible by Facebook's default built-in classification of post types (Links, Status updates, Photos, Videos, and Events). Thus, when comparing the five types used on the Facebook campaign page, we found a number of significant differences, pointing towards the idea that they indeed played different roles on the page.

The posts made by page administrators had received on average, 139 likes and 19.2 comments. The heavy usage of photos is evident; photos comprised 44% of the overall composition of posts types, where they received 359.5 likes and 32.3 comments on average. This finding is in line with similar research that concluded that the frequent usage of visual hooks (photos or videos) is often found to be emotionally rousing and thus particularly appealing to individuals. The majority of the posts which contained photos often included them as an evidence of the success of the campaign either by showing how the women responded to the calls of the campaign by driving in the streets or by sharing photos which visualize instances of transnational solidarity from other women around the globe.

Links were also widely used, which involved the inclusion of direct links to newspaper articles citing and reporting the activities of the campaign in various news sources such as www.english.alarabiya.net or www.arabnews.com. The links comprised 33% of the sample and managed to receive 63.4 likes and 10.5 comments on average. This was followed by the usage of videos (14%) which contained recorded video footages of women who have responded to the calls of the campaign by driving in the streets of Saudi Arabia, and status updates (7%), which are often short comments about the campaign or propositions inviting users to react. The administrators often used this post type to engage in a dialogue with the page users, either by posting calls for action, asking for users' opinions and feedback. The category of events were the least used, as it comprised (2%) of the sample.

Conducting Qualitative Content Analysis

A further in-depth qualitative content analysis of the types of Facebook (FB) posts was undertaken for the posts that were written by page administrators starting from the launch of the FB page till the end of the second round of the campaign. This specific method was chosen because of its characteristics as "a systematic, rule-guided technique for examining information and content, in written or symbolic materials" (Neuman, 1997, 426).

The content of the social media page (Facebook in this instance) was the unit of analysis (Graneheim & Lundman, 2004) while the individual posts by the administrators of the page were the coding units. Overall 449 posts made by the page administrators were collected via Netvizz v1.44 and read several times before being coded. I used a manual, inductive open coding approach based on the analysis of posts' intents and content. First, I identified the major themes that emerged from the intents and content of the sample. These themes were then coded into one or more categories according to the coding scheme. Posts that did not fit the codes formed new categories and some earlier categories were also merged and refined. This approach is in line with the classification scheme developed by Qu, Wu, and Wang (2009), and Miles and Huberman's (2004) recommendations for iterative coding.

The analysis revealed four relevant categories of posts, explained by 15 other subcategories and their traits. The four broader categories of posts were: information-related, action-related, feminist-related, and emotion-related. One other category of posts-others-was also identified but was omitted in the analysis.

Results and Discussion

The results of the content analysis as shown in Table 8.1 demonstrates the detailed breakdown of the FB posts per general category, sub-category, and their percentage. We can see from the Table that information-related posts constituted 37.8% of the overall sample at hand, closely followed by the feminist-related posts (33.1%). The posts that carried action-related content accounted for (17.3%) of the sample, followed by the emotion-related and user engagement broader category which constituted 7.5% of the overall collected posts. Finally, only 4% of the sample belonged to the "other" topics category.

The results point out that the Facebook page played an informative role, through broadly distributing and circulating information. This dissemination included (1) circulating campaign-related news or information from various news sources; (2) sharing of other general local news articles that are related to the Saudi context; (3) sharing of other international news articles which is usually followed by the inclusion of links of the materials it references; (4) providing social sociopolitical commentary and critique; and (5) sharing personal testimonies and statements of support from the supporters of the campaign.

Facebook has been used instrumentally in this regard as a low-cost channel for circulating information and sharing real-life updates about the campaign (Earl & Kimport, 2011). Moreover, when analyzing the content of the informative posts we witnessed the usage of a highly charged critical tone towards some state-officials and the religious establishment, which is demonstrated in the following posts:

Table 8.1 General Classification Scheme

Category	Number of posts	(%)
A *Information-related*	*170*	*36.6*
1 Providing/sharing campaign-related news or information	49	10.9
2 Sharing of news articles on local issues	16	3.5
3 Sharing of news articles on international issues	38	8.4
4 Providing sociopolitical commentary/critique	57	12.6
5 Sharing personal testimonies	10	2.2
B *Action-related*	*76*	*16.7*
6 On-ground mobilization	11	2.4
7 Online action	12	2.6
8 Transnational solidarity and support	44	9.7
9 Providing evidence of success	9	2.0
C *Feminist-related*	*149*	*33.0*
10 Sharing general feminist-related news or articles	74	16.4
11 Saudi women's achievements	53	11.8
12 Empowerment and motivation	22	4.8
D *Emotion-related/ user engagement*	*34*	*7.5*
13 Expressing gratitude	6	1.3
14 Expressing solidarity	5	1.1
15 Occasional greetings	23	5.1
E *Other*	*18*	*4.0*
Total posts	449	100.0

I'm a Saudi girl and I say this country is a big joke. The regime is distracting people by women's and religious issues so they can steal as much as they want from the wealth of the country. We are just scapegoats!

Let me introduce you to our oppressors. The former minister of interior Prince Naif Bin Abdulaziz and his son Prince Mohammed Bin Naif the current minister of interior. They've been arresting torturing and jailing more than 30.000 people in Saudi Arabia for years without trials! If you ever seen the little criminal in your country please spit and throw eggs on him may he follow his dad to hell soon. Amen.

We can see from the above posts the page administrators' efforts to appeal to the public and evoke a collective identity in terms of framing their position "we are the people" and "we are the scapegoats." Moreover, what is noticeable is the diversity of the topics that are discussed within the Facebook page; they are no longer limited to the driving issues, but extend to human rights violations, political oppression, in addition to women's participation in the public sphere such as banning them from attending sport events.

Furthermore, it was also clear that the page administrators had adopted an anti-religious establishment stance which was reflected in the below extracts:

> This is Abdul Aziz al ash-Shaikh the current Grand Mufti of Saudi Arabia (pope) this hypocrite man has strongly opposed the idea of women in the Shura Council and then supported it when the king appointed 30 women in the Council!! He can solve all of our problems by some Fatwas! What do you want to say to him?
>
> How to beat your wife in London!! Mohammed Al Arifi is a Saudi preacher. He hates women and he doesn't like seeing women working in public to appear on tv or mix with men he wants us all covered up. This misogynistic preacher is enjoying his life traveling everywhere freely while we the women of Saudi Arabia can't do the same. He's in London to enjoy his summer break after he asked the Muslim youth to go and fight (Jihad) in Syria!! Why didn't he go and fight as well!! Please England kick him out he's too sick to be in a free country. This video shows him teaching some Saudi youth how to beat their wives!!

Thus, we can observe the strong language, which is used against several religious figures. What is also interesting in this case is the use of vocabulary that is clearly directed to the western audience which can be exemplified by the post in which the position of the "Grand Mufti of Saudi Arabia" has been translated to its western equivalent the "pope," and the call to expel the Saudi preacher Mohammed Al Arifi from London because he shouldn't be allowed to be present in a "free country."

This pattern should not be surprising because the western-based audience constitutes a larger percentage of the overall audience of the page with the largest proportion of audience based in the United States, followed by Saudi Arabia, and then the United Kingdom.

The posts which were under the emotion related/user engagement broader category carried expressive and emotive evaluations of the actors and events as they were mainly devoted to (1) expressing gratitude by thanking the supporters of the campaign for their enthusiasm and dedication; (2) expressing solidarity and evoking a "we-feeling" through the posts that offer moral and commends the dedication of the campaign's supporters; and (3) posting greetings during special occasions and events. Examples of that can be shown in the following extracts:

> Good morning friends. Much love and appreciation from your sisters in Saudi Arabia <3

> March 21st is mother s day in the Arab world. Happy mother's day to all those beautiful precious women in KSA Arab world and the whole world <3

This is not surprising and is in line with the results of some of the studies which have concluded that social media platforms such as Facebook and Twitter have a strong emotional aspect, and that "digital, among other media, sustain effective feedback loops that generate and reproduce affective patterns of relating to others" (Papacharissi, 2014, p. 65) while bolstering the level of emotional solidarity. Thus, the social media and emotions nexus is particularly important in the case of grassroots campaigns.

Also, communication on Facebook catalyzes mobilization, and that was clear in the posts under the action-related category as they were either (a) calling for on-ground mobilization by asking Saudi women to drive in the streets in challenge to the ban, (b) calling for online action by urging the users to use the web to spread the message by sharing the link to the page, or sending collective emails to the members of the Shura "consultation" council in Saudi Arabia, (c) showing acts of transnational solidarity and support through the circulation of support messages/organizing international marches near the Saudi embassy in many countries around the globe, or (d) providing evidence of the success of the campaign by posting footages and videos of the driving rallies. Examples of these forms of mobilization are below:

> We are creating a petition to be sent to the international organizations and media. The Saudi Government did sign on the CEDAW yet didn't make any efforts to stop the violence and discrimination against Saudi Women! We hope they will be penalized. We just need your suggestions now and signatures later. Thanks.
>
> Civil disobedience or social activism or whatever you call it WE DID IT. Women of all ages went out and drove their cars on Oct 26. 15 violation tickets were given to some women. We appreciate your help and support thanks to our supporters around the world. And the fight is still on.

What was also notable is the focus on the transnational aspect of the campaign by encouraging the international supports and empathizers to perform symbolic acts of solidarity like contacting or honking near the Saudi embassies and consulates in their respective countries. The following posts demonstrate this transnational solidarity:

> Dear friends now we are close to June 17th. Could you please email the Saudi embassies. Let Women Drive in Saudi Arabia so we can

get their attention? You can find all of the emails in the link below.
Thank you http://embassy.goabroad.com/embassies-of/saudi-arabia
Some Italian ladies honked for us this year too. Grazie ladies <3

Through the formation of transnational ties and the ability to promote offline events, the Saudi Women2Drive page demonstrates the potential capabilities that online spaces offer when it comes to the creation of feminist alliances with women all over the world. These attempts to attain international support were pursued for the sake of giving the campaign external legitimacy and acknowledgment, and to disseminate its claims and practices beyond the local scope. The use of the page to organize offline events and actions also contributes to the development of a grassroots movement and shows us that offline action is considered to be a critical part of the collective movement. This clearly shows that Facebook is being pragmatically used to create new dimensions and opportunities of action.

The feminist-related posts were mainly concerned with (a) posting and disseminating general feminist-related news or articles that draw attention to the ubiquity of sexism, misogyny, and violence against women, (b) covering the news that relates to Saudi women's achievements in particular, (c) posting of status messages that carry empowerment and motivational content. Examples of the posts that embody these characteristics are shown below:

> Saudi Arabia has one of the lowest female participation rates in the work force in the region a recent World Bank report has found this. www.arabnews.com/news/445991.
> After three years of petitioning the Ministry of Justice Arwa Al-Hujaili 25 has finally received her registration to practice as a trainee lawyer the first woman to do so.
> We are mothers we are teachers we are beautiful creatures.

A large majority of the posts that belonged to this category either contained links to articles or videos relating to topics of concern for women and feminists from news sources, feminist publications and personal blogs from all over the world. The topics of these posts were diverse, including women's political representation, their participation in the labor force, and domestic violence.

The Discursive Construction of Secular-Feminist Thoughts

The reliance on and influence of secular feminist thought was clearly evident while analyzing the content of the English-speaking Women2DriveKSA Facebook page, as it appeared that the page administrators based their rationale of feminism on the "all inclusive human-rights" strand of it.

In light of that and given its mutability, secular feminist thoughts in and outside Islam have been comprised of a cluster of discursive strands, including secular nationalist as well as the more generic universalist human rights and democratic strand of it (Moghadam, 2003)—that was observed in this instance—though there is often an overlap among them as well.

A clear manifestation of that can be observed in the description page of the campaign, which reads: "*dedicated to the* citizens of the world *who support women's freedom in Saudi Arabia, starting by allowing them to drive*." This universalist discourse and display of inclusivity is the same approach used by secular feminists, which moves away from using religion as a framework to define gender roles, while basing their rationale for women's rights on universalist and human rights discourses to enable and empower women. Thus, women's rights and human rights are thought to be best promoted and protected in an environment of secular thought and secular institutions, including a state that defends the rights of all its citizens.

Also, the emphasis on secular thought was manifested through the posting of direct quotes by founder of the modern Turkish Republic Mustafa Kemal Atatürk, who governed Turkey by strictly secular principles. The administrator has defended her choice of quoting him by stressing that there is a need for such as a secular extremist in Saudi Arabia as there is no time for slow change.

Additionally, page administrators wove a humanitarian discourse into their feminist articulation in calling for the demands of equality and emancipation that secular feminists usually call for. Thus, the framing of demands around "rights" and the reliance on secular universal discourses for gender equality reveals a liberal ontology that reproduces an approach to feminism assuming an individualistic premise, which is a key part of the secular metanarrative that informs feminist scholarship today.

The page also announced its support for marriage equality on the premise that equality is a basic human right, although it was careful in clarifying that marriage equality is not directly related to women's issues in Saudi Arabia nor in the Arab World—but instead emphasized that equality is a basic principle that should be fully integrated and respected.

Although attempting to bypass the stable (and binary) gender definition through demonstrating transnational solidarity, and facilitating conversations about homosexuality and marriage equality that are often absent from discussions due to the lack of support for LGBT issues, this topic remains a taboo that is rarely featured and discussed in the Saudi public sphere.

In light of this, such particular notions of inclusiveness seem to be premised on a desire to accommodate women of different statuses, ethnoracial backgrounds and socio-economic positions which overall appears to be motivated by the concept of intersectionality.

Intersectionality was first coined by Crenshaw in 1989 as an approach addressing the multiples locations of oppression such as gender, class, age, sexual orientation, and religion, among others. The basic premise underlying intersectionality theory is that systems of oppression cannot be understood in isolation from one another; each of these types of inequalities is in fact interconnected and interlocking.

In other words, an intersectional approach to one's identity rejects the notion that gender is the primary criterion upon which feminist approaches should be based, and instead strives to achieve an understanding of how the myriad differences in women's lives and facets of one's identity intersect (rather than accumulate) to construct their social positioning(s). Accordingly, some attempts of demonstrating intersectional ties of feminist solidarity and enabling new kinds of intersectional conversations were relatively apparent in the English language page of Women2Drive, in the posts which were calling for the protection of rights of domestic workers in the Arab Gulf and Lebanon, and others calling for abolishing discriminatory gender laws in Jordan.

Conclusion

The analysis of the content of the posts in the "Women2Drive" Facebook page offers a great example of how the Internet can be used effectively to create and support a grassroots feminist campaign, how the use of online spaces can promote free expression, deconstruct the stereotypical image of Saudi Arabia, embrace and participate in transnational feminisms, and organize and promote offline events, and how women can shape their own version of feminism in challenge to the patriarchal norms imposed on them through various institutions. Additionally, it appears throughout the analyzed textual material, that there is an active attempt to move away from Islamic feminism expressed in a single or paramount religiously grounded discourse with the Quran as its central text towards new forms of Saudi feminism that is based on human-rights discourse inspired by the transnational flow of feminist ideas, politics, and protests.

However, what was noticeable is the constant preoccupation of the Western secular model (in all its complexities and contradictions) as the primary referent and the uncritical assumption of its direct applicability and strict correspondence to the context. Hence, secular feminism was treated as if it holds positional superiority and was depicted as being modern and progressive as opposed to the backward and traditional "other" models that can be found in that context. Also, despite the reliance of this page on the concept of intersectionality, religion received relatively little attention within the intersectionality framework as an axis of difference and was never conceptualized as positionality, but was disregarded otherwise. The downplay of the role of religion points to the fact that despite the recent wave of scholarship on intersectionality, feminist research has yet to adequately engage with the role of religion within discussions of intersectionality, other than to occasionally list religion as one in a list of relevant differences among the other collection of social divisions (gender, race, class) that are typically taken into account.

This pushes us to renew the call for forging new critical engagement with secular, feminist, and religious thought as normative principles especially in such complex settings where the secular and religious both intersect and diverge, while acknowledging the need for a more inclusive and cross-cultural understanding of feminism in the context of the global women's movement.

References

Abu-Nasr, D. (2011, June 22). Saudi women call on progressive subaru to leave kingdom over driving ban. *Bloomberg*. Retrieved from www.bloomberg.com/news/articles/2011-06-22/saudi-women-call-on-subaru-to-leave-kingdom-over-driving-ban

Doaiji, N. (2017). Saudi women's online activism: One year of the-I am my own guardian-campaign. *The Arab Gulf States Institute*. Retrieved from www.agsiw.org/wp-content/uploads/2017/10/Doaiji_Saudi-Guardianship-System_ONLINE.pdf

Doaiji, N. (2012, May 14). Saudi feminism: Between Mama Amreeka and Baba Abdullah. *Jadaliyya*. Retrieved from www.jadaliyya.com/pages/index/5516/saudi-feminism_between-mama-amreeka-and-baba-abdul

Doumato, E. (1992). Gender, monarchy, and national identity in Saudi Arabia. *British Journal of Middle Eastern Studies*, *19*(1), 31–47.

Doumato, E. (1999). The Saudis and the Gulf War: Gender, power and the revival of the religious right. In A. Abdelkarim (Ed.), *Change and development in the Gulf* (pp. 184–210). London, UK: Macmillan.

Earl, J., & Kimport, K. (2011). *Digitally enabled social change: Activism in the Internet age* (1st ed.). Cambridge, MA: MIT Press.

Graneheim, H., & Lundman, B. (2004). Qualitative content analysis in nursing research: Concepts, procedures and measures to achieve trustworthiness. *Nurse Education Today*, *24*, 105–112.

Human Rights Watch. (2013, December 17). *Challenging the red lines stories of rights activists in Saudi Arabia*. Retrieved from www.hrw.org/report/2013/12/17/challenging-red-lines/stories-rights-activists-saudi-arabia

Ibrahim, Y. M. (1990, November 7). Mideast tensions: Saudi women take driver's seat in a rare protest for the right to travel. *The New York Times*. Retrieved from www.nytimes.com/1990/11/07/world/mideast-tensions-saudi-women-take-driver-s-seat-rare-protest-for-right-travel.html?pagewanted=all

MacFarquhar, N., & Amer, D. (2011, June 17). In a scattered protest, Saudi women take the wheel. *The New York Times*. Retrieved from www.nytimes.com/2011/06/18/world/middleeast/18saudi.html

Medeiros, J. (2013, January 28). Dangerous driver: Manal al-Sharif after defying Saudi ban on women driving. *Wired*. Retrieved from www.wired.co.uk/magazine/archive/2013/01/start/dangerous-driver

Miles, B., & Huberman, A. (2004). *Qualitative data analysis: An expanded sourcebook* (2nd ed.). Thousand Oaks, CA: Sage Publications.

Moghadam, V. (2003). The emergence of Islamic feminism. In V. Moghadam (Ed.), *Modernizing women: Gender and social change in the Middle East* (2nd ed.). (pp. 215–220). Boulder, CO: L. Rienner.

NBC Washington. (2011, June 15). *Protesters Want Saudi Arabia to allow women to drive.* Retrieved from www.nbcwashington.com/news/local/Afternoon-protest-planned-at-Saudi-Embassy-123916649.html

Neuman, W. L. (1997). *Social research methods, qualitative and quantitative approaches* (3rd ed.). Boston, MA: Allyn and Bacon.

Papacharissi, Z. (2014). *Affective publics.* New York, NY: Oxford University Press.

Qu, Y., Wu, P. F., & Wang, X. (2009). *Online community response to major disaster: A study of tianya forumin the 2008 sichuan earthquake.* Proceedings of the 2009 Hawaii International Conference on System Sciences. IEEE Computer Society (pp. 1–11).

Rieder, B. (2013). Studying Facebook via data extraction: The Netvizz application. In *Proceedings of the 5th annual ACM web science conference: WebSci '13* (pp. 346–355). New York: ACM. http://dx.doi.org/10.1145/2464464.2464475

Saudi Women to Drive. (2011). *Facebook* [Women2DriveKSA]. Retrieved June 28, 2016, from www.facebook.com/Women2DriveKSA/www.facebook.com/specificpageURL

Shmuluvitz, S. (2011, July 26). The Saudi Women2Drive campaign: Just another protest in the Arab spring? *Telaviv Notes, 5*(14), 1–4.

9 "Does This Lab Coat Make Me Look #DistractinglySexy?"

A Critical Discourse Analysis of a Feminist Hashtag Campaign

Alex Rister and Jennifer Sandoval

Sir Richard Timothy Hunt works as a biochemist in England. His research specializes on the cell cycle, and he won the 2001 Nobel Prize for his contributions to physiology and medicine. On June 9, 2015, Hunt spoke at the 2015 World Conference of Science Journalists in Seoul, South Korea. A transcript reveals Hunt said, "Let me tell you about my trouble with girls. Three things happen when they are in the lab: you fall in love with them, they fall in love with you, and when you criticize them, they cry" (Saul, 2015, para. 3). In response to Hunt, the hashtag "#distractinglysexy" was first used on Twitter on June 10, 2015. Soon, hundreds of tweets used the hashtag; some mocked Hunt's words while others shared experiences of real women in science.

While women have made significant contributions to science throughout history, some view science as inherently masculine. Fewer women than men earn PhDs, fewer women than men work in scientific fields, and women earn lower salaries than men in the workplace (Pollack, 2013). Moss-Racusin, Dovidio, Brescoll, Graham, and Handelsman (2013) found a gender bias against women in science in a study asking science faculty to rate the applications for a laboratory position. As a result of the double-blind study, participants "rated the male applicant as more competent and more hirable than the (identical) female applicant;" "selected a higher starting salary" to the male applicant; and "offered more career mentoring to the male applicant" (p. 16474). These results indicate continued unequal treatment and prejudiced opinions of women in employment opportunity generally as well as employment in science specifically.

Due to unequal treatment of women in the workplace, women offer stories to share their experiences. According to Rickett (2014), stories emerge that "tell us of the less than trouble-free manner in which women take up, and progress in, employment in male-dominated organizations" (p. 161). These stories are often told on social media, which is an important space for online activism related to feminist causes. For example, although the Me Too movement originated with Tarana Burke in 2006, #MeToo went viral on social media after a tweet by Alyssa Milano in

October, 2017, revealing the widespread issue of sexual assault and harassment. Due to the use of hashtags, Twitter is an important medium for studying stories told by women. Hashtags can become interactive and create a dialogue about an experience or event, as with #MeToo. According to Conley (2014), "hashtags represent evidence of women and people of color resistiny authority, opting out of confirming to the status quo, and seeking liberation, all by way of documentation in digital spaces (p. 1111). "#distractinglysexy" is another important example of a hashtag displaying narrative resistance against Hunt's comments and telling counter-stories of women in science. What did tweets utilizing the #distractinglysexy hashtag reveal about women in science? How do those tweets resist socio-cultural norms about women in science? This chapter seeks to uncover the assumptions about women scientists through the #distractinglysexy hashtag as well as the assertions about women scientists made by the hashtag.

Literature Review

Twitter

Created in 2006, Twitter quickly became one of the most popular social media sites on the Internet. When #distractinglysexy first appeared in 2015, Twitter boasted 316 million active users posting 500 million tweets per day (Twitter, 2015). Twitter allows users to compose, share, and read short messages of 280 characters called tweets which may include images, tags of other users, links, or hashtags. When reading tweets, users may "favorite" a tweet or "retweet" to share on their own pages. Twitter profiles may be public, open and accessible to anyone with the link, or protected, private and accessible only to users who have been manually approved to view the page.

To comply with the 280-character limit, tweets often contain abbreviated language. Scott (2015) explains that Twitter's character limit adds to the conversational and relaxed tone of the platform. Despite an overall casual tone, tweets share mundane as well as important updates; for example, tweets may explain what a user ate for breakfast, may share content in the classroom environment, or may connect people in an emergency (Honeycutt & Herring, 2009). Additionally, some tweets "go viral," a term associated with content online that quickly spreads and gains popularity. For example, the hashtag #MeToo went viral after being tweeted by Alyssa Milano on October 15, 2017; within 24 hours, the phrase had been repeated more than 500,000 times on Twitter (France, 2017).

Sharing information is one primary aim of posting on Twitter (Chen, 2015; Johnson & Yang, 2009). With approximately 500 million tweets per day, the hashtag serves as a search tool that allows users to find that information on Twitter. A hashtag utilizes the "#" symbol followed by a word or phrase. "Hashtags function primarily as metadata tags facilitating the retrieval of content from the site" (Scott, 2015, p. 8). This hashtag becomes a hyperlink, and users who click on the link will view all other tweets featuring the same hashtag. News organizations use Twitter to share news quickly with links incorporated so that followers can be directed to read more at a particular website (Armstrong & Gao, 2011). Businesses and companies use hashtags to promote products and services. Tufekci (2017) cites Twitter as the organizing force behind the Gezi Park protests in Turkey in 2013, revealing the importance of connection through hashtags. The use of a hashtag allows for live information sharing by multiple users at various locations around the globe which can lead to online activism, such as #MeToo's raising awareness of sexual assault and sexual harassment, as well as offline action, such as the Gezi Park protests.

Twitter and Women

More women than men use social media websites overall (Duggan, Ellison, Lampe, Lenhart, & Madden, 2015). Megarry (2014) argues that despite the prevalence of women using social networking, "this has not resulted in a feminist transformation of digital technologies" (p. 46). In fact, many studies reveal communication online can "perpetuate the prejudices and hostilities of the offline world," including sexism against women (Fox, Cruz, & Lee, 2015, p. 436). This proves especially true on Twitter. For the first time, in 2014, Twitter saw slightly more men than women users (Duggan et al., 2015). In addition to the increase of men users, Heil and Piskorski (2009) conducted a study that revealed a skew toward men on Twitter. While men and women Twitter users follow about the same amount of people and tweet at about the same rate, men had more followers than women (Heil & Piskorski, 2009). Armstrong and Gao (2011) found, "Given that our finding demonstrated there were more tweets and news from news organizations emphasizing men, it seems possible the news delivery and news consumption on Twitter will be increasingly male-skewed, providing less space for female perspectives and certainly not attracting more female followers" (p. 501). Additionally, outright discrimination against women can be seen on Twitter through the use of sexist hashtags; some examples include #LiesToldByFemales and #ThatsWhatSlutsDo. In addition to #MeToo, hashtags such as #HeForShe and #YesAllWomen highlight and attempt to combat sexism. #HowToSpotAFeminist is an example of a hashtag originally utilized for a sexist purpose but later reclaimed by feminists to emphasize the importance of equal rights for women in America.

The anonymity associated with the online environment can lead to increased sexist language. The online disinhibition effect indicates people are more likely to communicate offensive and negative content online versus in person. People feel free and uninhibited when using online communication channels; thus, they are more likely to communicate things online that they would not dare to say in person (Lapidot-Lefler, 2012). One example of the online disinhibition effect is the communication of sexist content. Fox et al. (2015) found that "interacting with sexist content anonymously promotes greater hostile sexism that interacting with it using an identified account" (p. 440). Unfortunately, these online attitudes do not always remain online, as Fox et al. (2015) also reported that experiencing online sexist content may translate to offline sexist attitudes.

Acts of Narrative Resistance by Women

Storytelling pre-dates written language and serves as a powerful medium for communicating information (Duarte, 2010). Stories convey best practices and connect people through shared experiences. "Stories connected to the lives of people enacted in stories are located in a socio-political context of power, knowledge, and culture" (Tursunova, 2014, p. 2). Narratives teach cultural lessons and pass down important customs. "We turn to life narratives in part to see what they might teach us about how individuals in different cultures experience their sense of being an 'I'" (Beard, 2009, p. 1). In addition to helping us understand our place in our own culture, the universal emotions conveyed in a story allow us to understand other cultures as well.

However, stories often reflect the dominant ideas of a culture, and this proves problematic for marginalized populations. "Dominant features of the current political climate in the West (such as neoliberalism, patriarchy, and scientism) prop up particular discourses/narratives that serve the interests of some at the expense of others" (Lafrance & McKenzie-Mohr, 2014, p. 4). Narrative resistance involves speaking against the dominant story with a counter-story. Since the dominant discourse in America is androcentric, it is important that women narrate their own experiences to include women's experiences in the conversation and to ensure those experiences are autobiographical as opposed to being communicated from a man's perspective (Beard, 2009; Lafrance & McKenzie-Moh, 2014). Narrative resistance allows audiences to achieve a clearer and more accurate picture of a particular society and to balance the dominant view with views from those who may be marginalized. These stories also allow audiences to contemplate or even challenge cultural values and norms. Some researchers label the dominant experience "the story" with the narrative resistance acting as the "counter story." Considering narrative resistance utilizing "this framework offers a powerful way to conceptualize the power and politics of storytelling, in the suggestion that new stories are crafted in opposition to existing ones" (Devault, 2014, p. 26).

Hashtag Activism as Acts of Narrative Resistance

Acts of narrative resistance can occur in any medium, including Twitter. Radio host Doc Thompson created the #HowToSpotAFeminist hashtag in a tweet on May 3, 2015. Thompson tweeted, "Any tips on #HowToSpotAFeminist??? We'll discuss tomorrow TheBlaze.com/Radio" (twitter.com/docthompsonshow). After many sexist responses using the hashtag, feminists reclaimed #HowToSpotAFeminist. "Some made poignant statements about feminism being about equality between the sexes, about equal pay and breaking down stereotypes" while others used humor and sarcasm (Regan, 2015, para. 3). This reclaiming of #HowToSpotA-Feminist displays just one example of narrative resistance on Twitter.

Around the world, hashtag activism brings awareness to feminist causes. In 2014, the Turkish hashtag campaign #KadinKatliamiVar, or "there is a massacre of women," trended after its creation by the Urgent Action Group against Murders (Altinay, 2014). Also in 2014, #YesAllWomen," was a hashtag campaign originating from German feminists (Baer, 2015). Most popularly, #MeToo served as a hashtag campaign to raise awareness of sexual assault and sexual harassment against women. Participants utilizing these hashtags sought to raise awareness to women's issues, specifically violence against women, and to change the discourse surrounding these issues (Altinay, 2014; Baer, 2015). However, many scholars argue that hashtag activism alone is not enough.

In examining the #BringBackOurGirls campaign designed to bring attention to returning kidnapped Nigerian girls, Chiluwa and Ifukor (2015) found that hashtags may be impactful but only if accompanied by actions offline. Similarly, Guha (2015) studied the hashtag #VictimBlaming about rape culture in India. While a hashtag allows for discourse on a particular topic, simultaneous news and media coverage was needed to inspire policy-making and true change (Guha, 2015). In the case of #MeToo, online awareness was, in fact, accompanied by offline action. Social activist and community organizer Tarana Burke, attributed as the founder of the phrase "me too" in 2006, not only uses the hashtag #MeToo online but also wears "me too" shirts while speaking at marches and rallies and discusses the movement in national interviews and in town halls.

While offline action is important, hashtag activism online does allow for acts of narrative resistance that otherwise would not be heard. For example, #StandWithJada sought justice for a teenage girl named Jada whose rape was photographed and published on social media. Williams (2015) argues that "Twitter is often a site of resistance where black feminists challenge violence committed against women of color, and they leverage the power of Black Twitter to bring attention and justice to women who rarely receive either" (p. 343). Narrative resistance seeks to challenge the dominant story to shift and change it, and the dominant story encompasses privilege based not only on male dominance but also based on race, class, and sexual orientation. According to Beard (2009), narrative resistance may allow us to better understand privilege and oppression in order to determine how to work toward social change. While successfully achieving that change may not always occur, highlighting the oppression by providing a counter-story is another goal of narrative resistance. "In naming their own identities as part of their struggles to challenge domination, the women employing these genres create autobiographical acts of political and narrative resistance" (Beard, 2009, pp. 1–2). In addition to shifting and changing the dominant story, narrative resistance also seeks to combat sexism and discrimination against women. "Feminist researchers stress the importance of voice, authenticity, interpretive authority and representation whereby women" tell the stories of their own lives (Tursunova, 2014, p. 2). Even if major change against oppressive voices cannot be achieved, the resistance narrative itself becomes important to give a voice to the oppressed. Lafrance and McKenzie-Mohr (2014) believe that "while it is essential to understand the ways in which women have been oppressed by hegemonic discourses, it is equally essential to understand the ways in which they resist" (p. 6). The stories of how and why women engage in narrative resistance prove just as important as the oppression itself; these stories allow for a deeper understanding of hegemony. However, telling one's personal story often seems difficult due to the language in which the narrative is constructed, which reflects the dominance and power embedded in patriarchal institutions, including the English language itself (Devault, 2014). Critical discourse analysis provides one lens through which to examine these stories despite the challenges of the patriarchal system of language.

Critical Discourse Analysis

Critical discourse analysis (CDA) investigates language to reveal hegemony and power relations. Van Dijk (2001) says CDA "studies the way social power abuse, dominance, and inequality are enacted, reproduced, and resisted by text and talk" (p. 352). When examining stories of narrative resistance, the CDA methodology allows for an analysis of those counter-stories while considering the patriarchal limitations of the language in which those stories are told.

Fairclough developed a model for CDA which explains that "every instance of language use is a communicative event consisting of three dimensions: it is a text (speech, writing, visual image, or combination of these); it is a discursive practice which involves the production and consumption of texts; and it is a social practice" (Jorgenson & Phillips, 2002, p. 68). CDA studies more than just the text itself; an examination of how that text relates to culture and society must also be considered. CDA examines "the relationship between language and society" as well as "the relationship between analysis and the practices analyzed" (Fairclough & Wodak, 1997, p. 258). CDA analyzes spoken and written language as well as visuals, cinematic and digital; this is important for understanding narrative resistance multimodal online environments like Twitter.

CDA becomes especially helpful when researching issues involving power such as women's acts of narrative resistance against the dominant discourse. CDA serves as a tool to explore the power embedded in language, and this becomes important in research of narrative resistance because the language itself being used and studied may possess a gender bias and derive from the most powerful group (Van Dijk, 2001). For example, sexism in the English language reflects the historically dominant group: white men. If the language available for women to use in acts of narrative resistance is androcentric, communicating a woman's story from woman's perspective becomes challenging. Studying a feminist issue utilizing CDA allows for a deeper analysis of how power works in the context of knowledge, experience, and reality (Mengibar, 2015). An act of narrative resistance must negotiate the language used which transmits a particular societal knowledge and ascribed identity for various groups.

CDA of Social Media

Social media posts, updates, and tweets blend written text, images, sounds, and videos, and CDA proves an effective tool for analyzing the hybrid nature of new media (Lee, 2011). Since social media changed the way public information is created, distributed, and consumed, the kinds of information presented have also changed. Social media is also constantly changing itself. For example, older platforms are decreasing in popularity as newer platforms emerge which influences the type of content shared.

As a social media platform, the most research has been conducted on Twitter due to the large number of public profiles and easier access to information. Additionally, researchers find benefits for information sharing on Twitter. Demirhan and Cakir-Demirhan (2015) believe "Twitter has a number of positive effects on developing freedom, equality and democracy" (p. 308). Twitter is free and promotes freedom of speech, which can allow marginalized voices to be heard; for example, "Black Twitter" is a term used to describe the virtual community of black users on Twitter. Hashtags popularized by Black Twitter include #BlackLivesMatter, which raised awareness of unfair treatment by law enforcement, and #OscarsSoWhite, which called attention to the lack of diversity in Oscar nominations. When communicating acts of narrative resistance, Twitter itself as a platform may provide beneficial in ensuring the story is heard, and CDA ensures that the language is analyzed in a way that uncovers power dynamics. CDA has been used to study hashtags that serve as acts of narrative resistance including Jackson and Welles's (2015) qualitative discourse analysis of #myNYPD.

Social media does pose problems for discourse. According to Demirhan and Cakir-Demirhan (2015), Twitter does "contribute to the patriarchal discourse on women" and has a "limited number of alternative views to produce alternative discourses" (p. 308). Still, the potential for expressing alternative views exists, as seen with the feminist reclaiming of a particular hashtag. Mengibar (2015) believes the study of texts will not, by itself, understand and change privilege and oppression. However, the voices that are included on Twitter and the conversations happening via tweets and hashtags can allow for important issues to be communicated and recognized. Twitter's blend of text, image, audio, and video may provide rich objects to investigate, and while studying tweets may never completely eliminate social inequality, Twitter's potential to challenge and change power relations remains. Careless (2015) writes:

> Because the construction, reconstruction, and deconstruction of social media discourse depends on users, and because their structure is non-hierarchical and widely accessible, the discursive practice of social media may indeed be useful in facilitating critical discourse—providing a space for talking or "typing back" to dominant power systems in society.
>
> (p. 52)

The present study seeks to examine the dominant power structure and an act of narrative resistance on Twitter utilizing "#distractinglysexy." CDA provides a method for exploring the socio-cultural assumptions about gender and science as well as the impact of an alternative narrative that emerged in the summer of 2015.

#distractinglysexy

Hunt's comments on June 9, 2015, inspired a hashtag seeking to provide a counter-story. The Vagenda Team first used "#distractinglysexy" on June 10, 2015. *The Vagenda* is an online feminist magazine founded in 2012 and currently run by British journalists Holly Baxter and Rhiannon Lucy Cosslett. This tweet read: "Call for all female scientists to upload pictures of themselves at work with the hashtag #distractinglysexy" (twitter.com/vagendamagazine). "#distractinglysexy" went viral and was used over 400 times on the day of its first appearance. Within the next week, the hashtag amassed thousands of tweets.

While some tweets responded to the hashtag with a picture of themselves at work, many users posted photos of women in science. This is important because research has not yet been conducted "on the experiences and stories of women in everyday male-dominated work, particularly those working in the lower ranks of organizations, since these appear to represent the bulk of women working in fields previously dominated by men" (Rickett, 2014, p. 162). This includes women in science.

Many tweets contained sarcasm; however, identifying sarcasm in a social media post proves difficult. In a study of human versus automatic coding of sarcasm on Twitter, Gonzalez-Ibanez, Muresan, and Wacholder (2011) discovered low accuracy in both. To help identify sarcasm, a bigger picture may be necessary. Justo, Corcoran, Lukin, Walker, and Torres (2014) suggest, "Sarcastic language is often subtle and requires world knowledge to recognize" (p. 131).

To contribute to the literature on acts of narrative resistance, the present study asks two primary research questions:

RQ1: What did tweets utilizing the hashtag #distractinglysexy communicate about women in science?

RQ2: How do those tweets resist socio-cultural norms about women in science?

Method

To answer the study's research questions, the researchers conducted a thematic analysis and then a critical discourse analysis of public tweets containing the hashtag "#distractinglysexy" posted on Twitter on June 10, 2015.

Data

First, the source of the "#distractinglysexy" hashtag was identified. The research team isolated a tweet first using the hashtag posted on June 10, 2015, by The Vagenda Team, @VagendaMagazine on Twitter. After finding the first appearance of the hashtag in a tweet, an advanced search in Twitter was conducted of all tweets written in English using the hashtag "#distractinglysexy" on June 10, 2015. This search resulted in 462 public tweets using the hashtag; many tweets included both image and text. This advanced search in Twitter was saved as a 90-page PDF including all 462 tweets and images. For initial data management, the research team analyzed the tweets for themes. Following the initial thematic analysis, a critical discourse analysis was conducted to understand the situated meanings in context and how the tweets contributed to a resistance narrative.

Data Analysis

Thematic Analysis

After reviewing the 462 public tweets posted on June 10, 2015, four primary themes emerged. These four themes included: personal photos by women in science conducting mundane, gross, or funny tasks on the job; historical photos of important women in science; humorous responses to Hunt's remarks; and opinion and judgment of Hunt based on his remarks.

Personal Photos by Women in Science

In response to "#distractinglysexy," many Twitter users posted personal photos of women in science, sometimes photos of themselves, depicting women scientists conducting mundane, gross, or humorous tasks on the job. For example, one user posted, "I hope the smell of the mouse urine I'm mixing with 2-mercaptoethanol isn't too #distractinglysexy" along with a picture of herself performing those very actions in a lab setting. Another user posted, "Pretty sure I was never/rarely #distractinglysexy in the lab. Even when I actually sort of tried" accompanied by a personal photo of herself working in the lab.

Some of the tweets not only included personal photos but also utilized humor and sarcasm. For example, one user posted, "Stopped crying long enough to upload this #distractinglysexy #TimHunt" with a photo of herself dressed in an animal costume and holding a test tube. Another user wrote, "How do the poor men in my faculty get any work done?" along with a group photo of herself with her colleagues. A user posted, "Here's me being #distractinglysexy with my frizzy hair+0 sleep as I submit my Hons [sic] thesis. Fall in love with me." The accompanying photo depicts what appears to be the Twitter user herself holding a physical copy of her thesis: "Localization and Expression of the *BPIFCL* gene in the Zebrafish Brain."

Historical Photos of Women in Science

Another response utilized through the "#distractinglysexy" hashtag was to post historical photos of important women in science. For example, one user posted a photo of Irish astrophysicist Jocelyn Bell Burnell accompanied by the hashtag, and another user posted a photo accompanied by this tweet: "Mary Sherman Morgan, inventor of the fuel used in the Juno I rocket. #distractinglysexy." These tweets served to highlight the important contributions of women in science.

Some users posted both photos of historical women scientists accompanied by text citing these women as their personal and/or professional heroes. For example, a photo of Rita Levi-Monalcini with the following tweet was posted, "Neurobiologist and badass—Rita Levi-Monalcini was #distractinglysexy! My hero—PhD was done in her old lab space." 1986 Nobel Prize winner Rita Levi-Monalcini was the user's hero, and the user actually conducted her doctoral work in the neurobiologist's former work area. Similarly, another user also posted a photo of an historical woman scientist who served as her hero. The image posted was of Barbara McClintock accompanied by the following tweet, "#distractinglysexy and my personal science shero [sic]." Barbara McClintock earned a PhD in botany and was awarded a 1983 Nobel Prize.

Humorous Responses to Hunt's Remarks

Many tweets included humorous responses to Hunt's remarks. One line of humorous tweets referenced Hunt's comments about falling in love with women in the lab. One user wrote, "I'm going to run a qPCR later . . . hope no one falls in love with me! #distractinglysexy #TimHunt." Another user posted, "I plan on spending my morning being #distractinglysexy in my locked office while I try and finish these grants. No one fall in love, now." Another tweet read, "I just hope no one accidentally falls in love with me whilst I'm dissecting tissues later #TimHunt #distractinglysexy." These particular humorous tweets juxtaposed falling in love with a mundane day in the life of a scientist running a test, applying for grants, or dissecting.

Another line of humorous tweets referenced conducting distractingly sexy tasks while in the lab or in the field. One user wrote, "When I worked in a lab, the men always crowded around to watch me smear my plates with E. coli bc I was so #distractinglysexy #TimHunt." Another user tweeted, "Helping my lab mate get some data. Hope my brain waves weren't too #distractinglysexy #womeninscience #TimHunt" accompanied by a picture of a woman in a lab wearing a blue cap and wires to test brain wave activity. These humorous tweets juxtaposed being distractingly sexy with a mundane day in the life of a scientist running a test or collecting data.

A third line of humorous tweets referenced Hunt's remarks about women crying. One user wrote, "If any of you women out there missed #distractinglysexy it is probably because you are off crying in your labs." Another user wrote a post to a fellow Twitter user: "How did we do it?! Just managed a whole day in the lab not crying AND I didn't get asked out on any dates!"

Opinion and Judgment of Hunt

Finally, many tweets offered personal opinions on Hunt as well as judgment of the scientist based on his remarks. One user wrote, "Sort of seems to me that women being #distractinglysexy goes away with the absence of #TimHunt." Another more extreme example comes from this post: "Tim Hunt shows why old men should be banned from science." Judgment of Hunt proved largely negative as opposed to tweets defending Hunt's comments, reporting his words were taken out of context, or providing evidence to support Hunt's claims.

One line of tweets offered judgment of Hunt for his sexist and heteronormative views. One user wrote, "Why just men? Ladies think I'm sexy too. . . . Dear god how does anyone in my dept even function with me around?? #distractinglysexy." This user's perspective highlights Hunt's comments as not only sexist but also single-minded; women are not only found attractive by men but can be considered sexy by other women, too. Another user wrote, "Only women can be #distractinglysexy? That's so unfair I think I'll just cry." These two users' posts highlight not only the sexism but also the heteronormativity in Hunt's comments.

Another line of tweets sought to shine a light on sexism in the past as well as today in the science, technology, engineering, and mathematics (abbreviated as "STEM") fields. For example, one tweet read, "Ironic that 50 yrs ago #archaeology argued that women were too #distractinglysexy for the field but welcome in the lab? #TimHunt #science." This particular user's post highlights the history of sexism in a specific field of science. Another user wrote, "Dear #STEM, if you want to encourage girls to be scientists, you need to teach boys to treat them better than #distractinglysexy"

Critical Discourse Analysis

After analyzing four emerging themes from the tweets, the research team conducted a critical discourse analysis of the original list of 462 tweets posted on June 10, 2015. The four areas of analysis included intertextuality, hyperbole, presupposition, and functionalization of #distractinglysexy tweets.

Intertextuality

According to Gee (2011), "When we speak or write, we often quote or allude to what others have said" (p. 165). These references are known as intertextuality. Gee (2011) refers to intertextuality as a "tool of inquiry." As a tool of inquiry, intertextuality may guide deeper understanding of a text due to emerging questions about not only the text being analyzed but also previous texts. First, determining whether the intertextuality is purposeful is essential. Second, it is important to consider how and why previous texts were incorporated in the text being analyzed.

Many tweets using the hashtag #distractinglysexy referenced Tim Hunt's comments directly using a variety of tones. One user wrote, "Personally, I always did [my] best work completely alone in the lab without anybody distracting me regardless of gender." This particular user used Hunt's words purposefully and in a sensible and straightforward tone to highlight a personal work choice. The user referenced Hunt's words to comment on a work style or preference—to work alone despite the gender of other scientists. Another example of intertextuality was the reaction of another user who wrote, "I really hope I won't have to tell my daughter she can't have a career in science because she will be too #DistractinglySexy." The mother's emotional connection with her daughter emerged as well as the mother's hope that gender inequality did not exist for her daughter in the future. The tone of this mother's tweet was pensive and disappointed as it referenced the future she hoped for her daughter, a future not restricted by sexism in the workplace. Again, the reference to Hunt's words was purposeful which indicates the user heard about and considered Hunt's remarks before composing her response.

Some users displayed a more disappointed tone. A tweet read, "2015 and obviously still a long way to go for equality." This particular user accompanied the tweet with a link to an article referencing Hunt's comments. Juxtaposing the text containing Hunt's exact comments with the text of personal disappointment, the user also highlights the bigger picture: the inherent hegemony in science.

Other users found the narrative resistance displayed via the hashtag empowering and positive. A user posted: "Check out #distractinglysexy & #TimHunt tweets. Proof you shouldn't say stupid shit out loud abt [sic] smart chicks." This user sees the hashtag as a successful act of narrative resistance by "smart chicks," indicating her view that #distractinglysexy is a sort-of victory in response to Hunt. Another woman in science communicated a sense of pride in her post: "Am LOVING the #distractinglysexy hashtag. Way to take back an issue! #womeninscience #proud." Rather than allowing Hunt to lead the dialogue on women in science, this user believes the hashtag campaign effectively resists those views by reclaiming and redefining the conversation. The hashtag "#proud" in this tweet indicates the user feels glad and appreciative about the hashtag's act of narrative resistance against Hunt.

Hyperbole

Hyperbole refers to exaggerated language to create emphasis or to demonstrate humor. Claridge (2010) says that hyperbolic language is characterized by deliberate, purposeful exaggeration for the purpose of "the expression of an emotional attitude and the presentation of an appropriate 'image' of oneself" (p. 264). Some #distractinglysexy tweets used exaggerated language to make fun of and to mock Hunt's comments. One user wrote, "Like all lady PhDs, I frequently ask myself, 'How could I be sexier?'" The user exaggerates that all women with PhDs routinely focus on being sexy and becoming sexier as opposed to research or work in the lab or in the field. The user not only referenced Hunt in a humorous, hyperbolic way but also added a link to a Huffington Post Science article on Hunt in her tweet. The world knowledge inserted in the tweet through the link to Hunt's comments supports Justo et al. (2014) who tell us sarcastic language can be interpreted best with world knowledge.

Many hyperbolic tweets referencing Hunt focused on women scientists crying at work. One user referenced an online friend and posted, "How do we do it?! Just managed a whole day in the lab not crying AND I didn't get asked out on any dates!" The user's clearly exaggerated language can be identified through her use of punctuation and capitalization for emphasis. By including another Twitter handle, this user exaggerates her daily routine with a fellow scientist which indicates both are in on the joke.

Presupposition

According to Machin and Mayr (2012), presupposition refers to "what kinds of meanings are assumed as given in a text," or the baggage or preconceived notions that may come with words or phrases (p. 153). Many tweets take note of the sexism and heteronormativity associated with Hunt's comments. One man wrote, "Hey Tim, I've cried in the lab before. What does that say about me as a scientist?" This user shows that crying in the lab is not exclusively linked to women. Similarly, another user tweeted about crying in the lab: "last time I cried in lab was when I accidentally swallowed a soap/mud solution trying to measure sediment size." This user defended crying in the lab as a direct result of performing routine tasks on the job. Another user wrote, "It's true, we also have lab dance offs in my nearly all-female lab." The user indicates science is not always a male-dominated field; in her case, her lab contains almost all women scientists. Additionally, the user points out that science does not have to always be serious; crying can occur, and so can dancing. By injecting emotion—in this case, the fun and silliness that comes with a dance off—the user states that science does not have to always be sterile and solemn.

Functionalization

Functionalization, also known as nomination, serves as a representational strategy that depicts people based on what they do (Machin & Mayr, 2012). In response to Hunt's comments, many users sought to define themselves not as women but as scientists. In a pushback to the stereotype of women crying and falling in love in the lab, users connected the hashtag to pictures of themselves conducting actual scientific work in the lab or in the field. One tweet read: "Working in the cleanroom, culturing dendritic cells. Hope I'm not #distractinglysexy." The image accompanying the tweet showed a figure dressed in an all-white lab suit with a hood, a hairnet, and a face mask in an all-white, sterile room. Only the eyes could be seen in the photo, showing a scientist, not man or a woman. The user sought to depict herself not as a woman scientist but merely as a scientist doing her job. Another user wrote, "Does this lab coat make me look #distractinglysexy? #TimHunt If it doesn't please don't criticize me. I would cry." The corresponding image depicts the scientist in a lab coat with her name on the front. She works at a desk, holding and standing in front of equipment a layperson would associate with a scientific laboratory. The image shows a scientist at work which serves to depict her not as a woman doing science but as a scientist.

Conclusion

According to Launius and Hassel (2015), "Feminist activism has increasingly moved online and has demonstrated that it can produce tangible results" (p. 158). Online activists successfully use social media tools to raise awareness of an issue, to organize protests, and to build community. From #MeToo to #BlackLivesMatter, power and privilege are highlighted using hashtags to raise consciousness of important issues and to seek political and social change. Additionally, these hashtags inspire a sense of community, a group of people who can share stories together about a shared experience, Additionally, engaging with the hashtag creates a new shared experience: collaborating with like-minded others on social media and being a part of a trend in the moment.

As an act of narrative resistance, tweets using the hashtag #distractinglysexy sought to do many things: to display personal photos of women in science conducting mundane, gross, or funny tasks on the job; to show historical photos of important women in science; to respond to Hunt's comments in a humorous way; and to offer judgment and opinion of Hunt based on his remarks. In addition, four areas of critical discourse analysis including intertextuality, hyperbole, presupposition, and functionalization revealed that women in science used the hashtag #distractinglysexy as an act of narrative resistance to challenge the dominant story of women in science offered by Hunt and to shift and change that story. Milan (2015) highlights the importance of social media to contribute to the conversation, and often to the debate, happening at all levels of society—local and international—as well as to take the lead on that conversation. The #distractinglysexy hashtag motivated real scientists to protest the sexist comments made by Hunt, to combat the story being told about women in science, and to share a counter-story focused on the reality of scientists' lives. Using a unified hashtag on Twitter allowed #distractinglysexy to gain visibility on a larger scale, resulting in not only public participation in the United States and United Kingdom but also news coverage by outlets such as NPR and the BBC.

Tufekci (2017) discusses online activist culture and how movements are often leaderless, how they quickly gain popularity before just as quickly fading into oblivion, and how they inspire participation. Certainly, this movement began with an initial call made by a leader: the Vagenda Team's tweet requesting women in science to upload a photo of themselves at work with the hashtag #distractinglysexy." However, the immediate participation by so many unique users transformed the intent of the original tweet into its own leaderless movement, a #distractinglysexy not only about personal photos of women at work but also of historical photos of inspiring women scientists, humor and funny quips, as well as harsh judgment of Hunt and his remarks. As Baym and boyd (2012) point out, human beings have long utilized the media to create identity—identity for self, identity for other, and identity for group. Ultimately, #distractinglysexy revealed a protest of sexism using social media and a specific hashtag to create a public identity for a particular group: women in science. Tweets using #distractinglysexy resisted socio-cultural norms about women in science by responding to the sexist notions by Hunt's in serious, humorous, and disappointed ways.

The participatory nature of the original tweet calling for action around #distractinglysexy galvanized people to respond, and according to Tufekci (2017), people participate in protests in order to express themselves, to rebel, and to have fun. The mix of serious and humorous responses was also seen in the hijacked hashtag #myNYPD in the study conducted by Jackson and Welles (2015), as people used both comedy and outrage in tweets to protest police brutality. In the case of #distractinglysexy, users sought to highlight the sexist of Hunt's comments by sharing what women scientists actually do in the lab—much of it mundane and sometimes even gross—using a mix of comedy and outrage. Users also called attention to the heteronormative nature of Hunt's remarks by sharing that women can fall in love with women in the lab and that men in science can cry, too—again, using a combination of approaches. Finally, participating in the protest itself is often as important as the overarching outcomes of that protest (Tufekci, 2017). In the case of #distractinglysexy, use of the hashtag indicated not only a desire to share everyday stories about women in science but also a desire to participate in the conversation online.

References

Altinay, R. E. (2014). "There is a massacre of women": Violence against women, feminist activism, and hashtags in Turkey. *Feminist Media Studies, 14*(6), 1102–1103. doi:10.1080/14680777.2014.975445

Armstrong, C., & Gao, F. (2011). Gender, Twitter, and news content: An examination across platforms and coverage areas. *Journalism Studies, 12*(4), 490–505.

Baer, H. (2015). Redoing feminism: Digital activism, body politics, and neoliberalism. *Feminist Media Studies, 16*(1), 17–34. doi: 10.1080/14680777.2015.1093070

Baym, N. K., & boyd, d. (2012). Socially mediated publicness: An introduction. *Journal of Broadcasting & Electronic Media, 56*(3), 320–329. doi:10.1080/08 838151.2012.705200

Beard, L. J. (2009). *Acts of narrative resistance: Women's autobiographical writings in the Americas.* Charlottesville, VA: University of Virginia Press.

Careless, E. (2015). Perspective in AE: "Typing back": Social media as space for critical discourse. *New Horizons in Adult Education & Human Resource Development, 27*(3), 50–55. doi:10.1002/nha3.20111

Chen, G. (2015). Why do women bloggers use social media? Recreation and information motivations outweigh engagement motivations. *New Media & Society*, 17(1), 24–40. doi:10.1177/1461444813504269

Chiluwa, I., & Ifukor, P. (2015). "War against our children": Stance and evaluation in #BringBackOurGirls campaign discourse on Twitter and Facebook. *Discourse & Society*, 26(3), 267–296. doi:10.1177/0957926514564735

Claridge, C. (2010). *Hyperbole in English: A Corpus-based study of exaggeration*. Retrieved from http://dx.doi.org/10.1017/CBO9780511779480

Conley, T. (2014). From #RenishaMcBride to #RememberRenisha: Locating our stories and finding justice. *Feminist Media Studies*, 14(6), 1111–1113. doi:10.1080/14680777.2014.975474

Demirhan, K., & Cakir-Demirhan, D. (2015). Gender and politics: Patriarchal discourse on social media. *Public Relations Review*, 41, 308–310. http://dx.doi.org/10.1016/j.pubrev.2014.11.010

Devault, M. L. (2014). Language and stories in motion. In S. McKenzie-Mohr & M. N. Lafrance (Eds.), *Women voicing resistance: Discursive and narrative explorations* (pp. 16–28). New York, NY: Routledge.

Duarte, N. (2010). *Resonate: Present visual stories that transform audiences*. Hoboken, NJ: John Wiley & Sons, Inc.

Duggan, M., Ellison, N., Lampe, C., Lenhart, A., & Madden, M. (2015). *Social media update 2014*. Retrieved from www.pewinternet.org/files/2015/01/PI_SocialMediaUpdate20144.pdf

Fairclough, N., & Wodak, R. (1997). Critical discourse analysis: A preliminary description. In T. A. van Dijk (Ed.), *Discourse as social interaction* (pp. 258–284). Thousand Oaks, CA: Sage Publications Ltd.

Fox, J., Cruz, C., & Lee, J. Y. (2015). Perpetuating online sexism offline: Anonymity, interactivity, and the effects of sexist hashtags on social media. *Computers in Human Behavior*, 52, 436–442. http://dx.doi.org/10.1016/j.chb.2015.06.024

France, L. R. (2017). #MeToo: Social media flooded with personal stories of assault. *CNN*. Retrieved from www.cnn.com/2017/10/15/entertainment/me-too-twitter-alyssa-milano/index.html

Gee, J. P. (2011). *How to do discourse analysis: A toolkit*. Milton Park, Oxfordshire: Routledge.

Gonzalez-Ibanez, R., Muresan, S., & Wacholder, N. (2011). *Identifying sarcasm in Twitter: A closer look*. Proceedings of the 49th Annual Meeting of the Association for Computational Linguistics, Portland, OR.

Guha, P. (2015). Hash tagging but not trending: The success and failure of the news media to engage with online feminist activism in India. *Feminist Media Studies*, 15(1), 155–157. doi:10.1080/14680777.2015.987424

Heil, B., & Piskorski, M. (2009). New Twitter research: Men follow men and nobody tweets. *Harvard Business Review*. Retrieved from https://hbr.org/2009/06/new-twitter-research-men-follo

Honeycutt, C., & Herring, S. (2009). *Beyond microblogging: Conversation and collaboration via Twitter*. Proceedings from the Forty-Second Hawaii International Conference on System Sciences (HICSS-42), IEEE Press, Los Alamitos, CA. Retrieved from http://info.ils.indiana.edu/~herring/honeycutt.herring.2009.pdf

Jackson, S. J., & Welles, B. F. (2015). Hijacking #myNYPD: Social media dissent and networked counterpublics. *Journal of Communication*, 65, 932–952. doi:10.1111/jcom.12185

Johnson, P. R., & Yang, S. (2009). *Uses and gratifications of Twitter: An exami-nation of user motives and satisfaction of Twitter use.* Communication Tech-nology Division of the Annual Convention of the Association for Education in Journalism and Mass Communication in Boston, MA. Retrieved from https://umdrive.memphis.edu/cbrown14/public/Mass%20Comm%20Theory/Week%207%20Uses%20and%20Gratifications/Johnson%20and%20Yang%202009%20Twitter%20uses%20and%20grats.pdf

Jorgenson, M., & Phillips, L. J. (2002). *Discourse analysis as theory and method.* London, UK: Sage, Ltd. http://dx.doi.org/10.4135/9781849208871.n3

Justo, R., Corcoran, T., Lukin, S. M., Walker, M., & Torres, M. I. (2014). Extract-ing relevant knowledge for the detection of sarcasm and nastiness in the social web. *Knowledge-Based Systems, 69,* 124–133. http://dx.doi.org/10.1016/j.knosys.2014.05.021

Lapidot-Lefler, N. (2012). Effects of anonymity, invisibility, and lack of eye-contact on toxic online disinhibition. *Computers in Human Behavior, 28*(2), 434–443.

Lafrance, M. N., & McKenzie-Mohr, S. (2014). Women counter-storying their lives. In S. McKenzie-Mohr & M. N. Lafrance (Eds.), *Women voicing resistance: Discursive and narrative explorations* (pp. 1–15). New York, NY: Routledge.

Launius, C., & Hassel, H. (2015). *Threshold concepts in women's and gender studies: Ways of seeing, thinking, and knowing.* New York, NY: Routledge.

Lee, C. (2011). Micro-blogging and status updates on Facebook: Texts and prac-tices. In C. Thurlow & K. Mroczek (Eds.), *Digital discourse: Language in the new media* (pp. 110–125). Oxford Scholarship. Online. doi:10.1093/acprof:oso/9780199795437.001.0001

Machin, D., & Mayr, A. (2012). *How to do critical discourse analysis: A multi-modal introduction.* Thousand Oaks, CA: Sage Publications.

Megarry, J. (2014). Online incivility or sexual harassment? Conceptualizing women's experiences in the digital age. *Women's Studies International Forum, 47,* 46–55. http://dx.doi.org/10.1016/j.wsif.2014.07.012

Mengibar, A. (2015). Critical discourse analysis in the study of representation, identity politics and power relations: A multi-method approach. *Communica-tion & Society, 28*(2), 39–54. doi:10.15581/003.28.2

Milan, S. (2015). Mobilizing in times of social media: From a politics of identity to a politics of visibility. In E. Dencik & O. Leistert's (Eds.), *Critical perspectives on social media and protest: Between control and emancipation* (pp. 53–72). New York, NY: Rowman & Littlefield International.

Moss-Racusin, C. A., Dovidio, J. F., Brescoll, V. L., Graham, M. J., & Handels-man, J. (2013). Science faculty's subtle gender biases favor male students. *Proceedings of the National Academy of Sciences of the United States of America, 41,* 16474–16479. Retrieved from www.pnas.org/cgi/doi/10.1073/pnas.1211286109

Pollack, E. (2013, October 3). Why are there still so few women in science? *The New York Times.* Retrieved from www.nytimes.com/2013/10/06/magazine/why-are-there-still-so-few-women-in-science.html?_r=2

Regan, H. (2015). Feminists are reclaiming the sexist hashtag #HowToSpotA-Feminist and it's glorious. *Time Magazine Online.* Retrieved from http://time.com/3848097/feminism-howtospotafeminist-feminist-twitter/

Rickett, B. (2014). Girly-girls, "scantily-clad ladies," and policewomen: Negotiating and resisting femininities in non-traditional work space. In S. McKenzie-Mohr & M. N. Lafrance (Eds.), *Women voicing resistance: Discursive and narrative explorations* (pp. 159–173). New York, NY: Routledge.

Saul, H. (2015). Richard Dawkins demands apology from Sir Tim Hunt's critics amid claims leaked transcript shows "sexist" comments were "light-hearted banter." *The Independent.* Retrieved from www.independent.co.uk/news/people/richard-dawkins-demands-apology-from-sir-tim-hunts-critics-and-claims-leaked-transcript-shows-sexist-comments-were-lighthearted-banter-10341160.html

Scott, K. (2015). The pragmatics of hashtags: Inference and conversational style on Twitter. *Journal of Pragmatics, 81,* 8–20. http://dx.doi.org/10.1016/j.pragma.2015.03.015

Tufekci, Z. (2017). *Twitter and tear gas: The power and fragility of networked protest.* New Haven, CT: Yale University Press.

Tursunova, Z. (2014). Women's narratives: Resistance to oppression and the empowerment of women in Uzbekistan. *Journal of Indigenous Social Development, 3*(2), 1–16.

Twitter. (2015). *Twitter usage: Company facts.* Retrieved July 25, 2015, from https://about.twitter.com/companyTwitter.com/docthompsonshow.Twitter.com/vagendamagazine

Van Dijk, T. A. (2001). Critical discourse analysis. In D. Schiffrin, D. Tannen, & H. E. Hamilton (Eds.), *The handbook of discourse analysis* (pp. 352–371). Malden, MA: Blackwell.

Williams, S. (2015). Digital defense: Black feminists resist violence with hashtag activism. *Feminist Media Studies, 15*(2), 341–344. doi:10.1080/14680777.2015.1008744

10 Papuan Political Resistance on Social Media

Regionalization and Internationalization of Papuan Identity

Yuyun W. I. Surya

This chapter explores the extent to which the articulation of Papuan identity becomes political and the way in which Papuans express it in the *Orang Papua* Facebook group through messages posted by members of the group. Facebook is an ideal platform because many Papuans use it. Facebook is not only popular among Papuans but its ubiquity and the ease with which groups can be established has made it a convenient forum for political expression for many groups. Conflict between Indonesia and West Papua is ongoing. Papuans' articulation of their identity is significant because the Indonesian government denied them the freedom to express their ethnic identity. On the other hand, the Indonesian government views the expression of Papuan identity as subversive and treats it with significant suspicion and concern. Indonesians generally regard Papuans as primitive and uncivilized. In accordance with their aims to integrate Papua in a greater national Indonesia, the government has consistently sought to make Papuans behave and appear more similar to Indonesians. They have attempted to achieve this by prohibiting traditional Papuan clothing, hindering traditional governance, and limiting cultural practices and symbols. In this sense, the expression of Papuan identity (Papuanness) became the core of their political struggle to form a nation separate from Indonesia.

The challenge to construct Papuan identity has taken place within the context of Indonesianization for almost 50 years. Papuans learned to be Indonesians through the education system, the media, economic development, and transmigration. These systematic programs aimed to incorporate the Papuan population into the Indonesian nation-state. Along with Indonesianization is the process of de-Papuanization, a transmigration program that resettled thousands of Javanese migrants in Papua, in an attempt to spread Javanese culture. . . . The de-Papuanization process also occurs through the spreading of Islam by building mosques in Christian-dominated Papuan villages (Trajano, 2010). There is strong indication that the Indonesian government has committed ethnic genocide against the Papuans. According to the United Nations Genocide Convention, ethnic genocide is defined as acts committed with intent to destroy, in whole or in part an ethnic group, It is based on evidence that Papuans constitute a group under the definition of genocide, the acts perpetrated by the Indonesians against the Papuans qualify as genocidal, and these acts can be inferred as an intent to destroy the West Papuans. Indonesia's oppression of Papuans represents a deliberate attack on the sustainability of the group. Webb-Gannon and Elmslie (2014) claim that an estimated 100,000 and 500,000 Papuans have been killed under the Indonesian occupation. Their horrific and frequent crimes against humanity have been largely ignored. Since 1957, there was the institutionalization of violence due to the increasing role of the military in politics and administration in Indonesia.

In the political history of Indonesia, social media have acted as cyber-civic spaces in which individuals and groups encourage collective activism online and translate it into movement offline. Social media have become spaces of resistance for Indonesians. With a remarkable growth in social media usage, along with the restrictions on mainstream media, and the lack of control mechanism on social media contents, I argue that Papuans use Facebook to express their ethnic solidarity and political criticism.

Online media became the viable means for Papuans to articulate their identity freely since mainstream media, education, and economic sectors are dominated by Indonesia and are still under the government's control. On social media, Papuans can post links, add comments, and likes, as well as share messages to develop the narrative of their identity. In this chapter, I claim that through Facebook, Papuans have the freedom to choose how they wish to present themselves and also how they express their political resistance. In this regard, the articulation of Papuan identity online plays a pivotal role in and is a part of their online activism. Papuans are strengthening their identity by raising their distinctive ethnic consciousness.

Papuans are also emphasizing their affiliation to the Melanesian race to show their ethnic distinctiveness and to contrast with Indonesians. The term Melanesia arose from a complicated colonial context. Melanesia refers to an ethnic category created by the colonial administration that imposed homogeneity and aimed at reducing indigenous people's reaction against colonial hegemony. In this sense, Melanesian-ness is an anticolonial identity discourse (Webb-Gannon & Elmslie, 2014). The strengthening of Papuan identity is indeed very crucial for the Papuans to come together and be united in liberating their homeland. Papuan ethnic consciousness is facilitated by Facebook which allows them to choose and post visual images and messages to support their preferred online identity. Furthermore, Facebook facilitates small groups like Papuans to integrate to larger communities such as Melanesian.

Papuans have transformed their Melanesian affiliation from a marker of identity into political alignment with other Melanesian countries. Papuans share visual images of the Indonesian armed forces torturing Papuans in an effort to regionalize Papuan resistance and raise international awareness of human rights abuses.

As this study is primarily concerned with the posts produced by members of the *Orang Papua* group, I use a multimodal discourse analysis as the research method. Social media is "multimodal" because it incorporates various modes including visual, audio, and moving images. This method pays attention to specific aspects of the medium and situation. It allows us to interpret and understand the significance of social media data. The main benefit of applying multimodal discourse to analyse social media text is it potentially includes all multimodalities of communication on social media.

In this study, the data-multimodal texts produced by members of the *Orang Papua* group-were collected over a six-month period. The group was accessed and posts were monitored daily. The 278 collected posts were then divided into categories. The categories in this study are based on the theme of political resistance. The theme was then categorized further into four sub-categories as can be seen in Table 10.1.

In analyzing each component of the collected posts, this study employed Jancsary, Hollerer and Meyer's (2016) analytical procedure of multimodal text. The spatiotemporal and sociocultural context of the multimodal text was analyzed by looking at different kinds of objects, actions, and settings of the visual images as well as the language and metaphors of a verbal text. The next section examines the way Papuans use Facebook to regionalize and internationalize their political movement.

Table 10.1 Categories of Orang Papua's Posts

Discourse strand (theme)	Discourse sub-strands	Examples of texts' components	Number of posts
Political resistance	Civil disobedience	Reject government policies (repressive approach-)	72
	Symbolic action	Create politically themed narrative (Papua as Indonesia's kitchen)	71
	Expressing identity	Ethnic identity-based solidarity and alignment (back to Melanesian family)	60
	Mobilizing protest	Invitation to join & organize protests (support ULMWP& MSG)	75
Total posts			278

Regionalization of Papuan Identity

Back to Melanesian Family

Papuans were encouraged to think of themselves as members of a broader entity by the Dutch, who colonized Papua in 1898 and remained in the region before the integration of Papua into Indonesia in 1963. The Dutch observed that there was little sense of national awareness among Papuans due to the topography and the ethnic diversity in Papua. Through education and political development initiated by the Dutch, Papuans were encouraged to envisage a future as an independent state, one that is more part of a Melanesian world of the Pacific rather than the Malay world of South-East Asia. Chauvel (2008) states that the Dutch objective was that "Papua shall in the future constitute part of greater Melanesian entity" (p. 42). Within this historical context, expression of Melanesian affiliation is now being cultivated by members of the *Orang Papua* group by raising the issue of the importance for Papuans to obtain political support from Melanesian countries. Papuan identity as Melanesian has been utilized for political mobilization. This politicization process tends to reinforce collective identity. For instance, a post that attempts to develop awareness is about a seminar announcement in one of the local universities in Papua and a media release from *AliansiMahasiswa Papua*/AMP (translated as Papuan Student Alliance). The posted message not only contained the seminar announcement, but also added a comment, "congratulations to the President of the Papuan students union (*Gempar Papua*) for conducting the seminar on Do Papuans belong to Melanesians? *Salam Revolusi* (the spirit of revolution)." This additional comment is important since it contextualizes the seminar announcement in terms of the current situation of Papuan resistance. The group member who posted this message has chosen the words "*salam revolusi*" (the spirit of revolution) that indicates the Papuan struggle to be recognized as Melanesian. The word "revolution" also indicates the readiness for a pervasive change. Within the context of Papuan struggle, it signposts political resistance, and directs Papuans "back to the (Melanesian) family," as written in the seminar announcement. It supports the argument that Papuans have much more in common with the rest of Melanesia than with Asia and Indonesia in particular. Furthermore, it endorses Papuans' chosen identity and signifies Papua's place regionally and internationally.

The words "back to the family" have been used by members of the *Orang Papua* group to express the significance of joining the Melanesian political bloc. This notion is emphasized by members of the group in several posted messages such as "AMP supports ULMWP: We Back to Family. AMP supports ULMWP to be part of Melanesian Spearhead Group from 1961 up till now. For more than 50 years Papuans are under Indonesian colonialism" and "keep the fighting spirit for the sake of Papuan identity. Let us pray and support ULMWP to be part of big Melanesian family (MSG)." These posted messages use the words "back to family" and "*keluarga besar Melanesia*" (the big Melanesian family). They indicate the importance for members of *Orang Papua* group to be aware of their Melanesianness. The words "bring West Papua back to the family" invoke kinship between Papua and Melanesia. The term kinship is used as a metaphor of shared geography, colonial histories, commonalities of culture between Pacific people, and a bond of affection that naturally links and interconnects Pacific people. Thus, affiliation to Melanesia captures both cultural and political aspiration of Papuans. The words "back to the family" also imply that Indonesians do not consider Papuans as close relations or kinsmen.

Papuans' enthusiastic outreach to Melanesia indicates an attempt to regionalize the conflict in opposition to Indonesia's claim that the Papua conflict is strictly an internal, domestic one. Indonesia resists any international gestures towards Papua since these have been perceived as undermining Indonesia's sovereignty. Papuans have participated actively in regional forums such as the Pacific Island Forum. The West Papua National Coalition for Liberation (WPNCL) for several years lobbied the Melanesian countries to support Papua's right to self-determination. The political support from the Melanesian countries is, in fact, crucial for Papua's political struggle. The Pacific countries' concern over self-determination and decolonization in Papua can be traced back to 1971 with the establishment of the South Pacific Forum. Since then the Melanesian countries, particularly through the Melanesian Spearhead Group (MSG), explicitly expressed their support to Papua's self-determination. MSG is a political and economic bloc of Pacific Island countries that support the Papuan movement to become an independent nation from Indonesia. It comprises four Melanesian states including Fiji, Papua New Guinea, Solomon Islands and Vanuatu, and New Caledonia. Melanesian countries also play an important role in unifying Papuan political factions. The United Liberation Movement for West Papua (ULMWP) was established in 2014 as a new umbrella organization for Papuans under an agreement signed in Vanuatu. Although Papua is considered the far eastern limit of Indonesian state, Papuans are "ontologically attached" to the Melanesian Pacific as a distinct and separate region from Indonesia's Asia (Webb-Gannon & Elmslie, 2014).

Facebook has become the most common entry to Papuan online activism (Titifanue, Tarai, Kany, & Finau, 2016). It has been used to disseminate a wide variety of information relating to Papua. Facebook provides a proper way to present news and views on Papua since the company imposes few political restrictions and becomes the key plank of civil resistance strategy (Chesterfield, 2011). *Orang Papua*, the Facebook group, could be considered a grassroots organization. As of February 2016, this site had more than 63,000 members.

Papuans have taken the opportunity to express their ethnic identity through Facebook and to use it as part of their political movement. Members of *Orang Papua* use the Facebook group to articulate Papuans' "political Melanesianhood" (Webb-Gannon & Elmslie, 2014). This term refers to the similarity with Melanesia in cultural background and political experiences, particularly regarding decolonization. Members of the *Orang Papua* group have utilized the Facebook page as a space to spread awareness of Papuans' political movement in Melanesia region and lead its members to believe in the importance of taking part in a Melanesian sub-regional political bloc.

Symbolic Action: Papua as the Kitchen of Indonesia

The feeling of being a second-class citizen in Indonesia became the second narrative developed by members of this group. In describing how the Indonesian government is taking advantage of Papuans, one of the posts uses the term Papua as "the kitchen of Indonesia." The word kitchen refers to the central place to store food, cook and process the food in a household. In the Indonesian context, a kitchen is a place hidden from guests. It is typically placed at the back part of the house. It is considered a private, domestic space. Despite providing family members and their guests with food, it is considered as an untidy, potentially dirty, and unsightly space. The spatial division of the house is based on two kinds of rooms: the front and the back of the house. The division of the rooms is apparent in the way they are perceived; the front as the daily served area, while the back is the daily supporting domain. The front domain has its center in the guest room, whereas the kitchen becomes the core of the back domain. Within the Indonesian context, the daily supporting domain is always associated with, "*orang belakang*" or the servants of the house. This notion suggests that the importance of kitchen is overlooked in relation to the guest room.

Thus, describing Papua as the kitchen of Indonesia implies the Papuans never benefit despite the fact that Papua has provided Indonesia with its abundant natural resources. The province of Papua also continues to have some of the highest poverty rates in Indonesia. High GDP rates in Papua, primarily as a result of the extraction of oil, timber, copper, gold and other precious minerals, have not resulted in greater prosperity for Papuans. Profits are not invested back into Papua's economy. Instead, revenues earned from natural resource extraction are controlled by foreign corporations and by the Indonesian government. A former governor of Papua province describes this situation by comparing Indonesia to a village, but complaining that "the people in the house called Papua feed those in the other houses but are themselves starving" (Schwarz, 1991 as cited in Webster, 2001, p. 524).

Mobilizing Protest: Support for ULMWP and MSG

Political institutions are part of the context that shapes ethnic identity. Political leaders use the emotional appeal of ethnic identity to mobilize mass support. The relevant identities for political mobilization entail a coalition of group identity with political claims. Furthermore, Gerbaudo (2012) argues that political mobilization becomes a means of obtaining power as an end, to secure group entitlement and reduce group anxieties. Within this context, the "back to Melanesian family" narrative has become a motivating force to mobilize Papuans to join the Melanesian regional political bloc: Melanesian Spearhead Group (MSG). MSG is a regional and an international platform for Papuans to support their political struggle to be an independent nation. The frequent use of messages containing MSG in *Orang Papua*'s posts indicates that MSG has become a new catch cry for members of the *Orang Papua* group. In this sense, the articulation of Papuan identity as Melanesian emphasized by members of the *Orang Papua* group is congruent with their narrative of regionalism: the movement to join Melanesia's regional political bloc. The "back to Melanesian family" narrative is thus supported by Facebook's platform that enables users to develop stories by adding links from other websites and by creating visual images. Through the *Orang Papua* Facebook group, Papuans establish connection with MSG. Social media, like Facebook, have also made visible the political struggles of ethnic groups such as Papuans to others. Within this context, it can be said that social media, especially Facebook, with its platforms have influenced the process of integration of Papuan into a broader Melanesian community.

Current investigation focuses on the relationship between social media and intercultural communication. There is a circumstance in which different communities have to readjust to develop mutual understanding with others in virtual interaction on social media (Allwood & Schroeder, 2000). Although face-to-face communication is replaced by computer-mediated communication, distinct cultural and social backgrounds that have a strong influence on individual and group behavior remained. Thus, whether individuals and groups communicate offline or online, they bring their culture and experiences with them (Uzun, 2014). A solid cultural identity is strengthened through social media as social media has intensified the relationship between people. Social media also remake the communal identity of the users (Arnett, 2002). Within the context of Papuans, social media, especially Facebook, has provided them a chance to become visible and to raise voices for their political struggle. Papuans have used social media to broaden their cultural alignment to Melanesian.

Members of the group repeatedly post messages with visual images that illustrate the significance of Papuans to join MSG. It is expected that through MSG, Papuans will get support for their independence movement. Previously, MSG had supported a pro-independence movement from New Caledonia (FLNKS) by accepting its membership (Cain, 2014). The prominent use of verbal messages and visual images containing MSG posted by members of the group is an indication of the necessity of joining this Melanesia's sub-regional political and trade bloc to support Papuans' political struggle. By selecting images in a patterned way, media have a strong impact by constructing social reality. The frame and narrative devices employed by members of the *Orang Papua* group can thus systematically affect how members come to understand the issue.

The need to be part of MSG has made different factions in the Papuan resistance group converge into a new umbrella organization: United Liberation Movement for West Papua (ULMWP). There are various factions and actors in the Papuan political landscape. Elmslie, Webb-Gannon, and King (2011) state that there are at least 31 different Papuan independence groups that are highly committed to achieve their goal of independence from Indonesia. They include influential activist groups, key NGOs, and student and youth groups.

In June 2015, MSG had rejected ULMWP full membership, and instead granted ULMWP observer status. This status implies that MSG members are not fully recognizing Papuan Melanesianess and support Papuans' political agenda. However, after over 50 years of political struggle, the observer status is Papuan's first step to full political recognition and is seen as the step toward addressing the human rights atrocities committed against Papuans by the Indonesian army. One of the MSG summit agendas in 2016 was to elevate the membership of ULMWP from the current observer status to full membership. Members of the *Orang Papua* group have taken this opportunity to mobilize political support further for ULMWP's attempt to get a full membership at MSG. Thus, members of the group frame it through tangible and less tangible elements. Tangible elements include political parties, staff, and events, which are in this case, the existence of ULMWP and the MSG. Less tangible elements consist of discourses and practices such as human rights violations, explained in the next section.

Visualizing Human Rights Violation

Webb-Gannon and Elmslie (2014) observe that there has been a tremendous increase in Papuan voices heard by the regional and international community. For instance, international interest has grown due to the continuing human rights violation in Papua. Nearly every year a variety of organizations publish new studies about human rights abuses in Papua. The Papuan pro-independence group is also constantly lobbying the UN Decolonization Committee to put Papua on the non-self-governing country list. Furthermore, members of the *Orang Papua* group use visual images to express their political resistance by raising international awareness of human rights abuses in Papua. For instance, members of the group post images of tortured bodies along with captions "Indonesia does not need Papuans. But Indonesia needs Papua's natural resources. What has been done in Papua is genocidal project" and "while Melanesians focused on MSG summit, Malays are killing Melanesian Papuans." The focus on human rights abuses is aimed to mobilize public opinion worldwide about what is happening in Papua. Neumayer and Svensson (2016) argue that the global solidarity shown through social media platforms is important in strengthening the movement. Members of the *Orang Papua* group focus on the nature of violence, perpetrated by the Indonesian armed forces, that has changed from massive open military operations to more covert operations that could be classified as Military Operations Other Than War (MOOTW). Even though the region is no longer considered a military operation zone, the authorities continue to use a repressive approach when dealing with Papuans. Indonesian armed forces are seen in public places in Papua. More often than not, political expressions, such as rallies conducted by Papuan activists, end up with the torture of activists by the armed forces. In one of the posts, members of the group uploaded images of civilians shot by Indonesian armed forces along with the narrative "Indonesian armed forces shot civilians in Paniai Papua. There are 13 people died. Three people [in the visual image pictures] were intentionally brought to the public area by the army. Indonesian intelligent agency [BIN], army and police are responsible for this violence." There has been a militarisation of the region. Thus, the use of visual images that predominantly focus on the tortured Papuans is an attempt to frame Indonesian military as heartless abusers of human rights.

Visual images as a form of expression of Indonesian violence were in fact used by Papuans long before the coming of the Internet. Abusive Indonesian security forces have long served as a rallying point for Papuan separatists. Chauvel (2006) argues that the Papuan loathing of Indonesians is a direct consequence of the way in which Indonesians have despised and belittled the Papuans. Papuans are simply thought of as possessions rather than as fellow citizens by Indonesians. Thus, it is not a surprise that members of the *Orang Papua* group exploited the images of bloodshed and torture to articulate their hatred of Indonesians. These images aim to perpetuate a negative stereotype of Indonesians, to provide a ground and a fundamental reason for Papuan political resistance as well as to draw international attention to Papua's plight. The trauma under Indonesian rule seems to keep cohesion among Papuans. The usage of visual image becomes the *Orang Papua* group's protest tactic since it symbolizes the oppressed struggle. Furthermore, it makes it easier for the members of the group to identify their orientation. Doerr, Mattoni, and Teune (2015) posit that visual materials are repositories of shared activist identities and cultures that are able to link different waves of contentions.

The ability to communicate in visual forms is especially important for Papuans. Besides the need to show and demonstrate the oppression, they also need to disseminate the importance of fighting against Indonesian government and reaching their political goal to become an independent nation. Thus, the need to be recognized and be "seen" has made members of *Orang Papua* group post images central to Papua's political struggle. These visual strategies echo political struggles elsewhere. For example, Khatib (2013), who studied the use of visual images in the Middle East, posits that the images are at the heart of the political struggle, which have become an endless process of images battling, reversing, erasing, and replacing other images. States, oppositional groups, and ordinary people are engaging in political struggle and deliberately using images to exert political influence. The desire to get rid of any image can be realized only through a new image. Thus, political struggle is a fight over presence and visibility. Further, Khatib (2013) argues that the key political moments in the last decade are mainly remembered as images. She cites the collapse of the Twin Towers and the toppling of the statue of Saddam Hussein in Baghdad as examples.

The dominant use of visually powerful messages framed by members of the *Orang Papua* group facilitates an emotional condensation of Papuans' anger at the Indonesian regime. Indonesian government regarded Papuans as primitive and uncivilized. Members of the group post visual images aimed to frame Indonesian government as being cruel and abusive. Thus, the visual forms, especially emotionally provocative ones, not only provide evidence of Indonesia's military's violence but also a useful and instant tool for political mobilization. Gerbaudo (2012) argues that emotions played a crucial role in the process of mobilization. He describes the role of social media to create the "choreography of assembly" as the symbolic construction process of public space that enables the circulation of an emotional narrative to maintain users' sense of togetherness. In the case of Papuans, online media have facilitated different political constituencies by creating spaces where they can develop a sense of community. A provocative post to explain the violence, with an appealing headline and simple narrative, is in line with the principles of the political campaign and mobilization via social media. Given the fact that Indonesian authority is tightly controlling international access to Papua, especially foreign media, Papuans take the opportunity provided by social media to expose this genocide and circulate it globally. Facebook plays an important role for members of the *Orang Papua* group to gain public visibility and shape public opinion. It offers places to post and share shocking images and add captions and comments to contextualize the images that fit into Papuan political framework. Images of blood/tortured Papuans along with Indonesian military members with guns are posted, aimed at showing random brutalization of Papuan civilians which often takes place in public places (MacLeod, 2015). Indonesian armed forces perform torture as a public event to terrify Papuan civilians. In response, members of the *Orang Papua* group display these crimes to end the human rights abuse and ultimately, achieve Papuan independence. These two goals are important since the abuses are still occurring. An end to human rights abuses is an even more vital claim than independence.

According to Khatib (2013), visual images are constructions infused with meanings, attributes and projected perceptions. As such, the posts containing the image of dozens of tortured dead bodies clearly show that there is massive and systematically organized massacre in Papua, and are aimed at generating the broad and universalized emotional resonance of injustice. Furthermore, the depiction of civilian casualties in the mosaic picture show the gap between the Indonesian government's peace rhetoric and the unchanged heavy-handed response (military approach) in Papua. However, the government has neither resolved any of the past human rights violations, nor provided any guarantee for non-recurrence given to the victims.

The individuals in the images of bloodied bodies can be considered as martyrs in Papuans' struggle for freedom. The images can also function as evidence of atrocities since the pictures will not be found in mainstream media in Indonesia. In this sense, posted images in the *Orang Papua* group become an issue intensifier, where members of the group highlight the issue of human rights abuse, blow up the reality, and exacerbate it. Furthermore, these posts are part of an attempt to show the Indonesian government's involvement in human rights abuses and violence against its own citizens. In 2003, the Indonesian National Commission on Human Rights declared that the military had committed gross abuses in Papua, but the perpetrators have not been punished (Crocombe, 2007).

Heidbuchel (2007) observes that in the Papuan context, bloody incidents are confronted with "a murky jigsaw consisting of rumors, facts, allegations, threats, political and economic interests" (p. 144). Rumors are considered as real as facts. Since there are only pictures without sources explaining who, why, when or how they have been murdered, one may doubt whether these Papuans who have been portrayed were all civilians and victims of the Indonesian's armed forces' violence due to their political activities.

Members of the group attempted to contextualize the images of bloodied bodies by adding a caption. The caption clearly identifies the bloodied body's identity (name, age, and location of the killing). The post that mentioned the victim's identity indicates an effort to convince the other members of the group that the posted image is real. Furthermore, to prove that it is a real event with a real civilian victim, the post includes the reason behind the murder. The message, "while Melanesians focused in MSG summit, Malays (Indonesians) are killing Melanesian Papuans" indicates Indonesian government political movement by diverting attention from the effort to be part of MSG to the above issue.

The presence, and relevance, of images in political mobilization is undeniable. Encounters with political movements have always been intrinsically tied to the visual sense. Political movements produce and evoke images, as a result of a planned, explicit, and strategic effort (Doerr et al., 2015). Furthermore, Khatib (2013) argues that the image-making can itself be a political act as "politics is not only about material interests but also about contests over the symbolic world" (p. 3). Images are used to support an argument that the Papuans' resentment of the Indonesian government is the result of the armed forces' brutality. Members of the *Orang Papua* group post images that emphasize the violence used by Indonesian armed forces to develop a visual narrative of resistance. The use of tortured bodies and a beaten man indicate an attempt to construct this narrative. To make the narrative stronger, members of the group post not only figures that present images of the tortured Papuans but also figures that display the Indonesian armed forces. The striking image of the officer who stomps his feet on the head of a Papuan, a group of Papuans sitting on the ground surrounded by Indonesian armed forces, along with a handcuffed and injured Papuan become visible evidence of the involvement of Indonesian government in the brutality. They function to reemphasize the argument that the Papuans' resentment is the result of the brutality.

Through these widespread victimization and injustice posts, members of the *Orang Papua* group try to get most Papuans who are not politically active to engage in the political movement. In this sense, images of tortured bodies have functioned as an expression of Papuans as victims and as means to fight against the oppressive actors. Thus, these visually dominant-posted pictures offer the justification of the struggle and reasons for Papuans to have political engagement and band together to reach the political goal. Doerr et al. (2015) argue that images are important resources for activists to express themselves and they have an impact on collective identities and emotions, as well as an important role in framing and representing action in the mobilization of resources. Images provide activists with a symbolic resource to attain resonance in the context of political discourse.

New media platforms became a key venue for the production, distribution and mobilization of images to support activists' causes (Doerr et al., 2015). Through online media, activists challenge mainstream media representations of the movement by highlighting images that are not covered by mainstream media. As the visual messages in the *Orang Papua* group aim to break the silence and reluctance of most Papuans to engage in political movement, interestingly, members of the *Orang Papua* group give a limited number of comments and likes. This fact is important since comments and likes are "the gestures of social media activism" and indicate groups' engagement (Miller, 2015, p. 13). For example, likes on Facebook indicate that members of the group are viewing the posts.

Comments show interactions as there are conversations between members of the group. Even though it is a mistake to assume that numbers of comments and likes imply members of the group's reluctance to engage actively in political movement, such forms of participation are important for the visibility and acknowledgement of activist demands. The limited number of comments and likes may indicate that members of the *Orang Papua* group still treat this group in a way similar to traditional media with their one-way communication and as passive receivers of messages. Neumayer and Svensson (2016) argue that in a narrow definition, all kinds of expressions of opinion, such as Facebook status updates and comments, are forms of political participation on social media. These forms of activist participation are sometimes referred to as lazy, with notions such as slacktivism (Morozov, 2011) due to their simplicity. Slacktivism is defined as the practice of supporting a political cause through social media. It implies little efforts or commitments since the act is done through online media. However, these forms of participation are still part of the broader repertoire of political action. Thus, regardless of a limited number of comments and likes, members of the *Orang Papua* group have shown their political participation and engagement.

Conclusion

In this chapter, I argue that social media, particularly Facebook, have been used as a means to amplify and foreground several aspects of Papuan political resistance. In the *Orang Papua* group, these elements are indicated by the creation of the narrative of regionalization and internationalization. In this sense, social media not only reshape political activities but also transform intercultural communication While members of the *Orang Papua* group create messages that emphasize their close ties to a regional community (Melanesian countries), they also develop messages to get attention from international community. Social media opened up the possibility for an intense mediated intercultural communication on individual and group levels. Facebook platforms facilitated members of the group to create a broader sense of community as indicated by the Papuan cultural and political affiliation to Melanesia, and to raise human rights violations to place Papuan issues internationally. This alignment is due to the politics of violence that have long defined Papua's relationship to Indonesia.

Papuan political resistance has been constructed as the struggle for self-determination and as a fight for human rights by members of the *Orang Papua* group. Members of the *Orang Papua* group have developed these narratives through visual images that coexist with narratives of political resistance, as Khatib (2013) argues that the image-making act can itself be a political act as images can implicitly diffuse political arguments. The use of visual images of violence are political, but they are also aimed at articulating human rights violations. As members of this group become increasingly adept at using social media to get their story out, they use stories of human rights violations to attract more international attention. According to Macleod (2015), propagating the issue of severe human rights violations in Papua is much more dangerous than violent resistance because they have "reached the outside world" (p. 66) Thus, social media have enabled Papuans to reach international audiences and to pay attention to human rights violations in Papua.

References

Allwood, J., & Schroeder, R. (2000). Intercultural communication in virtual environment. *Journal of Intercultural Communication*, 1–16.

Arnett, J. (2002). The psychology of globalization. *American Psychologist, 57*(10), 774–784.

Cain, T. (2014, March 14). The Melanesian spearhead group: What is it, and what does it do? *The Interpreter*.

Chauvel, R. (2006). Violence and governance in West Papua. In C. Coppel. (Ed.), *Violent conflict in Indonesia: Analysis, representation, resolution* (pp. 180–192). London, UK: Routledge.

Chauvel, R. (2008). Papuan political imaginings of the 1960s: International conflict and local nationalisms. In P. J. Drooglever (Ed.), *Papers presented at the seminar on the act of free choice* (pp. 39–59). The Hague, Netherland: Institute of Netherlands History.

Chesterfield, N. (2011). Free the people? Free the media! Broadcasting Papua's songs of freedom. In P. King, J. Elmslie, & C. Webb-Gannon (Eds.), *Comprehending West Papua* (pp. 29–36). Centre for Peace and Conflict Studies, University of Sydney.

Crocombe, R. (2007). *Asia in the Pacific Islands replacing the West*. Suva, Fiji: IPS Publications, The University of the South Pacific.

Doerr, A., Mattoni, A., & Teune, S. (2015). Toward a visual analysis of social movements, conflict, and political mobilisation. *Advances in the Visual Analysis of Social Movements, 35*, xi–xxvi.

Elmslie, J., Webb-Gannon, C., & King, P. (2011). *Anatomy of an occupation: The Indonesian military in West Papua*. Retrieved from http://sydney.edu.au/arts/peace_conflict/docs/Anatomy_for_print.pdf

Gerbaudo, P. (2012). *Tweets and the streets: Social media and contemporary activism*. London, UK: Pluto Press.

Heidbuchel, E. (2007). *The West Papua conflict in Indonesia*. Wettenberg, The Netherlands: Johannes Herrmann J & J-Verlag.

Jancsary, D., Hollerer, M., & Meyer, R. (2016). Critical analysis of visual and multimodal texts. In R. Wodak & M. Meyer (Eds.), *Methods of critical discourse studies* (3rd ed., pp. 180–204). London, UK: Sage Publications.

Khatib, L. (2013). *Image politics in the Middle East: The role of the visual in political struggle*. London, UK: I.B. Tauris & Co Ltd.

MacLeod, J. (2015). From the mountains and jungles to the villages and streets: Transitions from violent to nonviolent resistance in West Papua. In V. Dudouet (Ed.), *Civil resistance and conflict transformation: Transitions from armed to nonviolent struggle* (pp. 46–68). New York, NY: Routledge.

Miller, V. (2015). Phatic culture and the status quo: Reconsidering the purpose of social media activism. *Convergence: The International Journal of Research into New Media Technologies, 19*(3), 1–19.

Morozov, E. (2011). *The net delusion: The dark side of internet freedom.* New York, NY: Public Affairs.

Neumayer, C., & Svensson, J. (2016). Activism and radical politics in the digital age: Towards a typology. *Convergence: The International Journal of Research into New Media Technologies, 22*(2), 131–146.

Schwarz, A. (1991). Eastern Reproach. *Far Eastern Economic Review,* (11 July 1991), 1–24.

Titifanue, J., Tarai, J., Kany, R., & Finau, G. (2016). From social networking to activism: The role of social media in the free West Papua campaign. *Pacific Studies, 39*(3), 255–281.

Trajano, J. (2010, November). Ethnic nationalism and separatism in West Papua, Indonesia. *Journal of Peace, Conflict and Development, 16,* 12–35.

Uzun, L. (2014). Utilising technology for intercultural communication in virtual environment and the role of English. *Procedia-Social and Behavioral Science, 116,* 2407–2411.

Webb-Gannon, C., & Elmslie, J. (2014). MSG headache, West Papua heartache? Indonesia's Melanesian foray. *The Asia-Pacific Journal, 12*(47), 1–22.

Webster, D. (2001). Already sovereign as a people: A foundational moment in West Papuan nationalism. *Pacific Affairs, 74*(4), 507–528.

Index

Note: Page numbers in **bold** indicate a table on the corresponding page.

Printed in the United States
by Baker & Taylor Publisher Services